Impressions of the
NORTH CASCADES

Impressions of the
NORTH CASCADES

Essays about a
Northwest Landscape

Edited and Introduced by

John C. Miles

Illustrations by

Dale Hamilton

Published by
The Mountaineers
1001 SW Klickitat Way
Seattle, WA 98134

0 9 8 7 6
5 4 3 2 1

Published simultaneously in Canada by Douglas & McIntyre, Ltd., 1615 Venables Street, Vancouver, B.C. V5L 2H1

Published simultaneously in Great Britain by Cordee, 3a DeMontfort Street, Leicester, England, LE1 7HD

Manufactured in the United States of America

Edited by Deborah Kaufmann
Map by Green Rhino Graphics
Illustrations by Dale Hamilton
Cover design by Watson Graphics
Book design by Alice C. Merrill
Cover illustration and frontispiece by Dale Hamilton. Frontispiece: *North slopes of Mount Johannesburg*

Library of Congress Cataloging-in-Publication Data
    Impressions of the North Cascades : essays about a northwest landscape / edited and introduced by John C. Miles
        p. cm.
    Includes bibliographical references.
    ISBN 0-89886-484-4
    1. Cascade Range—Description and travel. 2. Landscape—Cascade Range. I. Miles, John C.
    F851.7.I47 1996
    917.95—dc20   96-30628
                                                                                  CIP

To the Memory and Unfinished Work of
WILLIAM LESTER
1942–1996

Park ranger, pioneer of the northwest revegetation, friend, mentor, husband, father, and uncompromising champion of wilderness and wilderness management.

Touch the wilderness gently . . .
and leave it better than you found it.

❖   ❖   ❖

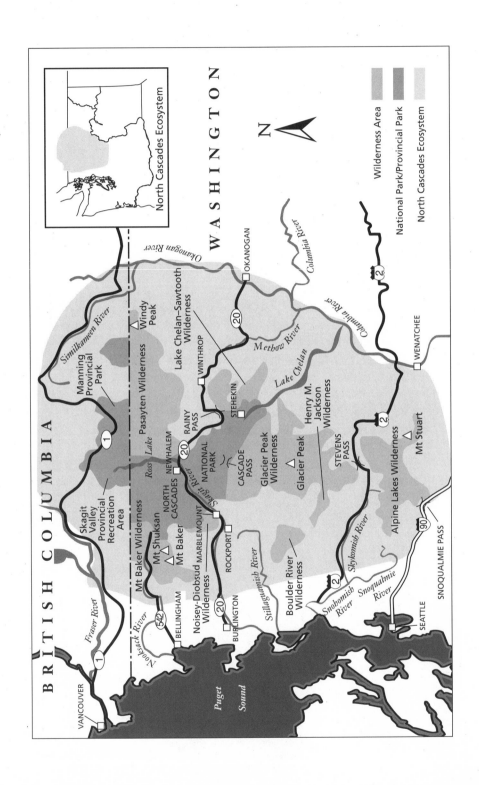

BRITISH COLUMBIA

WASHINGTON

North Cascades Ecosystem

N

Wilderness Area

National Park/Provincial Park

North Cascades Ecosystem

VANCOUVER

Fraser River

Nooksack River

BELLINGHAM

BURLINGTON

Puget Sound

SEATTLE

SNOQUALMIE PASS

Manning Provincial Park

Skagit Valley Provincial Recreation Area

Mt Baker Wilderness

Mt Shuksan

Mt Baker

Noisey-Diobsud Wilderness

MARBLEMOUNT

ROCKPORT

Stillaguamish River

Boulder River Wilderness

Snohomish River

Snoqualmie River

Skykomish River

Similkameen River

Okanogan River

Pasayten Wilderness

Windy Peak

Ross Lake

Skagit River

NEWHALEM

RAINY PASS

NORTH CASCADES NATIONAL PARK

CASCADE PASS

Glacier Peak Wilderness

Glacier Peak

STEVENS PASS

Lake Chelan–Sawtooth Wilderness

WINTHROP

STEHEKIN

Lake Chelan

Methow River

OKANOGAN

Columbia River

Columbia River

WENATCHEE

Henry M. Jackson Wilderness

Alpine Lakes Wilderness

Mt Stuart

SNOQUALMIE PASS

Contents

Acknowledgments

I have many people to thank for their assistance with this collection of essays. All the writers gave generously of their time and talent. They have donated their work to the cause of the educational programs of the North Cascades Institute. All were an editor's dream in that they quickly and willingly responded to my editorial concerns. Dale Hamilton embraced the project with enthusiasm; it is especially pleasing to me to include the artistic work of this long-time friend in this collection. Thanks also to Stephen Frenkel for helping me develop the concept of this book and to Margaret Foster of The Mountaineers Books for guidance and encouragement. Deborah Kaufmann, editor for the project, was most helpful. My deepest gratitude goes to my wife Rotha, who helped throughout with editing and handled the chores associated with preparing and formatting the manuscripts. I simply could not have completed this project without her help and constant support.

—*John C. Miles*

General Introduction

The landscape of the North Cascades is bounded by the Fraser River on the north, the Okanogan Highlands and Columbia Plateau on the east, Snoqualmie Pass to the south, and the Puget lowlands to the west. Mountains, rising nearly from sea level, are the signature of this magnificent place. Fifteen peaks tower over 9,000 feet while nearly 300 rise in elevation between 7,000 and 9,000 feet. Torrents of water fall as rain and snow here, and as a result, 519 glaciers cover over 90 square miles between Snoqualmie Pass and the Canadian border. Lakes nestle in tight pockets between sharp, often serrated ridges. Most of these lakes are natural, while a few are reservoirs behind dams. The North Cascades is a dramatic place of deep-green hillsides and rock faces raked by streamers of cloud, gleaming glaciers riven by crevasses, rivers racing under gray skies, and ravens rolling on the wind.

The essays in this book reflect upon this mountain range, looking at its place in space and time. The essays are organized into three sections that address what the North Cascades landscape has been in the past, what it is today, and what it might or should become in the future. We look at a place dominated by rock and ice and huge forests and think it has always looked like this, that it always will and probably should. Yet we know it has not always been as it is today, and will not be so in the future, despite our wishes. What, then, has it been, and what might it become? We learn that humans have been among these mountains for thousands of years; those of European descent not much more than a century. Tectonic plates, volcanoes, ice sheets, alpine glaciers, and indigenous peoples have formed this land. Transformation has continued in this century of dominance as pioneers and developers have gained power and built dams, bored tunnels, shaved trees off hills, drawn boundaries around forests and parks, and otherwise made their mark. This last hundred years of history raises questions about the consequences of our actions for both ourselves and the other beings with whom we share this place. In the concluding group of essays, we look to the future and reflect on what will be necessary to ensure that the North Cascades remains the rich and beautiful natural area it is today.

I use the term *landscape* in this work. What is a landscape? According to *Webster's Collegiate Dictionary*, in the usual sense associated with painting, landscape is the part of the geography we can see from one place. I can climb to the summit of Mount Baker or Glacier Peak and look out over row upon row of ridges and valleys. Mount Stuart stands sharply to the southeast while Mounts Daniel and Hinman, Chimney Rock, and Lemah Mountain dominate the southern horizon above Snoqualmie Pass.

Mounts Redoubt, Spickard, and Hozomeen stand up to the north. Jack Mountain looms to the east and Whitehorse and Three Fingers are prominent on the western edge of the range. Even from these highest points, I cannot truly see everything that makes up the North Cascades.

Another of *Webster's* definitions of landscape is "the landforms of a region in the aggregate." Ridges, summits, valleys, cirques, horns, and moraines are all landforms found in the North Cascades. Add meadows, lakes, swamps, snowfields, glaciers, rivers, creeks, waterfalls, scree and talus slopes, timberlines, and avalanche trim lines. Include also the plant and animal communities: the fir, cedar, hemlock, spruce, bumblebees, hummingbirds, marmots, pikas, and thousands of other forms of life. And the human creations: the roads, mines, dams, clearcuts, campgrounds, parking lots, buildings, communities, national parks and forests, recreation and wilderness areas, state forests, private lands. All of this forms the aggregate we call the landscape of the North Cascades.

A landscape is a complex entity of physical and cultural dimensions. This piece of Earth has a reality entirely separate from us, preceding our human experience and definition of it by billions of years. Over this immense journey through the eons this particular landscape has changed countless times in ways that we, with our growing body of analytical tools, are only beginning to glimpse and understand. The essays by Scott Babcock and Jon Riedel introduce this understanding. At the same time, we "create" places such as this, give them names, attach to them cultural, economic, political, and symbolic importance, and come to think of them as fixed and lasting entities. There are many versions of the North Cascades, and in these essays we identify and describe our experiences with some of them. Jeanne and Jeff Hardy offer anecdotes from their living and working in community and wilderness on the east slope of the range. Bob Keller reflects on the changes that have come to his property on the Cascade River. Wendy Walker describes living and teaching in the remote Lake Chelan village of Stehekin.

Landscapes such as the North Cascades also have an imaginary element. They evoke emotional responses from us, and as social and cultural contexts change, so do these responses. This place has come in and out of fashion. At one time little known, these "American Alps" were elevated in the imagination of the nation and made a special place. They became a national park in 1968; pieces of the area were designated part of the National Wilderness Preservation System in 1964, 1968, 1984, and 1988. Native Americans saw this land one way, as a source of sustenance and inspiration. National Park Service archaeologist Bob Mierendorf explains our growing knowledge of these early North Cascadians. Skagit Elder Vi Hilbert offers the perspective of a contemporary Native American born and raised in this landscape. Early trappers and explorers, bent on conquest and riches, imagined themselves engaged in a struggle against the physical powers of the place. Miners, settlers, sheepherders, and loggers similarly fought to bend the place to their will and desire, with varying degrees of success. Jim Harris and Charles Luckmann tell the stories of some of these conquerors. Politicians and government agents, trying to mediate growing conflicts between various groups with interests in the region, drew lines all over it, relegating this part to wild nature, that part to hydroelectric energy generation, yet another part to logging, and so forth. Mountain climbers, hikers, and tourists of various ilk, some searching for sport and challenge, others for a renewal of contact with nature, imagined the North Cascades to be a place filled with monumental scenery and the last remnants of pristine nature, a place to be protected from human engineering and manipulation. Tim McNulty describes these realities in his essay.

Our goal in these essays is to explore the North Cascades landscape in all its many dimensions, to delve into the meaning of what is observed and experienced in this corner of the Earth. We are asking "What is this place and what does it mean to us?" We approach this question by exploring what it was before we came to it, what we have made of it, and what we might make of it in the future. Every contributor to this book loves this landscape, identifies with it, and wants it to continue to be a wild, beautiful, and at the same time human place. We all wonder what it will take to keep it so.

Part I

Landscapes *of*
Memory

Introduction to Part I

The North Cascades is a wild landscape. Its wildness is its most distinguishing quality, since the surrounding land has been extensively sculpted by human activity. Gazing out from the summits of Mount Fury or Sahale Peak today, one sees little sign that humans have been active in this area. Appearances can be deceiving.

When we gaze upon such a wild landscape our thoughts turn to geologic time scales. Glaciers grind the bedrock up high, while meltwater gouges the hillsides and valley bottoms. For a moment we think that we see a place as it has always been, but of course this is not so. The landscape changes before our eyes. The mountains are wearing down, the glaciers retreating, the flora and fauna changing with the climate. The only constant here is inexorable change.

The North Cascades has a history that stretches back billions of years, and the trained eyes of the geologist and glaciologist are slowly unraveling the mysteries of this history. These people study a natural history of ancient seas, colliding tectonic plates, volcanic eruptions, and grinding ice sheets. The crash of colliding glaciers echoes down the ages. Animals and plants come and go. The trumpeting of mastodons and mammoths, the screams of saber-toothed cats, and the croak of the raven are heard above the rush of water and the roar of wind.

We look upon such landscapes as having no significant human history, defined as they are by their wildness. Yet human history also plays a part here. Native Americans came and lived on and with this land. They gathered huckleberries, hunted goat, elk, deer, and bear, fished for salmon in the rivers, and made a living. Their tools were few, but they had what they needed. They struggled and loved and, in ways that perhaps seem small from our modern perspective, made their mark upon the land.

The Native Americans yielded to a human power greater than theirs. They succumbed to diseases to which they had no resistance, were pushed aside by technological might beyond their imagining. European settlers came and trapped, prospected, mined, homesteaded, and logged. They built dams on the rivers to power their cities and created national parks and forests to preserve resources for human futures. They decreed that the core of this landscape would be park and wilderness in what Rebecca Solnit in *Savage Dreams*, has described as an attempt "to save a few places from the fate of the rest and to prepare an escape from the diminished beauty of the rest, a landscape of leisure apart from the landscapes of work."

This landscape of the North Cascades has many histories. We look first to the past, to memories of the landscapes we find in rocks, glaciers, and the minds of people who have lived long in this place.

Ancient Aires and Rock Romancing

SCOTT BABCOCK

My first exposure to the geology of the North Cascades was on a field trip with Peter Misch, the legendary University of Washington professor who, in his sixties, was still outlasting his graduate students on the ski slopes. Driving up the Skagit River Valley in his battered blue van, Peter provided a running commentary which gave familiar landmarks a whole new meaning in a geologic context. The towering cliffs of Sauk Mountain became an ancient sea floor thrust onto the continent by tectonic forces of unimaginable power. Diobsud Creek was no longer mundane, but rather a marker of the Straight Creek fault—a San Andreas–like structure that changed the nationality of rocks near Stevens Pass by moving them across the Canadian border to the vicinity of Harrison Lake. Fortunately the last movement on this fault was about forty million years ago, so the International Boundary Commission will not have to adjudicate.

By the time the trip was over, I had filled a notebook with revelations confirming my decision to abandon a career in art and architecture and start a romance with rocks. What I learned after years of study in the Skagit region was just how complicated a relationship with the rocks of the North Cascades can be.

Nowhere is this better illustrated than in the sorry saga of the Skagit Nuclear Power project. In the late 1970s Puget Sound Power and Light announced plans to locate a nuclear plant about 8 miles east of Sedro Woolley at a site on Bacus Hill declared to be the safest and best of hundreds of localities evaluated. The Bechtel Corporation, one of the most experienced engineering firms in the world, was hired to demonstrate the geologic feasibility required for site licensing by the Nuclear Regulatory Commission. The company spent millions on geologic research and hired several famous geologists as consultants. But in the end all this money and expertise did not come close to providing an adequate understanding of geologic features in and around the Skagit Valley. Because seismic safety could not be assured, the site was abandoned at a cost that customers of the utility continue to pay.

Geology also played a role in Seattle City Light's decision to abandon the Copper Creek Dam site and to curtail a plan for raising the height of Ross Dam on the Skagit River. Much research has been done by a long list of geologists. In addition to Peter Misch and his pioneering studies, others playing a major role in reading the rocks of the North Cascades include Ned Brown at Western Washington University, Joe Vance and Bernard Evans at the University of Washington, Bob Miller at San Jose State University, and Roland Tabor, Ralph Haugerud and Wes Hildreth of the United States Geological Survey. And then there are the legions of graduate students and field assistants who have put their hearts and minds on the line to thrash up a creek bed full of devil's club or lead a 5.10 route up an icy rock wall to get a close-up look at a critical outcrop.

So after years of additional research, including dozens of graduate theses and hundreds of technical publications, do we know enough about the North Cascades for a concise description of the materials and processes involved? The answer is no. But what I can offer in this brief essay is a progress report given in the form of a narrative field trip to three spectacular locales, each of which illustrates an important aspect of the geologic evolution of the North Cascades. The first will be a hiking traverse from Austin Pass to Lake Ann, revealing some "explosive" new data on the volcanic history of Mount Baker. The second will be a hike from Schreibers Meadow to Park Butte where we will examine some of the most ancient and some more recently formed rocks in the North Cascades. And, lastly, we will venture into the depths of the Skagit River Gorge where we will discover evidence of the cataclysmic events which formed the deepest, darkest roots of the mountain range.

❖ Austin Pass to Lake Ann ❖

Our first excursion begins at the end of State Route 542, the Mount Baker Highway, which runs 55 miles east of Bellingham into the heart of the North Cascades. From here a summer-only road runs through the Mount Baker Ski Area to Austin Pass, where we park and put on our day packs for an 8-mile round trip to Lake Ann.

This is an unusual Cascades hike because it begins with a steep *descent* of the headwall of a glacial cirque. From the trail we can see that the cirque lies between two steep ridges. To the north is Shuksan Arm. On the south is Kulshan Ridge, which is a finger of lava pointing toward the summit of Mount Shuksan, looming bright and white on the eastern horizon. The outcrops at Austin Pass and the surrounding promontories of Table Mountain and Kulshan Ridge are composed of andesite, named for the Andes Mountains in South America. This particular andesite has a polka-dot pattern of white feldspar crystals set in a gray background. The gray is formed by a mass of microscopic crystals and glass. As the proportion of glass increases, the background gets darker, eventually becoming jet black. Another variety of andesite has a red background produced by the oxidation of iron; this rock has literally rusted.

When the lavas around Austin Pass erupted, about 300,000 years ago, they flowed down valleys which have long since been removed by erosion. In fact, the flat top of Table Mountain at 5,742 feet was once in the bottom of a lava-filled valley. It now stands as a high plateau because the lava was much more resistant to erosion than the surrounding valley walls. Geologists call this process *topographic inversion*, and Kulshan Ridge is another example. It seems astonishing that the landscape could change to such an extent, but where geologic time is involved there is no such thing as the Rock of Ages.

The history of the Earth, according to some, can be read from the record of the rocks like the pages in a book. This may be partially true of places like the Grand Canyon, but about a quarter mile down the Lake Ann Trail is an outcrop demonstrating why the reading is so difficult in the Cascades. In a small streambed that crosses the trail, two distinctly different rock types occur. Upstream on the left is more of the andesite we saw above. On the right is a mottled green rock that belongs to the Chilliwack Group. This was originally part of a basaltic sea floor that existed 250–300 million years ago, possibly somewhere in the southeast Pacific. By the time the andesite erupted 300,000 years ago, the basalt had been cooked into a metamorphic greenstone, mashed against the North American continent, uplifted, and eroded to form a valley through which the lava flowed. Between the two rock types is an unconformity, a gap in time, tantamount to ripping most of the pages out of the rock record, leaving only a chapter near the beginning and another near the end of the story. What happened in between? We will have to go elsewhere to find out.

The switchbacks continue down the cirque headwall toward the headwaters of Swift Creek. Emerging from the forest onto the meadows of the valley floor, we see a jumble of rocks that rises at about a forty-five-degree angle to merge with the cliffs of Kulshan Ridge to the south. This is talus, blocks of rocks that have been pried off the ridge by gravity and freeze-thaw action. This freeze-thaw process involves innumerable cycles of water freezing to ice in fractures. Like pipes in a cold snap, the rock cracks and is slowly but surely pushed over the edge to tumble onto the slopes below.

As the trail wends its way through the talus, we discover that some of the blocks are greenstone rather than the andesite above. Careful scrutiny reveals there is a brigade of greenstone blocks that extends all the way across the valley. This is not talus, but rather a rockfall and avalanche that originated to the north, high on Shuksan Arm. The hurtling mass filled the valley floor and ran up the opposite side, creating a dam and a temporary lake which filled with sediments. The dam has now been breached, leaving only a few blocks on top and a flat valley floor as evidence of the catastrophe. Campers in the valley should cast a wary eye on the fractured rocks above and pray for seismic stability.

Continuing down the trail we reach a bridge over Swift Creek and discover that the rock here is neither greenstone nor andesite. Close examination reveals a mosaic pattern in tones of pink, white, gray, and black. The U.S. Geological Survey has informally named this rock the granodiorite of Lake Ann Stock. Granodiorite is composed of four minerals: the pink is potassium-feldspar; the white, sodium feldspar; the gray, quartz; and the black, either biotite or hornblende. This is a stock because the granodiorite extends only about 2 miles across the landscape—from here to Lake Ann (geologists name rocks for places where they are well exposed). The total area of exposure is only about 10 square miles—much less than the 40 square miles required to be designated a batholith like the Chilliwack Composite Batholith, which crops out from the Skagit River to the Canadian border. If *stock* and *batholith* are terms that do not fit into your memory bank, you can call this rock either a *pluton* or *plutonic rock*, after Pluto, the Greek god of the underworld—where these kinds of rocks crystallize from a molten state.

Plutonic rocks are common in the Cascades for the same reason that there has been lots of volcanic activity and earthquakes in the Pacific Northwest—the Cascadia Subduction Zone. We live on an active margin, where the Juan de Fuca Plate (a geological name for the sea floor) is moving towards a head-on collision with North America. But approximately 200 kilometers offshore, the sea floor takes a dive and moves under the edge of the continent. As it descends, it is transformed by metamorphism and, at a depth of about 40 miles, begins to suffer serious dehydration. The fluids expelled trigger massive melting in the sea floor slab and in overlying mantle rocks. Some of this molten rock (magma) makes it to the surface as volcanic activity. The rest is stuck in the crust to become the plutonic part of the story, which has been playing almost continuously in the Cascades theater for about 50 million years now.

What is most remarkable about the Lake Ann Stock is that it is only about 2.5 million years old. While inconceivably ancient on a human time scale, to a geologist this age is virtually instantaneous, and makes the Lake Ann Stock one of the youngest exposed plutons in the world. When the granodiorite crystallized, it was probably located at least 2 miles below the surface. So as we wade in the creek and cool our feet, we are walking on rock that required more than 10,000 feet of erosion to be exposed. This equates to an average uplift rate of about a half inch per year. This rate may not sound like much, but it is close to a world-record pace in mountain building.

Beyond the bridge, the trail continues through the woods until we reach the junction of the Baker Lake Trail. From here it is all uphill to Lake Ann. The first few switchbacks are still in the Lake Ann Stock, but as we traverse into another cirque below Lake Ann, yet another rock type appears. This stuff is bizarre. It looks as if somebody painted black and white stripes on a piece of cardboard and then, in a fit of rage, twisted it into a crumpled mess. The truth is, the stripes are layers of graphite- and quartz-rich sediment deposited on a sea floor approximately 150–160 million years ago. These layers sat peacefully for millions of years until they reached a plate margin (not necessarily North America) about 120–130 million years ago. Here the sediments were jammed down a subduction zone and squeezed into a metamorphic rock type called phyllite. At the same time the sea floor was converted to metabasalt. Then about 90 million years ago the plate smashed into the margin of North America, most likely at the latitude of Baja California. The phyllites and metabasalts were regurgitated by the Shuksan Thrust Fault, which involved even more twisting and recrystallization. Ultimately these rocks hitched a ride on a north-ward-moving oceanic plate and traveled as much as 2,500 kilometers to their present location, where the phyllites crop out along Shuksan Arm and the metabasalts comprise the upper massif of Mount Shuksan, which rises above us in all of its calendar-image glory.

So now it is time to reverse course and head back toward the trailhead where evidence of one of the most calamitous events in geologic history can be found. Between the bridge and talus slopes below Kulshan Ridge, we leave the trail and head about a quarter mile cross-country to the head of a rapidly deepening canyon. As we pick our way down the drainage we see that the walls of the canyon are composed of light gray to buff-colored material that looks like ash. It is ash, and in places it is more than 3,000 feet thick. The age of the ash has been measured at 1.15 million years (give or take 10,000). It apparently formed in a single explosion of incredible proportions. This focal point of the eruption was the Kulshan Caldera, where a section of earth about 4 miles long and 5 miles wide suddenly collapsed into an underlying mush of molten rock. This same process produced Crater Lake from Mount Mazama and has been responsible for the greatest volcanic eruptions ever observed on Earth. A comparable event at Krakatau, Java in 1883 cooled the entire planet to such an extent that all-time record-low temperatures were recorded for three subsequent winters in Europe and North America. A remarkable aspect of this caldera collapse was that it apparently happened beneath a sheet of glacial ice, so abundant steam was mixed with the ash, making the eruption even more explosive. Because of glacial erosion, we see few of the deposits from this eruption outside the source area, although a one-foot-thick deposit called the Lake Tapps Tephra can be found near Tacoma. It is mind boggling to consider the effects on the Puget Sound region if a similar eruption were to occur sometime in the future. I would not want to be living within 100 miles of the caldera, but there is always the hope that a strong wind would blow much of the ash toward uninhabited areas to the northeast.

Returning to the trailhead, we retrace our steps through time from the rockfall, which occurred less than a few thousand years ago, to the greenstone which flowed as lava hundreds of millions of years ago. As humans we have no basis for comprehending the pace of geologic time. In his book, *The Dragons of Eden*, Carl Sagan compared the age of the Earth to one calendar year and made the observation that on this geologic clock the time span since the birth of Jesus would be less than the last second before New Year's Day. Another way of putting it is that if you live to be 100 years old, your lifetime measured against the age of the Earth would be less than one snowflake on the 10,778-foot summit of Mount Baker—certainly a perspective to ponder.

❖   Schreibers Meadow to Park Butte   ❖

Our next excursion is about 120 miles by road, back to Bellingham, down Interstate 5, up Highway 20 (the North Cascades Highway), and along the Baker Lake Road to U.S. Forest Service Road 11 up the southwest flank of Mount Baker. The parking lot at the end of this 8-mile, dust-bowl route is one of the most popular places to be in the North Cascades and parking is limited, so come early during the summer or face a lengthy jaunt just to get to the trailhead. Crossing the bridge over Sulphur Creek and traversing Schreibers Meadow, we are surrounded by subtle evidence of two very recent catastrophic events related to Mount Baker. The first is a tree-covered hill to the south that rises a couple of hundred feet above the meadow. We depart the trail and head for the hill, grazing on seasonal berries and slapping at seasonal insects as we go. Being good campers we have brought along a small shovel which we use to dig an inconspicuous hole in the hillside. Beneath the thin soil a surprise awaits. This hill is composed of cinders and is the source of the ash layers we observed on the road coming in. The Schreibers Meadow cone formed during the most recent flank eruption on Mount Baker sometime between 7,600 and 12,000 years ago. We won't be able to get a precise age on this eruption until someone finds a well-preserved piece of charcoal among the volcanics. This eruptive event also featured a lava flow which moved down the Sulphur Creek Valley and probably reached the Baker River. Another young lava flow with an age of about 11,000 years can be seen at Crag View, just northeast of Schreibers Meadow.

Turning to the trail, we are now walking on evidence of the second catastrophe. The topography with lots of little lakes and hummocks is also a clue. Checking one of the drainage ditches along the trail, we see none of the ash or cinders that make up the cone. Instead, the surface is littered with blocks of andesite embedded in a mangled matrix of volcanic debris. This material originated high on the slopes of Mount Baker, probably near the rim of Sherman Crater. Here a large sector of the mountain collapsed and crashed downslope, first as a rock avalanche and later as a debris flow when the rock disintegrated and mixed with snow and ice. Another portion of this debris flow, which occurred approximately 6,800 years ago, roared down the Middle Fork of the Nooksack River and ran all the way to Bellingham Bay.

It takes little imagination to picture the devastation such an event would cause, and looking upward toward the east side of the crater, we can see a large mass of crumbly rock poised on the rim above Baker Lake. Geologists have named this outcrop Lahar Lookout, after the Indonesian name for a volcanic debris flow. All it would take to bring this down would be a steam blast or an earthquake. With this thought in mind we hurry across the meadow and into the woods on our way toward the aptly named Rocky Creek. Here again boulders clutter the landscape. However, snags of dead trees reaching skyward through the debris tell us that whatever happened here was not very long ago. A good guess is that it was a *jokulhlaups*. This is an Icelandic word for "ice burst flood." These happen when water accumulates under ice, like the Easton Glacier, which presently resides about a mile up slope. Considering the nature of Mount Baker, the water was probably produced by a steam vent under the glacier. When enough fluid had collected to float the terminus of the glacier upward, the torrent rushed downslope, destroying everything in its path. We pick up the pace a bit—this hike is turning into the Valley of the Shadow of Death!

A swaying suspension bridge presents a more immediate hazard—the embarrassing possibility of a clumsy fall into Rocky Creek. Then the ascent begins. Gently at first, we surmount morainal ridges formed less than 100 years ago when the Easton Glacier extended to at least this point. One piece of evidence for global warming is the rapid retreat of the Easton Glacier—more than a mile per century—which is matched or exceeded by many other ice sheets in the Cascades. Past the moraines the switchbacks get serious as we climb nearly 1,200 feet in little over a mile to Morovitz Meadows. The upper part of the ascent is one of the world's most dramatic transitions in landscape. The trail flattens out and we emerge from an Alaska yellow cedar and silver fir forest to the spectacle of an emerald-green meadow overarched by the brilliant white prominence of Mount Baker filling the skyline. Somebody starts singing the title song of *The Sound of Music* and it seems appropriate. For those who can tear their eyes off the skyline, there is a good geologic story in the ditches again. Interspersed with the mineral soil and peat that has collected over the centuries, there are black and cream-colored layers giving testimony to the recent volcanic history of the Pacific Northwest. The relatively thick black ash just below the surface is the product of the most recent eruption of Mount Baker which probably occurred in 1843. Other layers are from eruptions of Glacier Peak, Mount St. Helens and even Mount Mazama (now Crater Lake).

From here the trail diverges—the right branch leads up the climbing route to Railroad Grade and the left goes on to Park Butte. We choose the climbers' route because designated campsites, with a glorious view of Mount Baker and the meadows, are along the ridge just ahead. After setting up camp, the obvious afternoon excursion is a trip up to climbers' camp and beyond to the Deming Glacier overlook. A short hike brings us to the edge of the Railroad Grade. There are conflicting stories about the origin of this name, but the most plausible is that from a distance the lateral moraines formed during the rapid retreat of the Easton Glacier look like a pair of rails running up the mountainside. However, it is no gentle gradient up close on the edge where we now stand. The slope drops almost vertically to the floor of the great cavity drilled out of the mountain by the glacier when it was at its maximum stand in the late 1800s. We pick our way carefully upward along the knife edge of the moraine until we pass the present terminus and come alongside an expanse of blue-gray ice. Occasional cracks and groans are heard as the ice grinds downslope at the ponderous rate of a few inches per day. Those who carefully venture onto the ice can peer down bluish depths of crevasses that form where the glacier flows over ridges in the bedrock. Some of them seem bottomless, but the maximum depth of fractures in temperate glaciers is only about 100 feet. Below this the ice flows like silly putty to quickly heal any crack that opens.

From here we head cross-country through frost-shattered blocks of lava toward the Deming Glacier overlook, yet another extraordinary viewpoint. After about a mile of stumbling through scree and edging our way along steep, rocky inclines, we reach the edge of the abyss. This glacial trough makes Railroad Grade look like a drainage ditch. The terrain is so steep that the contours on a topographic map form a dark smear. Okay, the distance is not quite as far to fall as at Glacier Point in Yosemite, but it is definitely more spectacular because the neck-twisting views are not only down but up and all around. Even better, this is glacial geomorphology in action. You can almost feel the power surging in the immense mass of blue-white ice that looms directly above and plummets to the depths below. We wait, watch, and listen until the setting sun paints a rosy alpenglow, and then scurry back to our campsite in the meadows below.

We rise with the sun. Our agenda today is to follow a footpath familiar to thousands of Cascades hikers—the Park Butte Trail. Our purpose, however, is not the ascent, but reading the rocks and landforms along the way. The first geologic theme of note is a rounded ridge that runs across the lower end of Upper Morovitz Meadow. This is yet another moraine, one which formed at the terminus of a small cirque glacier and once completely enclosed the open end of the meadows. It has

Mount Baker from Sauk Mountain

now been breached by stream erosion, but on the lower slope of Castle Crags we find laminated clay deposits telling us that if we had been here a few centuries ago we would have been swimming in a lake at least 10 to 20 feet deep.

As the trail rises from the meadow, we encounter outcrops that look very different from the lava flows we have seen elsewhere. These rocks are twisted and gnarled, with a grain almost like that of wood. The rocks look ancient, and they are—they belong to the Yellow Aster Complex, the oldest unit in the Cascades. Dating is scattered and imprecise, but some parts of the Yellow Aster may be more than a billion years old. Their origin is problematic. We know these rocks are found only in the vicinity of the Shuksan Thrust Fault which runs from here to Lake Ann and beyond. The current theory is that the Yellow Aster Complex represents the sliced and diced remnants of an ancient continent shuffled into the deck of the

Cascades during some episode of mountain building lost in the mists of time and complex geology.

Onward and upward the trail winds through large talus blocks that have fallen off the cliffs rising above. At first glance this rock looks just like the andesite we have seen elsewhere, but radiometric dating indicates it is more than 700,000 years old and thus part of the early history of Mount Baker volcanism. The only visible clues that these flows are older are the presence of a few tiny green crystals of olivine and the topographic inversion that occurs here and at Cathedral Crags to the north.

Crossing a plateau at the top of the inverted lava ridge, we reach Pocket Lake—a textbook example of a cirque and tarn. There have been no detailed studies of the glacial history here, but it is a reasonable guess that glacial ice covered most of the landscape until the end of the Little Ice Age in the late 1800s.

Finally we reach the summit of Park Butte, occupied by one of the last, once numerous, Forest Service lookouts (this one is maintained in excellent condition by the Skagit Alpine Club). Toward the east is Mount Baker and Railroad Grade. To the west we see the U-shaped glacial valley of the Nooksack Middle Fork and a jagged mountain range that has an unusual orange color. This is the Twin Sisters Range which consists mostly of serpentine and dunite, rock types rarely found on the surface of the Earth. Indeed the Twin Sisters is claimed to be the largest single mass of this kind of rock in the world. The current geologic interpretation is that this rock was originally located 40 or more miles below the surface in the Earth's mantle. Like the Yellow Aster Complex it was thrust up to its present position by movement on the Shuksan Thrust Fault.

From Park Butte we also get a good look at the two volcanoes which developed to the southwest of the Kulshan Caldera. Looking directly north, the peaks of Lincoln and Colfax carve a dark, jagged edge on the skyline. These are part of the Black Buttes, a volcano active between about 500,000 and 300,000 years ago. The Black Buttes is composed predominantly of pyroclastic andesite, which indicates that most of the eruptions were explosive. However, there are at least a few extensive lava flows of the same vintage (for example, Table Mountain). What we see now at Black Buttes is only a portion of the original cone. Glacial erosion has removed the top and ripped into the sides, so at the head of the Deming Glacier we can see the vent structure in the core of the volcano.

Mount Baker is much younger, probably less than 50,000 years old, with the youngest flow less than 1,000 years ago. It also represents a change in volcanic venue because it is centered about 2 miles northeast of Black Buttes. However, because it is about twice the size of the Black Buttes, the two cones overlap, forming a saddle between the peaks. Between the summit (Grant Peak at 10,778 feet) and Sherman Peak to the south is Sherman Crater, where a sudden increase of steam vent activity occurred in 1975. This led to intensive monitoring of the mountain and the closure of Baker Lake, a popular recreation area. We now think the steam is probably due to a change in the plumbing system of the vent which allows meltwater to trickle to a greater depth where rocks hot enough to produce steam reside. There is no evidence that magma is moving upward to cause an eruption. It is unfortunate that the "cry wolf" aspect of the Mount Baker closures may have been responsible for the blasé attitude of the public and some government agencies that resulted in considerable loss of life during the 1980 eruption of Mount St. Helens. We now know enough about how Cascades volcanoes work to identify the steam activity at Mount Baker as non-threatening. But there can be no doubt that Mount Baker will erupt again. When it does, the Park Butte lookout could be an awesome and relatively safe place from which to watch it happen—unless the wind is blowing in a southerly direction or there is a south-directed lateral blast similar to Mount St. Helens.

One purpose of this excursion has been to justify the whimsical "Ancient Aires" part of the title. Despite considerable research effort, the Yellow Aster Complex remains a mystery. We do not know where it came from or where it has been on its torturous travel to end up as isolated fragments along great faults in the North Cascades. In fact we will probably never know the whole story of these rocks. That is the joy and frustration of geology. The joy is the opportunity for creative inter-pretation. Within the road rules of geology, I can say that the Yellow Aster came from the ancient supercontinent of Pangea and once existed at the geographic position of Australia. As Pangea broke up, some fragments became attached to the sea floor of the Proto-Pacific ocean and were transported like blocks on a conveyor belt across the sea to become North American immigrants. The frustration is that I cannot prove this is true. Rock types found in the Yellow Aster are not that uncom-mon and could match many other locales of similar age. Geologists have only a few small remnants of these ancient rocks, so reconstruction of the Earth's early history is as much an art as a science.

❖ The Skagit River Gorge ❖

Our last excursion begins in Newhalem, a village occupied mainly by people who run the Skagit River Hydroelectric Project for Seattle City Light. When I was doing my Ph.D. research on the Skagit Gneiss, this was my home for several summers. I ate (overate) at the Gorge Inn, swam in the old quarry down the road, climbed the rock walls north of town, and generally developed a special feeling for a dwelling place surrounded by mile-high mountains.

Driving east from Newhalem on the North Cascades Highway, we abruptly enter the Skagit River Gorge, one of the deepest canyons in North America. An ideal place to observe Gorge geomorphology is from the pullouts above Gorge Lake. Here we see that the bedrock walls descend from the adjacent peaks in a broad U-shape, except for the very bottom where a V-shaped notch has been cut. The notch in the bottom is the result of recent downcutting by the river. But the bulk of the canyon must have been cut by a glacier. One possibility is that ice pushed through here about 22,000 years ago during a period of extensive alpine glaciation called the Evan Creek Stade. Elsewhere this event was responsible for cutting the valleys now filled by Lakes Chelan, Keechelus, and Kachess. Another possibility is the continental ice sheet that crossed the Canadian border heading south about 20,000 years ago. During the maximum extent of this ice sheet about 15,000 years ago, the Puget Sound was filled with ice as far south as Olympia, and there is good evidence that a lobe of ice pushed up(!) the Skagit Valley at least as far as Newhalem. Landforms also indicate that the continental ice sheet pushed down the Skagit at least as far as Ross Dam. Whether or not these two segments linked up through the Gorge section is still a matter of speculation.

Another subtle, but significant, geologic feature to be seen from this turnout is the preponderance of boulders. They choke the tributaries and fill the bottom of the valley below Gorge Dam. (Incidentally, the reason there is almost never any water flowing here is that City Light converts the entire flow of the Skagit River to dollars by running it through a tunnel to the electrical generators in a powerhouse at Newhalem.) But back to the boulders, which are the verification that Newton's Laws apply here. The sheer walls and canyons are paths of potential energy that lead naturally from precipice to abyss. Potential becomes kinetic when rocks free-fall as blocks, shattering into progressively smaller splinters as they go. The splinters accumulated on the slope are merely resting a geologic moment, waiting for a downpour of rain or a slide of snow to trigger a massive mobilization. Rocks, soil, plants, animals, anything in the potential path turns into a slurry that hurtles downslope as one of the most destructive forces in nature. This is a debris torrent and anything in its way is flat out of luck. There have been fatalities in the Cascade River Valley to the south and several have rumbled into Diablo Lake near the North Cascades Environmental Learning Center.

Enough of doom and disaster and on to more metamorphism. Driving up the valley and across Thunder Arm, we reach John Pierce Falls. Just beyond the north end of the bridge is one of the better rock outcrops to be found anywhere. No gold, silver or diamonds, but another intriguing story of the North Cascades is readable here. Stand on the far side of the road and look back at the rocks in the outcrop. You will see black and white and gray stripes, but on a much larger scale than those at Lake Ann. The black parts are generally twisted and consist of tiny flakes or chunks all stretched out in the same direction. The flakes are biotite and form a rock type called schist. The chunks are hornblende and form amphibolite. The schist and amphibolite are interlayered with light layers of quartz and feldspar crystals with a few flakes of biotite that have also been stretched into a rock called pegmatitic gneiss. The schists were originally sand and clay and the amphibolites used to be lava flows.

By studying the composition of garnets and other rare crystals in nearby outcrops, we have learned that these rocks were once buried as deep as 80,000 feet within the earth! But there is no good evidence that this burial was related to subduction. So we have a major enigma here, and with every good geologic enigma comes the controversy of competing hypotheses.

One hypothesis is that about 90 million years ago this part of North America was the site of a collision with a microplate named Wrangellia (for the Wrangell Mountains in Alaska). In this collision, North America took the dive so that the Skagit rocks along the margin were buried to great depths where metamorphism occurred. An alternative is that the collision of Wrangellia was a sideswipe rather than a head-on. In this scenario, the burial of the Skagit was due to the loading of enormous amounts of granitic magma in the upper levels of the crust. The evidence available does not make a compelling case for either story, and it is possible that both are partially correct. We need a few more hardy graduate students who are willing to thrash through the devil's club and risk their lives on vertical walls to someday gather the definitive pieces of evidence.

So much for vignettes of the history of the North Cascades—what about the future? We have evidence that these mountains are still rising, perhaps as much as 1 millimeter per year. Multiply this by the geologically brief time interval of a million years and we have the potential for several thousand feet of uplift (minus erosion). We also know from satellite geodesy that convergence of the Juan de Fuca Plate with North America continues at an average rate of about 40 millimeters per year, so we can expect volcanism to continue, probably with greater frequency than during the last century. We can also anticipate great earthquakes because neither subduction nor uplift is a smooth process. The last magnitude 8 (or possibly 9!) earthquake in the Pacific Northwest was in 1700 A.D. Since then the subduction zone has locked in place, building up strain energy. Sometime in the next few hundred years—maybe much sooner—the oceanic plate will suddenly plunge 30 feet under the continent all at once and anyone climbing a Cascades peak will have to beware of falling rocks as the whole region shakes violently in another magnitude 8-plus earthquake. The largest (magnitude 7.2) historic earthquake in the Pacific Northwest occurred in 1872, with an epicenter near the Skagit Gorge. This was probably related to uplift, and quakes of similar size will undoubtedly happen in the near future.

Glaciers in the North Cascades are mostly in the unhappy condition of rapid retreat. This too will pass. We are currently in the latter stages of an interglacial period and climatic models point to another Ice Age within the next 10,000 years. Over the short term, global warming due to the greenhouse effect may shift the climate of the Pacific Northwest to a humid, subtropical condition. This would substantially increase the rates of stream erosion, flooding, and landslides in the mountains.

Finally, the long-range forecast for these mountains is that they will be gone. In about 20 million years the Cascadia Subduction Zone will have been "transformed" into a San Andreas–type fault and volcanism will shut down along with the compressional forces that cause uplift. The compensation for this loss is that Baja California will have moved northward on the Pacific Plate so that it will provide a great offshore view from the mountaintops left and we can contemplate the intriguing possibility of a future North Cascades Multinational Park.

❖ Epilogue ❖

The main impression to be conveyed by these field trips is that the only thing constant about the geology of the North Cascades is that it is constantly changing. We have seen evidence for many different incarnations of the landscape from the sea floor rocks of Mount Shuksan to the Himalayan-like collision zone recorded in the Skagit Gorge. The changes also vary immensely in rate from the supersonic blast of the Kulshan Caldera to the creeping crystallization of the Lake Ann Stock that might have taken 100,000 years or more to complete.

There is also the shifting paradigm of geologic science. When I first traveled with Peter Misch back in the 1960s, there was no such thing as plate tectonics, and even continental drift was viewed with great skepticism. The permanence of the continents and ocean basins was a prevailing concept and geology was interpreted accordingly. Now when I take students on field trips into the North Cascades, the simple message is that there is no such thing as *terra firma*. The older rocks of the North Cascades are foreign imports that have probably traveled thousands of kilometers from their birthplace to occupy this special part of North America. Most of the rocks younger than about 50 million years are bona fide Yankee residents, but sometime in the geologic future they too will become restless and move on to other parts of the world.

So as we sit on a high ridge looking over the magnificent vista of the North Cascades, we need to realize that this landscape will exist for only a brief moment in geologic time. We can count ourselves fortunate to have been here when a unique combination of tectonic forces and geomorphic agents created a mountain range of incredible beauty and diversity for us to appreciate and seek to understand.

SCOTT BABCOCK is a professor of geology at Western Washington University who has no expectation of ever completely understanding the rocks of the North Cascades. Appreciation, however, comes easily and is happily shared with others who venture into these magnificent mountains.

Keepers of the Beat

JON L. RIEDEL

❖ Introduction ❖

Jimmy Carter froze federal hiring in 1980, costing me an internship with the United States Geological Survey in Colorado. Election-year politics forced me to seek other employment. What I found was a volunteer position with the Student Conservation Association at North Cascades National Park. Little did I know, as my VW bug coasted into Colonial Creek Campground that June, that a very long chapter in my life had just begun.

When I think of seeing the Skagit Gorge and Jack Mountain that first day, I am reminded of Colin Fletcher's first impressions of the Grand Canyon.[1] He saw a mile of exposed rocks, some displaying brilliant color, others incredible detail of the past, tens of millions of years of earth history laid open like a book. After many days immersed in the Canyon, Fletcher wrote that "the rhythm of the rocks beats very slowly, that is all."

My first summer, the rhythms in the North Cascades seemed beyond comprehension. The easiest-to-reach rocks at lower elevations were obscured by dense vegetation. Well-exposed rock was a mile and a half straight up and surrounded by steep snow and ice. Only after fifteen years immersed in study of North Cascades glacial history can I begin to describe its rhythm of time and change.

The evidence of rock rhythms here is different than in the Grand Canyon because processes of landscape change are dominated by glaciers. Glaciers are elders of the landscape, having many stories to tell of rhythms spanning the past million years, tales written in glacial landforms and in the annual layers of glacial ice. The rhythms of the mountains recorded by glaciers are cycles of climatic change. They are the annual rhythm of seasons, climatic cycles spanning tens of thousands of years, the ultimate force shaping the mountains and causing change to land and life. The beats of these cycles could be so strong that they forced many creatures to abandon their homes as massive glaciers covered the landscape. Despite this power, the rhythms are imperceptible, the beat slow and complicated, but inexorable. They can be seen and heard only by those who take the time to look and listen for them. I have had the privilege and the resources, as a geologist, to listen and learn.

Let us journey to find these North Cascades rhythms. We begin at broad scales of space and time while exploring rhythms known as the great ice ages. These beats are marked by landforms of colossal, ice-age continental glaciers and alpine valley glaciers in the Fraser, Chilliwack, and Lower Depot Valleys. We move up Depot Creek to the Redoubt Glacier, traveling forward in time, and find the beat becoming more rapid as we come up to the present.

❖ *Stage One:* Fraser and Chilliwack Valleys ❖

Our search for the beat of the North Cascades begins from the northwest. We enter the mountains by way of the Fraser Valley, which is appropriate because the largest glaciers to occupy the North Cascades were born in this watershed. Landforms left by these glaciers reveal the rhythm of heating and cooling, of ice ages coming and going, of climate shaping the destiny of everything here.

Repeated periods of climatic cooling have been the dominant rhythms of the North Cascades, as deep cold has triggered ice ages at northern latitudes and high elevations. Massive glaciers grew during the ice ages, born of cooler summers that allowed snow and ice from previous winters to accumulate for thousands of years. The pulse of ice ages has been beating for at least 1 million years. Its rhythm is punctuated by periods of cooling that last 100,000 years, separated by periods of relative warmth lasting 10,000 years.[2]

Gazing across the lush, green expanse of vegetation surrounding the Fraser Valley today, we find it hard to believe that we may be at the end of the warm spell that allowed habitation of these mountains and on the verge of another ice age. Only 15,000 years ago, the entire Fraser watershed and half the North Cascades were covered by ice more than a mile thick.[3] This colossal glacier is known as the

Cordilleran Ice Sheet, which dwarfed alpine valley glaciers growing from the high summits of the North Cascades.

As we travel over the fertile floodplain and delta of the Fraser River, the scene 19,000 years ago when mammoths roamed this valley seems remote and scarcely possible. Sparse browse on cold, dusty, windswept tundra ended a few miles up the valley against the largest glacier this land had seen in 100,000 years. Change associated with these upheavals sealed the fate of many creatures; at least six waves of extinction are believed to have resulted from ice age changes. Between 12,000 and 10,000 years ago, at the end of the last ice age, at least fifty species of large mammals, including the mammoth, giant beaver, dire wolf, and saber-toothed cat became extinct.[4] At the mouth of Chilliwack Valley we pass the grave site of mammoths, whose bones were discovered beneath hundreds of feet of gravel on the north side of the road.[5]

The huge Cordilleran Ice Sheet had a tremendous impact on the landscape. At the international boundary, 6,000 feet of ice depressed the ground with its tremendous weight. The glacier was 600 feet thick near the mouth of the Chilliwack River.[6] This glacier was so massive that only the highest summits stood above its white expanse. For thousands of years during the ice ages, half the North Cascades mountain range slept beneath a 7,000-foot blanket of ice. Global growth of continental glaciers stored enough water to lower the sea level by several hundred feet, creating a land bridge between Alaska and Siberia that allowed humans to travel into North America from Asia. These nomads challenged mammoths and dodged saber-toothed tigers while migrating around the ice sheet. People came here with the last ice age—will they leave with the next?

The last ice age brought impressive change to the Chilliwack River. Before that, the river flowed southwest to join the Nooksack River. Deposition of a glacial moraine approximately 12,000 years ago in the nearby Columbia Valley blocked its former route, sending the Chilliwack north to the Fraser instead.[7] Salmon entering the Nooksack for the first time after the ice age found their home waters no longer accessible along the route their ancestors had used for thousands of years. It was a change the salmon adapted to often as glaciers rearranged the courses of rivers throughout this area with the passage of ice ages.

Following the path of the ice sheet, we continue into the North Cascades up the Chilliwack Valley. Along with the Skagit and Pasayten Valleys to the east, the Chilliwack was one of the major routes the ice sheet took to invade the mountains. A few years ago, I began to wonder about the impacts of glaciers flowing up these deep mountain valleys.

After years of investigation, I now know that the ice sheets created dams preventing drainage north to the Fraser and Similkameen Valleys, and flooding the upper Chilliwack, Skagit, and Pasayten Rivers. Lakes created by these dams

drained south across divides into the Skagit and Methow Rivers, cutting spectacular gorges along Lost River, Lightning Creek, Canyon Creek, and the Skagit
River. Over the course of many ice ages, this drainage system had astounding
effects.[8] Once-towering divides were reduced to valley-bottom swamps (Klesilkwa
Pass) or shallow lakes (Lightning Lakes and Hidden Lakes). Ultimately, erosion
at the outlets of these huge lakes caused the rearrangement of the drainage pattern of the entire area north of Newhalem. Indeed, the Pacific Crest of the northern North Cascades has shifted east at several locations. The largest shift may have
reversed drainage of the entire upper Skagit watershed above Gorge Dam. Incredibly, the upper Skagit River, as told in Native lore, used to flow north to the Fraser.
Like the glaciers and salmon, the original human inhabitants of these mountains
remembered the ancient rhythms.

Crossing the wood-plank bridge over Paleface Creek, I see few signs of the old
logging shacks that once stood here. I remember the old man and his son who called
this place home while logging the shores of Chilliwack Lake and its tributary valleys. Their Dobermans surprised me walking one night on the shore of Chilliwack
Lake. The encounter was worthwhile, however, as the dogs introduced me to the
only humans living in the upper valley. I was comforted on later trips to know they
were nearby and could help in case of an accident. Now the shacks and their friendly
inhabitants are gone. The only sound is the stream, and alder and oil-stained soil
are all that remain at the old logging site.

Vegetation change, associated with logging in this part of the valley, seems extreme. During the ice age, however, most plants moved far to the south to avoid the
advancing ice sheet. Forests in the upper Skagit and Chilliwack Valleys were overrun
and buried by the advancing ice.[9] This indicates that the ice age climate 20,000 years
ago within the mountains was not radically different from the present, and that the
turn toward a warmer climate had begun. Plant refuges from the ice sheet in this
region included several high peaks that stood above the great glacier, as well as all of
the southern North Cascades. What vegetation did survive on summits was certainly
sparse. On the northeastern flank of the range, tundra and permafrost probably dominated in a cold, windy, dust-swept zone near the ice.

At the ends of the ice ages, summer warmth rapidly melted the continental
glaciers, again bringing rapid change to the mountains. Landslides were large and
frequent on the unstable glacial deposits until the return of soil-stabilizing plants.
For several hundred years, at least, travel deep into the mountains would have been
extremely dangerous. Trees returned to the landscape at different rates, advancing
from a few hundred to a thousand or more feet per year in the wake of the retreating ice.[10] Mountain streams cut deeply into the glacial deposits, filling valleys. Eventually, stream channels stabilized and salmon returned to waters in which their
ancestors had last spawned thousands of years earlier.

The slow, strong ice age rhythm dominates the natural history of this region by creating landscapes, extinguishing the lives of animals, and forcing migration of plants and people. We exist here now between the glacial beats of the ice age drum. As we hike deeper into the mountains, we find that the landforms left by alpine glaciers growing from the mountains record yet more detail of Earth's beat.

❖ *Stage Two:* Up Depot Creek ❖

Fifteen miles of cross-country travel into one of America's great wilderness areas begins in a clearcut. Alder, fireweed, and other pioneer plants choke the old logging road. Many of these hill slopes have been stable since the end of the ice age, but logging has reactivated old landslides and started many new ones. Sediment surging down these valleys is part of a chain reaction felt all the way down to Chilliwack Lake. Evidence from the adjacent Silver-Hope Valley indicates that sedimentation of Silver Lake increased ten to a hundred times with the advent of clearcut logging.[11] The ancient rhythms seem to be muddled by the cadence of modern life.

After a mile or so in "alderland," the trail crosses the international boundary into North Cascades National Park. A single row of trees was spared on the south edge of the clearcut to define the north edge of the international boundary border cut. It seems the boundary clearcut would have been enough. Most of the remaining buffer strip of trees has fled to the United States, with the help of the wind. The panic also seems to have spread to many American trees. Wrestling through this border tangle provides time to reflect on the incredible contrast between the two sides of the border: hot, fly-infested clearcuts to the north, cool hemlock forest to the south. Dense vegetation on the west side of the North Cascades limits geologic interpretation of the landscape. On this hike, however, I welcome the physical comfort of the dense forest at the expense of geology—at least for a few strides.

In the forest permeated by the rumble of Depot Creek, my thoughts are drawn back to the ice age. The cold caused the expansion of glaciers in the mountains as well as in interior British Columbia. It triggered a relatively rapid reaction by the smaller, more sensitive alpine glaciers. They grew much more quickly than their continental-sized cousins because they were fed by abundant Pacific storms, in contrast to the dry interior plateaus that were the source of the ice sheet. Somewhere farther up the valley ahead of us, the continental and alpine glaciers collided. Discovering the exact location of the great crash is a continuing interest of mine. All I know right now is that it occurred closer to the head of this valley than its mouth because by the time the ice sheet was beginning to cross into what is now the United States, the alpine glaciers were retreating from their maximum down-valley positions.[12]

Nervous about a cross-country hike in a valley I had never seen, I barely took notice of a narrow ridge stretching across the valley floor on my first trip here in 1985. Eleven years and two dozen trips later, I am now convinced the ridge is an alpine glacial moraine. Its exact age is unknown, but I believe it represents the last advance of alpine glaciers, approximately 12,000 years ago, at the end of the most recent ice age. Other moraines from the Depot Valley glacier were probably obliterated by the ice sheet. A complete record of moraines from the last ice age is found in the Yakima and Wenatchee watersheds.

These moraines record rhythms of climate change more frequent than the 100,000-year ice age cycle. The moraines tell us that alpine glaciers advanced four times during the last ice age, and that retreat between at least one of the advances was significant. This geologic evidence indicates that the ice age climate was not uniformly cold, but was punctuated by brief periods of relative warmth. The elevation of these moraines also allows us to determine that average summer temperature was as much as 12°F colder 20,000 years ago.[13] This was enough to drop the snowline by 2,500 feet, which means skiing should be excellent in the next ice age.

Long tongues of blue glacier ice filled the upper reaches of nearly every North Cascades valley in the ice age cold. The largest valley glacier systems were fed by extensive ice caps and ice fields at a dozen locations scattered throughout the range. The alpine glaciers were long, but not as thick as the ice sheet. At this location, the Depot Creek Valley glacier was approximately 1,500 feet thick, only one fifth the thickness of the larger glacier.

The pattern of alpine glaciation is important to mountaineers and those interested in the varied climate of the North Cascades. Trails and well-planned, cross-country routes don't follow deep, winding, narrow canyons carved by streams. Preferred routes are the wide, flat-floored, straight, U-shaped valleys carved by glaciers. This valley up which we travel was glaciated from top to bottom, making the hike easy. The pattern of alpine valley glacier systems across the mountains also teaches us a great deal about the climate of the region. The glaciers in this valley were much larger than those in the Ross Lake drainage 15 miles to the east. This asymmetry was caused by the rapid decrease in precipitation across the North Cascades. Played out over many ice ages, this climatic wrinkle created two startlingly different landscapes on either side of Ross Lake.[14] Glaciers entering from the wetter west side were large and flowed all the way to the Skagit Valley. As a result, the west side valleys have classic U shapes for their entire lengths. Glaciers on the east side of Ross Lake were smaller and did not make it to the Skagit. As a result these valleys have narrow, V-shaped river canyons at their junction with the Skagit Valley.

A few miles past the moraine, the trail begins to climb steeply through a grove of huge cedars. The roar of Depot Creek is heard as it crashes 800 feet down a series of cliffs. At the base of the waterfall the sound is deafening. For hundreds of years these trees have listened patiently. On my first trip through here, I was not so patient, as the roar and icy blast spurred me to press ahead. Now, I enjoy this place as much as any on this journey, and often spend an hour or more listening to the sound of the water.

Above the waterfall, the route flattens out into a huge meadow covered by willow, alder, sedge, and grass. Towering above the meadow is the stunning north face of 8,985-foot Mount Redoubt. Ringed by blue glaciers, Redoubt is composed of many massive gray towers, flying buttresses, and steep, narrow couloirs. The desire for quick approaches to these inspiring peaks resulted in the cutting of an unofficial trail up this valley in the 1970s and 1980s. Similar expediency trails are beginning to scar many areas in the surrounding national park as people come in search of adventure, inspiration, and challenge.

Mount Redoubt is a testament to the legacy and powers of glaciers that have worked on this landscape for 2 million years and are alive today. This legacy defines the boundaries of the North Cascades Physiographic Province.[15] Unlike the Cascade Range south of Snoqualmie Pass, volcanic rocks have been mostly stripped from the North Cascades. Beneath the volcanic rocks, glaciers exposed the crystalline igneous and metamorphic rocks, seen on the flanks of Mount Redoubt, that form the backbone of the North Cascades.

Alpine glacial moraines record a more frequent beat emanating from deep within the mountains. Periods of glacial advance and retreat, recorded by lakes and moraines, identify at least four rhythms during the end of the last ice age. Superimposed on the slow, 100,000-year ice age rhythms, these more frequent cycles add tempo and complexity to the history of this place. The rhythms become more frequent and less powerful as we continue our climb higher and deeper into the mountains.

❖ *Stage Three:* On Mount Redoubt ❖

Sloshing along the flat meadow is a welcome change from the crawl up the waterfall. Adding to the comfort of this part of the journey is the solitude and warmth of the meadow, which contrasts sharply with the deafening sound and cold spray of the falls. This is a fitting place to reflect on the warming trend that caused the end of the last great ice age, which continued until approximately 4,000 years ago. In this 6,000-year warm spell, glaciers probably did not record climatic rhythms, as they disappeared from all but the high summits of Mount Baker and Glacier Peak.

Egyptians had built many of the great pyramids of Giza by the time glaciers again began to record the rhythms of these mountains. Pollen rained into lakes, and moraines shaped by readvancing glaciers provide evidence of colder and snowier periods between 4,000 and 3,000 years ago, 2,800 and 2,600 years ago, and within the last 800 years.[16] These shorter, more frequent cold climatic spells were caused by a 2,000-year cycle in sunspot activity, huge volcanic eruptions, and variations in global winds and sea-surface temperatures.

As our journey draws nearer to its conclusion, the glacial evidence we find is from the most recent cold wave, known as the Little Ice Age, when average annual temperatures were from 2°F to 3°F cooler than today.[17] The Little Ice Age began in the late thirteenth century and was known to people throughout the Northern

Hemisphere. It forced the Vikings from Greenland and caused famine in Europe, but also made life in the North Cascades difficult. Historic accounts from the late 1800s describe snow 12 feet deep at the mouth of Ruby Creek. In the last fifteen years, I have not seen more than 2 feet of snow anywhere along the shores of Ross Lake. Heavy Little Ice Age snow caused bigger rain-on-snow and spring snowmelt floods. Travel through the mountains was more dangerous because of bigger and more frequent snow avalanches. Stories are told of the Skagit River freezing over in the 1800s.

Vegetation also reacted to the changing Little Ice Age climate. Tree line dropped with heavier snowfall, causing shifts in the range of a larger community of plants and animals. Today, tree line is charging up slope, glaciers are in retreat, and willow and alder flourish in the barren expanses. Avalanche chutes once swept clear of trees are now dotted with small silver fir and other montane species. I currently can grow a wide variety of fruits and vegetables in Marblemount, something I could not have done during the Little Ice Age.

Skagit Gorge with Skagit River at flood

One hundred years ago, the geologist R. A. Daly stood near the south end of this meadow, his path up valley blocked by a massive glacier that covered the remainder of the valley to the summit of Mount Redoubt. This was the Redoubt Glacier, and it was a half-mile longer during the late 1800s than it is today.[18] To Daly and his team, the elongated Redoubt Glacier was stark evidence of a glacial beat in a climatic rhythm much faster than any we have encountered thus far on this journey. The beat is felt at time scales of mere hundreds of years.

At the same place today we see two long, stony glacial moraines deposited by the Redoubt Glacier. They record the fluctuations in the size of the Redoubt Glacier during the past several centuries. They illustrate that there were at least eight periods of glacial recession during the last 800 years.[19] The first moraine we crossed was deposited between 1760 and 1780. The glacier retreated from this position an unknown distance before finally depositing a second moraine 500 feet up slope between 1840 and 1860. When Daly's crew saw the glacier, it had retreated another 1,000 feet in fifty years, an average rate of 20 feet per year. After the surveyor's visit, retreat accelerated to 40 feet per year, and by 1947 the glacier had retreated a total of 2,000 feet. Between 1950 and 1990, a large mass of the glacier stagnated in a cirque, cut off from the main body of the Redoubt Glacier by a 400-foot headwall.

The moraines can be followed up the valley to a break in the slope of the valley wall where, above the lines of rocks, trees grow thickly. Below, a barren landscape composed of loose boulders and scoured bedrock stretches across the valley. Round rocks cover this 100-year-old landscape, making for tough travel with tired legs and a heavy pack. On one particularly long and arduous trip, I wondered if I had enough energy left to escape the glacier should it advance again down valley. Barren rock and glacial-till slopes like these throughout the North Cascades mark the extent of the last Little Ice Age glacial advance. In most cases, the change is astounding. What remains of the Little Ice Age Redoubt Glacier is a shallow puddle commonly known as Ouzel Lake. When I first visited here ten years ago, ice caves made Swiss cheese of the last part of the stagnant glacier. Today, there is no trace of the ice that covered the last half mile of our journey as little as fifty years ago.

We continue by climbing up the east wall of the cirque, the easiest way to gain access to the Redoubt Glacier. Granite, plucked and scoured by the glacier, makes a relatively easy climb. Finally, we stand on the glacier whose meltwater trail we have followed 50 miles into the mountains. Locked below our feet in annual ice layers is a record of the past 600 years: stories of cold, snowy winters and dry, fire-hazed summers. We hope to learn a great deal about the recent glacial rhythms of these mountains from a 600-foot-long ice core recently extracted from South Cascade Glacier. The age, memory, and beauty of all these glaciers command respect.

Throughout this area, glaciers have shrunk drastically since the end of the last century. The loss of these should not be taken lightly. As they melt, we lose a vital part of these mountains. Obelisks of time, elders of the landscape, glaciers add immeasurably to the North Cascades. In fact, the modern cover of glaciers defines the present boundaries of this region. Strung out like pearls on the backs of the mountains, the 700-plus glaciers in the North Cascades add greatly to the quality of our lives by providing challenge and inspiration, as well as consistent runoff for salmon runs, irrigation, and hydroelectricity.

We do not know if the glaciers will continue to wither, apparently in the heat of human consumption. Part of my current job is to monitor the health of four glaciers in North Cascades National Park. Silver Glacier, on the other side of the ridge, is one of the glaciers we visit three times a year. Since the late 1970s, there have been few good years for this glacier. Last year was the first in more than a decade that it gained more mass in winter snowfall than it lost in summer heat.

It is also possible that modern glaciers will stop shrinking and be the direct forebears of the next ice age. Many believe we are well on our way. It is estimated that a ten percent increase in winter precipitation or a 2°F to 3°F drop in average annual temperature would cause continual glacial expansion.[20] The glaciers are here, currently shrinking, but waiting to grow.

The rhythms of our lives may seem weak, especially in the din of the city. In these mountains the Earth's rhythm is strong, and its pattern is a big part of this place and our lives in it. Glaciers and their creations remind us of our helplessness in the face of ice ages, and of our dependence on the interglacial climate for food and the development of our civilizations and cultures. From this journey and place we can see very far in time and space. To Colin Fletcher I reply that the rhythm of the rocks in the North Cascades also beats slowly, but here we can find evidence of more rapid beats, recorded by the great dominance of glaciers in shaping this landscape. Here, the big ice ages dominate the rhythm at 100,000 year intervals. We exist here dependent on the warmth between ice ages. Fainter, less frequent beats remind us of other patterns to life here. Some come by the millennium, others the decade, but each is recorded in the glaciers and glacial landscapes of the North Cascades. They remind us of our past, and give perspective to our future.

JON L. RIEDEL has worked for the National Park Service in the North Cascades since 1980. He is a geologist at the North Cascades and other national parks in the Pacific Northwest. His professional interests include the glacial history and geology of the North Cascades, floodplain and geologic hazard management, and long-term monitoring of glaciers and streams.

Who Walks on the Ground

BOB MIERENDORF

❖ A "Ferocious Wildness" ❖

The scenic grandeur of the North Cascades will take your breath away, as it did
Henry Custer's on July 18, 1859. Perched on Middle Peak, above the Little Chilliwack River, the modest Custer became the first to write about this striking corner
of the range:

> I leave it to a better pen to describe the sublimity of true Mountain
> scenery in the Cascade Mts. . . . it can not be described. Nowhere do
> the Mountain masses and peaks present such strange, fantastic, dauntless,
> and startling outlines as here. Whoever wishes to see Nature in all its
> primitive glory and grandeur, in its almost feroci[o]us wildness, must go
> and visit these Mountain regions.

Working as a surveyor for the U.S. commission created to establish the international
boundary along the forty-ninth parallel, and guided throughout by Coast Salish
people familiar with these mountains, Custer left an account of his considerable

travels through subalpine and alpine terrain.[1] One hundred and fifty years later, the land is managed as National Park Service and United States Forest Service wilderness, where scenery and wildness are protected values.

But there is another, quite different view of this landscape. The spectacular scenery and raw wildness are only the outer wrapping that packages a story of bygone people and ancient landscapes spanning the last 11,000 years. The story is unwritten, yet it is chronicled, literally, underfoot—beneath the ground we walk on. This ground is the upper, biologically active mineral layer of the planet Earth, the foundation for the habitats of all terrestrial beings, including humans. Since our emergence and occupation of the planet, we have left evidence of our passing. We have built and modified and left our refuse everywhere, and the North Cascades is no exception. Here, in Custer's "ferocious wildness," we find in the ground a narrative of people deeply involved with this landscape for millennia.

The human story is not the only one found in this ground. Few are aware that today's Washington State was the native home of animals such as buffalo, camels, elephants, and giant ground sloth; that pronghorn antelope and mountain sheep were abundant in the arid lands east of the Cascades; that arctic tundra blanketed lowlands; or that a native nicotine tobacco grew widespread in areas of eastern Washington. Since before the last great ice advance 15,000 years ago, the landscape has evolved in a swirl of climatic shifts, geologic events, biological adaptations, and human interactions. Viewed from this time span, today's scenery is as ephemeral as the climate it echoes, but in the ground, virtually every being, whether it be plant, animal, insect, or human, leaves physical clues of its existence.

There are various ways to acquire knowledge about the Earth's past inhabitants and their relationship with their environment. One of the easiest would be to ask them, but this presents obvious difficulties. Much ancient knowledge has been passed down through Native American languages and traditions. A story of the ancient past of the Pacific Northwest is told by Native elders, embedded in their traditions of carving cedar, weaving bear grass, hunting whales, netting salmon, or through their mythology, which tells of great floods and the origin of the mountains. Their ancestors, they say, were here forever.

A vital contribution of archaeology as a method of exploring the human past is its ability to put the ancient environments back into the story, to recreate the scenery, to place past and present human–environment interactions into a connected whole to which we can relate. The archaeologist uses the logic and techniques of science to gather evidence and form conclusions, evidence that is often buried under the surface of the earth. We will never have complete knowledge, but the wisdom of Native culture, combined with archaeology and supporting studies from ecology, botany, biology, and earth sciences, offers the fullest picture yet of human occupation of the Pacific Northwest. In what follows, we will look under the grand North

Cascades scenery, pulling back layers of earth to distill images of a past we can never directly experience. This endeavor will take us to an assortment of archaeological sites, whose material remains and artifacts will show the interdependence of cultures and people with their environment. The fact of this interdependence will be accepted as a truism and requires no repetition. From each archaeological site we visit we will learn lessons for an enlightened understanding of the North Cascades landscape and the complex history of human–environment interactions. This understanding will help us live today and tomorrow as part of this wild place.

❖ Miskaiwhu ❖

One of the first places I explored in the North Cascades was the mouth of Goodell Creek in October 1984. As part of my job as archaeologist, I was asked to evaluate the condition of an archaeological site recorded by a colleague nine years earlier. On that first visit, the site appeared to me much as he had recorded it—a scatter of fragmented stone tools at the base of an eroded riverbank, certainly prehistoric in age, but with actual dates of occupation unclear. It had probably been a short-term campsite. In subsequent years, during frequent visits to the site to monitor the erosion, I began to develop a familiarity for this place and to appreciate its qualities: its access to the Skagit River, the salmon spawning along its shores, and the flood-wise cedars rooted in its banks. It had been more than just an ephemeral campsite, and I understood that it was not just another nameless riverbank. But how little I really knew at that time! It was not until 1991, when we excavated through ancient soils covered under layers of Skagit River flood sands, that I began to understand the story within the site.

Here we found four old soils, each marking what had been the ground that Upper Skagit people lived on until the next layer of flood sands buried it. We found artifacts extending to a depth of more than six feet below the modern ground. Each soil appeared as a black, charcoal-stained matrix full of charred salmon bones, cooking rocks fractured by heat, and chipped stone tools. A handful of the blackest, organic-rich matrix from one of the layers, when squeezed tightly in a fist, left a slippery film, a mixture of fish oil and campfire creosote. We had found the remains of an Indian fishing camp that had seen repeated use. Above each ancient ground surface had been a salmon-drying rack, long since disappeared but for the darkened stain where one of the rack posts had stuck in the ground. Radiocarbon dating of the charcoal indicated that salmon had been dried here for the last 660 years.

Who were the people who had smoked all those salmon? There are no written or oral accounts of people fishing or smoking salmon at this particular location, but Upper Skagit Indian elders told, over the years, of the Mis-skai-whwu (or Miskaiwhu), the name of the Upper Skagit band that permanently occupied the area in the nineteenth century and before. They were the Skagit Indian bands living farthest upriver, their villages scattered from the vicinity of today's Marblemount upstream on the Cascade River to near the mouth of Irene Creek, and upstream on the Skagit River to Newhalem. Little more is known about these people, but no doubt they are the descendants of those who smoked salmon at Goodell Creek hundreds of years ago.

The Miskaiwhu at Goodell Creek knew when the fish would be there, when the river would yield them. They knew much about the climatic muscle of the Cascades, and their vast experience of this place, if we could tap it, would tell us much about coping with that muscle. Our weather and flood records of a mere century are a start, but from archaeology we can gain more understanding of how to live with the powerful forces here. We are learning more about these Miskaiwhu who lived around Newhalem. We know they hunted mountain goats in these mountains 1,400 years ago, they carved decorative objects from the local varieties of Skagit soapstone, and they shaped wood with sharply ground adze blades. They manufactured some of their arrow tips from obsidian outcrops located in the surrounding mountains, yet they made others from obsidian taken from today's central Oregon hundreds of miles to the south. Remains of their ancient campsites and artifacts have been found throughout the adjacent mountains, well above tree line. Archaeology demonstrates, much to our surprise, that these early people traveled all over this rugged and, in our view, inhospitable landscape. They knew how to make their living from it.

But what happened to the Miskaiwhu? At the Port Elliott Treaty of January 22, 1855, convened by the territorial governor, Isaac Stevens, their chief, Ki-ya-hud, refused to sign. The Miskaiwhu band, as a member of an independent nation, never willingly gave its homeland to the territorial government that Stevens represented. As explained by Martin Sampson, "Early in the 1890s the remaining members of the upper river tribes, the Mis-skai-whwu and the Sauk people, under the leadership of Captain Moses Tiatmus and Chief Jim Brown, settled in the Suiattle Valley."[2] Today's Miskaiwhu descendants, along with those of the other ten Skagit River bands, continue to reside in their traditional Skagit River and Sauk River Valley homeland.

❖ Mountain Terrain ❖

The Miskaiwhu, as with all other Indian bands native to the Pacific Northwest, subsisted as foragers by fishing, hunting, and gathering from the variety of natural resources available in diverse environments. Societies that subsist through foraging, distinct from agricultural or industrial economies, are closely adjusted to natural cycles in the seasonal abundance and geographic distribution of the resources they rely on for food, clothing, shelter, tools, and medicines. As a result, each band or village necessarily develops an intimate knowledge of the natural history of its home territory, and accommodates itself to ecological conditions affecting its survival.

This means, also, that the economic adaptation of each band possesses unique qualities mirroring the particular environmental characteristics of its home territory. Given this dependency of foraging bands on their environment, we might expect great variability in how bands of the prehistoric past have adapted to the North Cascades. In this regard, one of the fascinating subjects of archaeological inquiry in the Pacific Northwest is the discovery of the sequence of cultural adaptations and transformations in Native societies during the changing climates of the last 11,000 years and across the diversity of Northwest landscapes. For the North Cascades, we are challenged to learn about human–environment interactions from the first inhabitants, whom Henry Custer (himself a mountaineer from the Swiss Alps) characterized as "true mountain Indians."

My interest in mountain people and their relationship to the North Cascades environment began about the same time that I initiated coursework toward a doctoral degree in anthropology. At the time, there was little known about human use of high-elevation and interior landscapes of the Cascade Range or other Pacific Northwest mountain ranges—they were prehistoric *terrae incognitae*. This is not surprising because the interest of professional anthropology and archaeology has historically focused on lowland, riverine, and coastal environments. There was no viable notion of Native mountain cultures—the recognition that some Native American groups might be so mountain oriented as to deviate from the classic characterizations of Northwest Coast or Columbia Plateau culture types. Although a few archaeologists had worked previously in the North Cascades, only a handful of prehistoric sites had been found and documented. The combined wisdom gleaned from ethnographic and historic documents was hardly better, with much of it contradictory. Yet, humans are known to have inhabited all but the most severe climatic zones of the world. I felt the urge to acquire a familiarity with the mountains that can only come from living and working in them, and walking on the ground of the Miskaiwhu and numerous other bands. In a sense, pursuing my degree had been getting in the way of my education; I left graduate school and moved to the North Cascades.

Although all cultures leave signs of their presence in the earth, the signs can be difficult to find and decipher. Tangible remains of pre-A.D. 1750 foraging cultures of the densely forested Cascades are, most often, concealed by vegetation. At their most subtle, the remains are visible, for example, as a handful of sharp-edged, flaked stone pieces marking a hunting station used a few thousand years ago. Occasionally the evidence is conspicuous, as at quarries where the ground surface is piled with shattered stone and broken hammerstones, or at pictographs along Lake Chelan, the most prominent of which is an array of figures guarding the mouth of the Stehekin River. Doing archaeology in these mountains, as I learned in the systematic searches I began in the 1980s, was strenuous—the ground yielded signs only to much patience and sweat. Soon, the demands of the work itself became the lesson. Places like this exact much from their human occupants, no less of archaeologists or hikers than of the early people whose paths we follow.

One dimension of the North Cascades that affects all who travel there, now or in earlier times, is terrain. By *terrain* I mean not just the ground we walk on, but the surrounding topography and all that grows and resides on it. All terrestrial mammals, including humans, must cope with the variables of terrain, and as we study how this coping has occurred we understand the adaptations, social and otherwise, of many species. For foraging human beings, and later non-Indian explorers, trappers, miners, and modern travelers such as tourists and archaeologists, the challenge has been how to move themselves and whatever they valued through deep, rocky gorges, around cliffs, and over high passes in snow, rain, wind, heat, and cold. All who would travel here must experiment with the many subtleties underfoot—rock slope and texture, hardness of snow and tenacity of brush, and with prodigious barriers of fallen old-growth tree trunks, and cliff faces, and raging streams. The prehistory and history of travel across this landscape is revisited through labor and exertion. For well-being, we all learn to choose terrain that requires the least amount of energy expenditure now, saving some for later. It is best not to rush, or to expect too much. Alexander Ross expected it would be easier, and I consider his July 29, 1814 comment an historic awakening to the North Cascades terrain. His first-recorded, trans-Cascades crossing was an unpleasant experience. Heading west, descending into Bridge Creek Valley from the Tw isp River Valley, he wrote, " . . . forests almost impervious, with fallen as well as standing timber. A more difficult route to travel never fell to man's lot. . . . The surface of the earth appeared in perfect confusion; and the rocks and yawning chasms gave the whole an air of solemn gloom and undisturbed silence."[3]

We are, in a sense, taught how to behave by the environment we encounter in a place like these mountains. The lessons learned by ancient travelers, or explorers like Ross, differ from those that come to travelers today. Our notions about travel through the North Cascades reflect our experiences, each varying according to our mode of locomotion, be it along Highway 20 at 50 miles per hour, or above in a jetliner approaching Sea-Tac Airport, or from hiking a trail. These experiences forge a perception and context through which we assess our own and others' capabilities in traveling these mountains. For most, hiking today in the Pacific Northwest is done across a landscape of maintained trails, with designated campsites, freeze-dried foods, high-tech camping gear, and most recently, a radio backup. We are destined to perceive terrain and to cognitively map the landscape differently, each according to our experience. How different from the modern perspective is that of a forager, especially one who traveled lightly with simple gear made from plant and animal materials, and used stone tools; a traveler who manufactured and repaired

*Old cottonwood near
the Cascade River*

gear along the way, and used inherited, ancient cultural recipes and wisdom for preparation of food and medicines acquired from the immediate environment. We should remind ourselves that, regardless of ethnic or cultural heritage, we all descended from forager ancestors mentored by wilderness terrains.

In considering what prehistoric travel and camping in the North Cascades must have been like, we must look at the social and technological strategies humans devise to get across terrain. We are foremost a species of terrestrial travelers. For simplicity, envision two extremes that encompass the full range of accommodations made by traveling parties to achieve certain levels of mobility. Social considerations often include age, gender, kinship, and purpose of the trip. Material considerations include the supplies and gear needed to sustain the traveling party, anticipated modes of travel, and any surpluses. A knowledge of the terrain is a highly valued commodity.

The first kind of traveling party is the slowest and most secure of the two. It consists of a foraging group characterized by mixed gender and age—members of nuclear and extended families, grandparents to grandchildren—who come together to spend a part of the summer to get berries, roots, trout, and basket materials, and to hunt deer, elk, bear, and birds. Such groups must have traveled with deliberation, most often choosing the paths of least resistance, with careful selection of overnight camps. They carried with them most of the tools for processing resources, and baskets and leather bags for gathering and transporting what they processed. Always important was the need to be opportunistic, be it for the chance encounter with a herd of elk or to heed an abrupt weather change forcing a bivouac for extra days. For such a group, the rate of travel was unimportant; cooking, consuming, or packaging the products of hunting, gathering, or fishing forays were of primary importance. So also was the passing to younger generations of traditional knowledge carried by the elders.

Much in contrast, the second kind of traveling party is small and highly mobile, carrying relatively little gear. Such a party consists of one or a few members, spanning one or two generations, with gender composition dependent on the purpose of the trip. A group of women, for example, depart a base camp in the river valley, ascend a ridgeline a few thousand feet to subalpine meadows, where they collect wild lily bulbs and medicinal plants, returning to their camp in the evening. Or a husband and wife travel over Cascade Pass to visit relatives, carrying dried food and gear sufficient for them to move steadily between any suitable overnight stops along the way. If they carry too much, and find that their snowshoes are not needed, they cache them under a pile of rocks in talus, awaiting the return trip.

A war party constitutes another kind of travel party. In actuality, there existed any number of travel party combinations, each accommodated to purpose and terrain, and exploiting a large social and technological repertoire of adaptive techniques. Consider mats, for example: made by sewing together or weaving reeds, they were used to line canoes, as bedding, to cover gear, and to cover huts; a rolled mat was a ubiquitous traveling item.[4] For mountain travel, leather clothing provided the most protection against thick brush. For descending steep snow slopes, a stick dragged in the snow was used to control the slide (long before today's equivalent glissade with ice axe!). Much of the archaeological record in the North Cascades reflects human involvement with terrain, which leaves telltale signs in the discarded stone tools used for manufacture and repair of gear, and the abandoned hearths where food was prepared and consumed.

The interaction of humans and terrain is apt to leave its mark in diverse ways. An archaeologist studies each terrain to reveal the combination of events that express the unique cultural and geological history of a place. All places are part of a cultural landscape. In the core of the North Cascades, strewn about the mountainsides above today's Ross Lake, is a cultural landscape marked by prehistoric rock quarries used for thousands of years by various Indian bands. The variety of quartz from these quarries, called chert, was used to manufacture an assortment of tools for cutting, piercing, scraping, drilling, and engraving. In the decade since the discovery of these quarries, this Hozomeen chert has been found in archaeological sites throughout the region. It was well known for millennia to all the bands who visited the North Cascades. Artifacts made from it were carried by these people to the head of Lake Chelan, across Cascade Pass, and to Puget Sound. There is a geography in these chert tools, scattered across a part of the Cascades, that validates only one of a myriad of cultural landscapes of the past. As further validation, a linguistic fragment of this landscape endures today as the word *Hozomeen*, which is derived from the Nlakɑpamux (Lower Thompson) language, and means "sharp, like a knife."[5] Now it names a mountain, a lake, a creek, and the stone that was used to make knives.

Our investigations showed that the quarries had been worked for at least 8,000 years, with the heaviest use occurring between 5,000 and 3,500 years ago. At the largest of these quarries, five distinctive terrain types revealed how the quarry was used. The most common terrain here is the steep, forested, brush-covered slopes where the stoneworkers searched for usable boulders of chert. Another terrain is bumpy and bouldery where an earthslide buried a 4,500-year-old workshop in which the chert was shaped into rough, unfinished blanks; other workshops are on small flats here and there on the mountainside. A smooth bedrock overlook served as an overnight campsite 300 years ago. But the most conspicuous terrain is one whose origin is due exclusively to human activity. It consists of thick deposits left over from cleaning and shaping chert fragments. In one place this debris measured 6 feet deep—a tightly packed mass of discarded chert, hammerstones, and broken tools, all mixed together with small pockets of soft, dusty sand of the Holocene. The radiocarbon age of the charcoal from this depth is 7,600 years old; this is the oldest date from an archaeological site anywhere in the North Cascades.[6]

The origin of the dust and sand is uncertain, but it may derive from a period when the Pacific Northwest climate was warmer and drier than any time since written records have been kept. The evidence for climatic changes during the span of time that people used the quarry is irrefutable. In rhythm with the climate, the terrain changed, but the people continued to come for the chert. We have yet to understand the extent to which mountain lifestyles were affected by the changed climate and why use of the quarry seems to have accelerated starting about 5,000 years ago. Only in the last couple of hundred years was the quarry abandoned, its stone replaced with metal introduced by people from across the oceans.

❖ Holocene Cultural Landscapes ❖

A most engrossing problem in Northwest archaeology involves tracing the evolution of cultural adaptations, which are woven through a fabric of changing Holocene landscapes. This word *Holocene* is applied to the last 10,000 or so years to denote the time period following the retreat of glacial ice that had covered Puget Sound and most of the North Cascades. Although the Holocene persists to the present, it has experienced climatic shifts that by today's standards are dynamic. Just as dramatic are the configurations that cultures have adopted in response to landscape changes initiated by major climatic events. The Native foraging adaptations observed by the first European people are not the same as those of 3,000 or 10,000 years ago. Instead, there occurred successive transformations in the cultural relationships among bands, to each other, and to their environments.

One of the most fascinating of these cultural phenomena occurred as the Holocene began—the initial occupation and exploration of the Pacific Northwest by nomadic hunters in the newly deglaciated landscape. The Pacific Northwest at the close of the last ice age sustained herds of now-extinct herbivores, including elephants (mammoths and mastodons) and buffalo (more correctly, bison), that in turn supported sizeable populations of large predators, including wolves, cats, and bear.[7] The land was open, much of it nurturing steppe and savannah, and at higher elevations, a patchwork of conifer forest and tundra; the large old-growth forests of today did not exist.[8] Not surprisingly, subalpine and alpine areas of the North Cascades are the closest modern analogs we have to experience what it must have felt like to travel through such a landscape.

These first nomadic hunters are an enigma in the evolution of Cascade mountain cultures. An astounding discovery was made in 1987 in an East Wenatchee orchard, tucked down in the lowlands along the southeast foothills of the North Cascades. Only a few feet below ground level, packed in the sand-swept top of a late-glacial riverbed, was an undisturbed cache of bone and stone tools of Clovis hunters—*Clovis* being the name given by archaeologists to one of the earliest documented

New World cultures—who roamed North America between 10,500 and 12,000 years ago. Their bone tools, of uncertain function, had been made from the leg bones of mammoth. Stone knives, spear points, and scrapers had been shaped from gemlike, brightly colored agates. The distinctive Clovis knives and points from this site are the largest known to North America, and there is no such Clovis site recorded elsewhere in Washington. Yet, the widespread presence of these people is marked by a scatter of isolated Clovis points found here and there, on either side of the Cascades, suggesting they hunted across the range. A single Clovis point found on the ground near Cle Elum supports this suggestion.[9] A characteristic of the Clovis lifestyle was great mobility. Individual bands traveled many hundreds of miles across vast areas of land. Another is the gemlike quality of rock types they used, and the workmanship of the tools made from them. What happened to the Clovis people is unknown, and their relationship to subsequent Pacific Northwest cultures is a mystery. All that is certain is that, with the extinction of the large, late-glacial herbivores, this specialized hunting economy did not sustain itself. These hunters were probably the first to visit the North Cascades wilderness.

Following Clovis, a more diversified hunting lifestyle persisted for thousands of years. Native cultures of the Cascades between 5,000 and 10,000 years ago subsisted in a climate significantly drier and warmer than now, unlike any modern equivalent. It was a time when the relative positions of the sun and earth were skewed by today's standards, resulting in warmer summers and colder winters.[10] Early Holocene forests west of the Cascade Crest were open and parklike, with large prairies and savannah, a favorable environment for herds of ungulates such as deer and elk and the foragers who hunted them. Archaeologists have struggled in their attempts to understand this cultural pattern because of poor preservation of the sites they occupied. Time, weathering, and all the processes that scar the Earth's surface have ravaged these sites left by small, nomadic groups of people. They hunted and gathered the year around, with no reliance on stored food. Their residences were small and temporary, leaving relatively little in the ground for study but tools of stone: spears, knives, scrapers, hammerstones, and the debris from their manufacture. Although their overall population density was low, groups practicing this economy left sign across the whole range of landscapes—coastal, mountain, and intermountain. By 5,000 or so years ago, they began to adopt strategies fine-tuned to specific marine, riverine, grassland, and montane ecosystems. A major cultural revolution was beginning.

Prior to 6,000 years ago, old-growth Douglas-fir and hemlock forests did not exist in the Pacific Northwest, but since a cooler and wetter climate set in 5,000 years ago, prairies have shrunk in the Puget lowlands at the same time alpine glaciers have enlarged in the North Cascades, and continuous forest has extended for the first time across most of the Pacific slopes of the Cascades. Adjusting to population growth and a decrease in prime ungulate habitat, foraging peoples resorted to entirely new social accommodations, and the relationships between culture and environment were transformed. The most fundamental change was from a nomadic lifestyle to one that was much more sedentary, along with a heavy reliance on stored food for winter survival.

To better understand this change, compress the last 11,000 years of cultural activity into a ten-minute time lapse, and these last few minutes will appear to erupt in a frenzy of human activity. The Northwest soilscape today is littered with the physical remains of this Holocene legacy, encompassing a fluorescence of technologies unlike any before. These remains include the first substantial dwellings, large shell middens, cooking pits and campfires, and storage facilities. Large villages and communities appeared. Populations adopted a wider variety of social and cultural accommodations, many of them typical of complex cultures, including class and rank, craft specialization, and sophisticated art styles. Exchange was intensified; foods, utensils, raw materials, shell money, and slaves became items of commerce. The landscape became more intensively lived on, with more people subsisting on a wider range of resources from within a smaller geographic space. Viewed across the entire Holocene, the relative recentness of this sedentary lifestyle renders its remains more visible, closer to the surface, less altered by the past, and yet more susceptible to the earth-moving ravages of the present. In the North Cascades, much of the mountain terrain where such Holocene cultural transformations took place is preserved underneath magnificent mountain forests, designated wilderness by an act of Congress. Ironically, the complexities of eleven millennia of human habitation on the landscape were far removed from the legal minds that established this wilderness.

Finally we reach the brief period in this landscape known as recorded history, which begins with seafaring expeditions of the eighteenth century. This period marks the most revolutionary transformation in Native cultures of the New World. From an anthropological perspective, prehistory ended when old-world peoples entered the Pacific Northwest in force, beginning about A.D. 1780, just in the last 15 seconds of the time-compressed Holocene. Shortly thereafter the cultural landscape underwent one of the most dramatic transformations seen in recent world history. The Pacific Northwest is richly endowed with historic documents, written and photographic, of the ensuing colonization and upheaval of Native cultures. So endowed too are the earth's ancient landforms, where introduced technologies and exotic adaptations must necessarily leave their droppings, curated within the topsoil. First to appear are iron and glass artifacts in the form of knives and trade beads, thimbles, bells, brass buttons, horse bones, lead balls, and Indian mass burials, followed somewhat later by tin and ceramic, cans and cookware, chisels and gold pans, plows and harness buckles—and on to the artifacts of the present.

❖ Wilderness Past and Present ❖

During his 1850s travels through the Cascades, George Gibbs was a keen observer of Native peoples and terrain. Although he saw only a fleeting part of this major cultural transformation, his record of the interaction of the Native people with the North Cascades environment are precious. Most revealing, in my view, are his direct observations from the 1850s about the effects of European trade on travel and trails in the mountains:

> In former times, before the diminution of the tribes and the diversion of trade to the posts, there were numerous trails across the Cascades by which the Indians of the interior obtained access to the western district. Of late, many of these have fallen into disuse, becoming obstructed with timber and underbrush. . . . In fact all their trails through the forest, though originally well selected, have become excessively tortuous, an Indian riding around the fallen trunks of tree after tree sooner than clear out a road which he seldom uses.[11]

In essence, Gibbs recognized a relatively subtle effect on the mountain terrain after hardly 100 years of European contact. His use of "riding" was certainly intended, as by this time Indian people from both sides of the Cascades were regularly crossing the crest on horseback. One who did this, in August 1882, was explorer Henry Pierce, who came up the Stehekin River Valley and over Cascade Pass; he descended the Cascade River to the site of today's Marblemount. Here, the party was ferried across the Skagit River in the dugout canoes of an elderly Indian and his family. Pierce recorded the reaction of the Indians to his arrival:

> They refused at first to believe that we had arrived from the summit, the old man, apparently 70 years of age, claiming that he had never seen a white man go or come that way, and that it was impossible for any one but an Indian to keep the trail.[12]

This statement provides us with a cultural metaphor for past and present wilderness—Native American and European. Barely 100 years after these thoughts about "keeping the trail" were expressed, and with little awareness that the land had a prior cultural heritage, a new nation's government designated the land wilderness because it was perceived as "unspoiled by the hand of Man." To my knowledge, there is no Salish linguistic combination comparable to *wilderness*. It is unlikely a linguistic counterpart would have been necessary, considering that the entire Northwest cultural landscape, extending far beyond the Cascade mountains, had evolved in response to wilderness ecosystems over the previous 11,000 years. If we truly seek to understand wilderness, we must become open to the existence of many past cultural landscapes, and we must regain the knowledge of lost ethnoecologies built on a heritage of wilderness living.

My archaeological explorations of this landscape yield many lessons, but the most important involves scale of human activity, and it is widely overlooked by people who today interact with the North Cascades. The lesson is that the scale of human population here and manipulation of the landscape determine how we understand the nature of this place. When foraging people lived on this land, their numbers were low and their impacts minor. Today, though few live on the landscape and know it intimately, the scale of human activity around it, and the perception of it as a natural resource, have effected profound change. For 11,000 years human alteration of the landscape was minimal—a quarry, path, village, or fishing site here and there. But in the past 100 years the scale of human activity has grown, and the cumulative effects of our industrial technology have altered fundamental components of the ecosystem. The water, forests, wildlife communities, even the air have been profoundly changed. Natural events such as floods, droughts, wildfires, and earthquakes have taken on new significance as population density has grown. People have coped with such events for over ten millennia, but today the scale has changed. Our relationship with the landscape is more uneasy than it has ever been.

Wilderness keeps open a window to the past. Considering terrain, in another way, links past and present wildernesses, if only because traveling through it appeals to our direct experiences. And we need to experience it lest we forget our hominid upbringing, for no matter who we are and where our ancestors came from, we are all descended from foraging peoples adapted to the Earth's surface. From infancy, each of us is equipped by heritage with the ability to "map on" to the terrain immediately surrounding us. To experience travel in the North Cascades wilderness is a realization that natural landscapes are where humans can reaffirm an innate awareness and appreciation for the ecological complexities of plant and animal communities in which we hold a lifelong membership. Traveling across North Cascades terrains dictates that we will adhere to the rules imposed on us by forest, slope, and glacier. There is a universality to the human living experience in this landscape, for it transcends time and culture.

❖ Old Earth ❖

Along the Skagit River, near my house, I walk about on new brown sand dropped by the November 1995 flood. Unlike the 1990 floods, this one advanced and peaked so quickly, and so much snowmelt flushed down the mountainsides, that it carried trees, gravels, and soil together. Although the fall's leaves on this day lie thick on the floor of forests above the flood level, hours after the flood subsided I stroll the floodplain on a soft carpet of sand, its thickness leveling the uneven forest floor in some places, and in others mounding streamlined sandbars. This new terrain is hardly 24 hours old, with not an autumn leaf visible on the fresh sand ripples. Salmon parts and carcasses are strewn about and dangle from branches above the ground, imparting an overriding aroma to the scene. The wet leaves hang like laundry on the branches of alder and salmonberry, marking the height of the flood waters, over 6 feet above the forest floor. I begin to feel this is only a subtle reminder of the magnitude of floods of the prehistoric past.

I think of the Miskaiwhu people, for it would be to our great benefit to know their experiences with the great floods. Such floods are believed to have occurred during the Little Ice Age, a climatic event that, glaciologists tell us, began sometime in the fourteenth century and lasted for roughly 500 years. Our modern climate records, upon which many land-use plans and decisions are based, were compiled after the Little Ice Age had ended, about A.D. 1850. Around the world, high mountain regions at this time, including the North Cascades and the European Alps, experienced a significant expansion of alpine glaciers, in some cases a greater expansion than any time since the beginning of the Holocene. Historic records from European mountain communities indicate that the magnitude and frequency of Little Ice Age floods and avalanches far exceeded those of modern and medieval times. No doubt the same occurred in the North Cascades, where the Miskaiwhu ancestors thrived, and buried beneath the sands deposited by Little Ice Age streams are the ancient soils upon which they dried and smoked salmon. We have much to learn. We must not, as a culture, treat the brief snapshot of the last hundred years as representative of what environments always were, or will be. We must look more at the ground.

BOB MIERENDORF is a National Park Service archaeologist and has been working in North Cascades National Park since 1987. His work has drastically changed thinking about the interactions of prehistoric peoples with the North Cascades landscape. He is a specialist in the adaptations of mountain peoples.

A Home for the Spirits

An Interview with

VI HILBERT

Vi Hilbert (*taqʷsəblu*) was born in 1918 to Louise and Charley Anderson, traditional Skagit and Upper Skagit Indians. She attended over a dozen schools, including the Chemawa and Tulalip boarding schools, and later worked in Portland, Seattle, Tacoma, Tahola, and Everson. After meeting the linguist Thomas Hess in 1967, Vi Hilbert devoted her life to preserving and teaching Salish culture, including Lushootseed, her native tongue. Hilbert taught courses in Lushootseed for fifteen years at the University of Washington, published a Salish dictionary, and translated two volumes of stories, titled *Haboo*,[1] plus several volumes of oral history.

Writings About Vi Hilbert,[2] a collection of essays edited by Janet Koder, pays tribute to Hilbert and reveals her influence on others. For further reading, several other books of note provide background information about Skagit Indian culture, including Annie Dillard's *The Living*,[3] Wayne Suttles's scholarly *West Coast Salish Essays*,[4] June M. Collins's *Valley of the Spirits: The Upper Skagit Indians*,[5] and Nels Bruseth's *Indian Stories and Legends of the Stillaguamish, Sauks and Allied Tribes*.[6]

Bob Keller interviewed Hilbert at her Seattle home on March 21, 1996.

Bob Keller: How did you learn Lushootseed?

Vi Hilbert: Well, my parents spoke it and all of their friends spoke it.

Keller: Was it your first language?

Hilbert: Oh, yes. My mother had eight children and I was the only one who lived. So I went everywhere with them and that was part of my training. You don't run around outside and play—"You come with us and you sit right there and you listen." No nonsense allowed.[7] This meant discipline and listening skills. I was obliged, I didn't have any choice, and I knew it. Sometimes it was pretty boring, hour after hour after hour, but every now and then something important would be said that's still in my computer. When people push my mental buttons, it just comes out, important Lushootseed words left for me to pass on.

Keller: Where did you grow up?

Hilbert: We lived up and down the Skagit River, every place my dad could find a job in a logging camp or put a short net in the river.[8] We never had a home. We lived hither and yon in chicken houses and empty garages, any kind of a shack with a roof over it. My mother could make any place home, always a nice one because she never complained about it. We didn't have money but I never felt poor. My dad's little leather coin purse had all the money we lived on. I saw paper bills once in a blue moon but most of the time it was silver coins. I always had access to that leather coin purse: "Can I count our money, Dad?"

Keller: Where was your parents' traditional homeland?

Hilbert: All the territory up and down the Skagit River, the mountains, the river and its tributaries all the way down to the saltwater.

Keller: North into Canada?

Hilbert: They knew their territory. They went over the mountains into Yakima and Lake Chelan. Some of Dad's people were from Chelan who knew that trail as well as they knew the river because they went back and forth so often.

Keller: Can you describe their route through the mountains?

Hilbert: Beats me. It was something I never asked my dad about, but he told my husband. When Dad used a wagon he had to take it apart and carry it over the steep places. Dad could describe every important landmark, special trees, and what was in the lake. In order not to get lost, my dad had to memorize the space. I didn't get that gift, never had to, because self-preservation never made me find my way in the forest.

Keller: What places in the Skagit country especially stood out for your people?

Hilbert: Well, Ilabot Creek was my dad's territory. His father had a longhouse at Hamilton, as did four or five other leading men. Hamilton was sort of headquarters for his group, but they went up beyond Rockport, too.[9]

Keller: How did your people travel back then?

Hilbert: By canoe. Dad was a canoe carver who made many, many river canoes as I grew up.

Keller: Let's discuss the natural environment and its role in traditional culture. First, the river. How did Skagits like your father and mother look upon the river? How did they think and feel about it?

Hilbert: We always considered the river a living and a home. It's our highway. It's home for the spirits that we access. It's important as a pantry, a highway, and as a living being.

Keller: A pantry?

Hilbert: A food source, a spiritual source, a road.

Keller: How is a river spiritual?

Hilbert: Well, anything with life also has spirit. My people have been given access to that knowledge. It's one of the things that remains a mystery for Europeans and always will, because we will never try to explain it.

Keller: Has that changed today?

Hilbert: No, no! The reverence is still very, very beautiful. It touched me deeply this year when I joined the tribe as they did a blessing for the fishery. This is something that they observe at the beginning of the season when a prayer is said for fishermen and for the fishery itself. Spiritual people went out on the water with plates of food to thank the spirits that live there.

Keller: If the river is so friendly, how did your people react to the floods?

Hilbert: A Lummi friend said that the Skagit was ugly, was always going over its banks. Well, it never flooded while we lived on it. My parents were not afraid because they understood the river so well. My dad could tell what was underneath by just looking at the surface and the motion of the current. He understood. If it was about to rain when we were near the river, we'd just move back. It was never a big deal to my family.

Keller: Were forests as important as the river?

Hilbert: Trees have life. They have spirit, so they're embodied with something that we revere. Our people will go into the forest to talk to the trees and there is a camaraderie that is very real because the trees are so ancient. If they have been left to grow long enough they can communicate with us.

Keller: Are certain trees more important than others?

Hilbert: Of course. The cedar, naturally, is one of our most precious trees. Now they're so few. It's pitiful that the entire Skagit Valley used to be a forest of cedar trees that were cut down and burned because they stood in the way.

Keller: I assume that your father used cedar for his canoes.

Hilbert: Yes. And he always chose a female cedar. I asked, "Why, Dad? Why a female?" " 'Cause the grain is finest so it would be stronger." How could he tell, I asked. "By the bark, of course." I've asked forestry people if they can point out a female tree. "No." See if you can find out how to identify one. The female cedar probably has different cones.

Keller: Do you recall going into the old stands?

Hilbert: Oh yes, we lived up in the Rockport/Darrington area where I used to walk to school, walked to the school in Darrington during wintertime and I remember how desperately cold it was. The snow would get deep, colder than anyplace else, and my mother would wake up real early in the morning and put potatoes in the oven to bake, then she would put her hand-knit wool socks over my shoes and put hot baked potatoes in my coat pockets for hand warmers. My wool socks would gather up a lot of snow until I'd be walking ten inches taller by the time I got to school. It was beautiful in the trees even if I had to walk in the cold.

Keller: How does the area seem to you today?

Hilbert: I haven't been back there since I was a girl in school. When I was three years old my mother took me to a hot spring. My dad was on the Baker River in charge of a boat crew and my mother was a cook for the crew. In her spare time—I don't know how in the world she ever found any spare time—she walked me to a hot spring and put me in. She didn't get in herself, but she put me in. She wanted me to have that experience.[10] I did go back there with a cousin for a television program.

Keller: What were the most important native plants in the Skagits' territory?

Hilbert: My mom utilized everything in the forest that she could gather because we had no money. She knew what to gather for vegetables along the streams, something that she used for greens, like a spinach. She would steam them and it was yummy. Then she would pick fern fronds when they were newly coming up, then sprouts from different berries. Many things were used for medicinal purposes. If Dad or I had a problem, we'd go out to gather medicine. Mom learned this from her parents, but everyone knew, it was just common knowledge.

Keller: Did she use nettles?

Hilbert: Oh, certainly. My mother took nettles and rubbed them all over her skin. I couldn't do that, but she could.

Keller: What did your people think about mountains, the high peaks to the east?

Hilbert: It is part of the spirituality of our people that the isolated areas, places uncontaminated by other humans, are where you found the strongest spiritual help. The mountain goat, for example, could give you some very strong spiritual help.

Keller: Did people go in groups?

Hilbert: No! No! They went one at a time and isolated themselves and called on the spirits for help.

Keller: How long?

Hilbert: Each person, each family, had a different set of secret rules. There was no one way people were sent out to quest. Every family gave directions and instructions to the young people, then kind of checked on them. If the vision and the spirit revealed itself, the young person could come home and the family would know it had been successful. Some people never received spirit help.

Keller: Well, if they went where mountain goats lived, they certainly climbed to high elevations and reached inaccessible places.

Hilbert: Yes, and they also hunted goats for food.

Keller: They didn't consider that inconsistent or irreverent?

Hilbert: No, the Creator gave us ways to utilize the animals that He had given life to. We spoke to animals who were created for food so their lives were honored; their spirits would be addressed and prayed for, and we would ask for permission to take their life. It was very honorable. We never, ever did things for "sport."

Keller: From what you say about the vision quest and about your father crossing the North Cascades to Lake Chelan, it seems that native people were not fearful of mountains or mountain spirits, as has been said of the Olympics and about Yellowstone National Park, as a way for whites to justify taking the land. It's been claimed that Indians never used it, that they were afraid of wild areas.

Hilbert: You see, this is how the English language gets people in trouble. Reverence and fear are sometimes thought to be synonymous, but the reverence that we feel for life and nature is something akin to respect. Some people just don't know about it.

Keller: You've already mentioned the role of salmon in your culture as a food source. But what else?

Hilbert: Salmon were people. They were always thought of as people, as tribes of people given life so that we might live. They were created to be food for us and it was never a casual thing to take the life of a salmon. It was something I lived with while growing up. Anytime my dad could catch one salmon and bring it home, there was joy in the home and a reverence in this act of taking a salmon from the river to our house. My mother never took it for granted. She would greet that salmon with the affection of a newborn child sometimes. Anytime I watched my parents respect that gift, I felt that it was coming to us from the earth. You never take it for granted. Every bit of that salmon was used.

Keller: Eagles?

Hilbert: Eagles have vision. They were much respected because of vision. If people were lucky enough to receive the spirit of the eagle, why, they became very, very powerful medicine. With that vision they could find the illness of the patient. The same with the owl, vision that the owl had because he could turn his head all the way around.

Keller: Elk and bear?

Hilbert: Elk were revered because they brought food to many people and their hides were respected by all because they made good warm covers. Bears were abundant, but not something that my dad hunted because they were one of his spirit guides. Other people did. My mother would never eat it because she knew it was my dad's spirit guide.

Keller: All bears, including the grizzly?

Hilbert: I don't recall seeing a grizzly. I saw lots of brown bear. When out on the Baker River, my mother and I wandered quite often in the woods because she loved to explore. I was never afraid, my mother was never afraid that some animal might pounce out and kill us. There were cougars and bobcats as well, and they too were part of my dad's spirit guides.

Keller: Let's see, any animal could be a spirit guide and that's part of what a person needed to discover in the mountains.

Hilbert: Correct, but not only animals. Inanimate things—trees, bushes, the wind, the water. There's no end to gifts. My Aunt Susie[11] talks about the power of a spirit guide that's in two tree limbs rubbing together. The raccoon, of course, was quite plentiful and the skunk, some grouse. My dad was a good shot and could spot grouse to bring home wonderful meat for our table.

Keller: So you think that Upper Skagits today, especially young people, have these attitudes?

Hilbert: I hear it anytime people get together. I hear the reverence for all these things that have been a part of our culture, and it's taught in the home and it's lived in the home.

Keller: How do you compare European attitudes toward nature with those of Skagits?

Hilbert: It's pitiful. I say that because people are so ignorant, and I mean that in all of its implications. They haven't taken time to understand how important earth is, how it is to be shared, because it's been grabbed. "This is mine! And now you can't have it." The area where my dad's longhouse sat is now fenced off: "PRIVATE PROPERTY, KEEP OUT!" and that was very hurtful when I went there this year to film the documentary. But we went near and I said I want my children and my friends to know that we're as close as we can get to the place of their grandfather's longhouse and where all the leaders of the Skagit tribe at one time gathered. A fence says we can't even step into that property. And that doesn't feel fair to me. I was taught never to hold bitterness or anger because it's counterproductive. It only reflects back on myself. But I *can* speak that. It's a fact! I don't need to be angry about it, only it feels sad. But when I say that the Europeans are ignorant about what importance land has to native people, I mean that they don't know the history of how respected every bit of this land is, how it has a memory for us. It has a sacredness that's important to us. The Creator gave us access to knowledge about the spirits of the land that was given life, and a lot of people were given access to how to use those spirits. This is something that Europeans will never know. They have no respect for the land, therefore it could never be revealed to them.

Keller: Given that, how do you feel about logging or dams?

Hilbert: Sacrilege! It's just sacrilegious. People do not think seven generations ahead as my people have always been advised to do. What effect is our action going to have seven generations from now? What will result from acting like this? Very wise people made that rule of thumb many years ago. I heard a statement from a wise, wise speaker, Russell Jim of the Yakima Tribe, at a conference. He said, "You have to constantly protect yourselves from the logic of the uninformed." I thought, boy, that's beautiful, so elegant, and exactly what we mean when we say people don't think, when they have a tiny bit of information and not the whole picture.

Keller: One thing which white people and Indians share is love of hunting. Do Europeans hunt differently than your father did?

Hilbert: They're out hunting for sport, not because they're hungry and not because they can't buy something at a supermarket. It's sport. It was not sport to my people. It was survival. Sure, the first people can do things wrong also—I've seen that. Once I was allowed to join a hunt on the Quinault Reservation. We paddled up the Quinault River in a canoe. Now these were Indian people, for it's not only Europeans who do things wrong. These hunters told us where to go and wait on the river, a certain place where the deer was going to come out and cross the water. So, all right, we sat quietly by the side of the river in the bushes and I heard dogs barking and pretty soon a frightened doe jumps out of the forest and heads for the stream. I stood up and started screaming at the deer: "Run, run! Get away, go away!" It didn't get shot—that time, anyway. The man with the dogs was absolutely furious. I didn't care. I thought it was ugly, nothing fair about it. An animal needs a chance.

Keller: What are your opinions about the North Cascades National Park and the Park Service?

Hilbert: I hope there might always be beautiful, pristine areas so that my great-great-grandchildren could come and see moss growing on a tree, see wildflowers growing in a forest. I want something here forever, some giant old-growth trees allowed to survive so that their progeny could give life to all the things in a forest. Parks are needed because we must protect ancient trees that are a bosom, the nursemaid which nurtures all other plants and creatures that depend on trees that have existed for centuries. The National Park Service, if it takes the long view of things instead of shortsighted profit, can protect that. I hope it will always be true.

Keller: What changes in this century have most affected your people?

Hilbert: The dams, I think. Dams have done a lot to make our salmon almost a thing of the past. Pulp mills have polluted the water, of course, and logging has done its damage.

Keller: Yet wasn't your father involved in that?

Hilbert: Yes, of course, but people were not aware of how they were affecting rivers by the logging, done in ignorance because most people were too greedy to stop and think about what they did. My dad was a logger. An illiterate person in the academic sense, he couldn't go and fill out an application to get a job anyplace, but he did what he could do and he was good at it. He worked in the logging camps. My mother was illiterate also, but of course intelligence and illiteracy have no correlation. Instead my people had memory and they practiced what they remembered, everything that was important.

Keller: Of all the changes, do you consider dams the most significant for Indians?

Hilbert: I think so. They've decimated our salmon runs. And, of course, the highways. And the diet. Changes in our diet, I think, have had a severe effect on many people. My mother didn't have diabetes and I don't have it, but a lot of our people do.

Keller: A final question: you speak of hopes for great-great-grandchildren. What is your vision of the future, of the Skagit River and the North Cascades? What will happen in the next century?

Hilbert: Had you asked me ten years ago, I would have painted a very bleak picture. But, you know, I have a little hope that more and more sincere people are looking at the damage that has been done and are becoming thoughtfully aware of what can be done to reverse things at this point in time. With cooperative effort by all people, we can indeed make things a little healthier. I doubt that I will ever drink the Skagit River again, like when I was a child, but I think we can certainly make it better than the present if people become more aware. My mother used to take buckets and go places where she found good, sweet springwater. That was nectar. I'm a person with lots of faith that human beings aren't completely stupid. I think we will eventually come to a realization that the end result of greed, of thoughtlessly using up everything, is to cause the human race to disappear. I think it can happen. I really do.

Keller: Thank you very much for meeting with me to share your memories and ideas.

My Place in the Mountains

Jim Harris

❖ From Across the River ❖

My earliest memories, my reference to the rest of the world, were from across the Skagit River beyond the tiny town of Rockport, Washington. That place, framed by the Skagit and Sauk Rivers and the mountains beyond, was the landscape I knew and loved. This bit of the Cascades was my home, a place of security and wonder, a place that fixed the vivid impressions of childhood.

Woodlands and meadows, interspersed with meandering water courses, ran from our log house to the Skagit and Sauk Rivers. I spent boyhood days in this setting, exploring glades and sloughs, reveling in the wildflowers and berries that flourished on loamy river bottoms. This was a time of trusted neighbors and childhood friends. We roamed the woods, swam our first strokes in cold backwaters, and knew the excitement and colors of changing seasons.

Family livelihoods came from logging, small ranches, river, and woods. With "woods savvy," a garden, a cow, and a few fruit trees, there was little need for steady cash incomes. Jars of salmon, venison ("vine maple beef"), and bear meat were hidden away for winter behind the fruit and vegetables. Fresh meat, whether from the pasture, woods, or river, was shared with neighbors. A full root cellar, stacks of firewood, and a barn stuffed with hay were measures of industriousness to ensure wellbeing. I have more bitter memories of the sack of cascara bark put up for our spring tonics.

Our life was centered on the land around us. A walk in the woods or a picnic by the river was a special family event. I remember hunting with my father for a new mother and calf by lantern light on a cold, rainy night. I recall the first time I harnessed the team by myself, standing on the manger, pushing the collar up over Jerry's great head, trying not to pinch his ears. I remember well the feel of sun and showers, the rich, mingling odors of sweating horses, freshly worked soil, and the sweet scent of erupting cottonwood buds as I trudged behind team and harrow. Are these just bits of nostalgia, memories of a more innocent time? In reflection, those experiences were much, much more—they were the weaving of a fiber which still connects me to the land.

We sometimes shared berry patches and overgrown orchards with wild residents. One summer evening I watched from our yard as my older brother toted milk pails down the meadow to the barn. The fun began as a big black bear ambled from the woods toward a wild strawberry patch on a collision course with my brother. It was the best real-life cartoon I ever saw as boy met bear. There were two speed records set that night—my brother bolting for the barn, milk pails clanging, and the bear nearly somersaulting as it woofed and tore for the woods.

Neighbors often dropped by on weekends, and I was delighted when they would stay for the evening. Our log living room with open fireplace was an inviting setting for storytelling. On such special nights and without complaint, I would stack in a big pile of wood and curl up by the fire to hear the best stories a boy could imagine. These were stories of people and the land—stories of hidden gold mines high in the Cascades, beautiful mountain lakes and meadows, and isolated stream valleys where a person could live well with ax, traps, and gun. There were accounts of prospectors and trappers who never returned from the hills. Bear and cougar stories were riveting and led to hesitancy on my part about carrying the lantern to visit our outhouse at the edge of the woods.

To get to town, we walked or drove our old truck to the ferry landing. If the ferryman was in his cabin on the far side, we gonged the saw hanging from the maple which clung to the river's bank. I hoped that old Frank would not come too soon. There were flat rocks to skip, but often I would be quiet and listen to the murmur of the river and wonder at its origin and timelessness. In late summer, through the dusk and wafting mists, I could hear the slap of water as the great salmon made their way upstream. My Indian friends knew there were spirits in all things—I too could hear spirit voices in those gently swirling waters.

Frank would often stand on the ferry and look up the river, as if transfixed by its flow or perhaps by the high Cascades beyond. I wondered if he had returned to the past—a time and place on the river which I would have loved to have known. One morning, when our small school bus arrived at the ferry, an engine had been mounted, replacing the spoked hand wheels which had powered the ferry's winches. A stranger, a white man, was at the controls. As the engine roared and the ferry swung into the Skagit, I saw Frank's canoe a ways downriver, the old Indian watching, leaning on his pole against the current. I felt deeply for this old river man and wondered about his past and our future.

Sixteen years later, a steel bridge spanned the spot where the ferry and Frank Tom's weathered canoe shed had been, the same year I returned to the Upper Valley to teach school.

❖ A Harder Reality ❖

By the time I was an adolescent, days of playing were few—hard days in the fields and woods were reality. My father worked very hard toward his dream of an independent ranch life, but it was logging that kept our family in groceries and shoes. Ironically, my father, who loved the natural woods, spent much of his life cutting trees and clearing land.

I remember the stream tumbling down through the old forest on the hillside above our ranch, spreading through the maple and cedar flats on our place. There my father taught me how to maneuver through devil's-club thickets, find cascara trees, and look for the first spring blooms of trillium and bleeding heart. We worked on that flat selecting cedar poles and short logs, pulled out on narrow trails by our horses.

One day we heard a 'dozer pushing a road onto the mountainside above us and soon felt the crash of great old Douglas-fir and cedar. Heavy equipment moved in and stripped that virgin stand in a few weeks. This was being done by people we knew, men making a living in the woods. Their crew got across our line, supposedly by mistake, and cut much of our maple flat. My father declined the logger's offer to buy the timber from us. We rigged a small spar tree and skyline to yard the stuff with our horses. My dad, my brother, and our horses, old Jerry and Queeny, worked to get the maple out before it cracked in the summer heat. I was proud of our effort. I was becoming a logger. That winter the stream washed its load of dirt and logging debris off the mountain. By early the next summer the "creek" was a dry, barren gully.

❖ Corked Boots and Copenhagen ❖

We too began logging with power equipment. Our first chain saw was an outdated, heavy old Mall which my father gained on a trade for a heifer. In time we had more efficient saws, a "donkey," and a D7 Cat. I learned woods skills of that place and time. By the time I was out of high school, I was a logger. Working summers, and sometimes laying out of school to go back to work when the woods opened up, I alternated between an education on college campuses and an education of corked boots, "widowmakers," and "sling'n riggen." One fall, my employer raised my wages and offered a bonus if I would stay "till the snow flied."

I have often joked that I left the woods because I couldn't handle snoose and whiskey and cuss like a real man. But there were other factors. One of the most beautiful places I have ever experienced was the Baker Lake Basin. Groves of moss- and fern-draped forest covered the mountainsides and ravines running down to the natural lake. In the mid-1950s the Upper Baker Dam project was in progress to greatly enlarge the lake, and logs started pouring from the clearing. My outfit logged the shoreline on the east side of the basin. I remember standing in a beautiful, old cedar and Douglas-fir grove at the mouth of Anderson Creek. A few days later I hooked the last of the big trunks and followed it up the muddy skid road to the landing.

The summer of 1958 was hot and dry. Our logging crew was sent to fight fire in the Upper Skagit country. For years, a buddy and I had debated which part of the Cascades was the grandest. I championed the Mount Baker area. My friend, from an Upper Skagit family, said that I hadn't seen anything yet. That summer my views were expanded.

We rode the City Light tugboat up the clear, deep waters of Ross Lake. For my first time, I saw the rock-walled side canyons and Nohokomeen Glacier high on Jack Mountain. Glacier-fed streams fell from pristine hanging valleys. After we were dumped off at Little Beaver Landing, we headed up the trail, at first on an exposed ridge, and then into cool valley forests of great cedars. By dark we were working our way up a faint, moss-covered trace along Perry Creek.

After a cold dip and a few hours' rest, we began our climb up the ridge. Sunrise on that high ridge was unforgettable. I could not absorb the beauty fast enough. To the west, rising out of dark valleys through layers of sun-tinted fog and smoke, was an unbelievable array of icy, jagged peaks. To the east, across the reflecting waters of Ross Lake, were the spires of Hozomeen, and the meadowed dome of Desolation. Into the distance flowed the ridges and mountains of the Pasayten. My crew, men toughened by hard work and an often harder life, stood in silence, as moved as I was by that scene.

❖ Country Teacher ❖

I returned up valley to teach school in Marblemount in 1961. With a love for the outdoors and a brand-new degree in biology, I looked forward to teaching in that country setting. My students studied ecology in nearby natural surroundings. We read the stories of predator and prey printed in snowy woods. A fun project was observing and recording life in and around a pond throughout the seasons.

My class struck up a friendship with Lenora and Rocky Wilson, a couple who had prospected, hunted, and fished the Cascades for over forty years. We visited them in their cabin on the Upper Cascade, explored their mine, and heard wonderful stories of horse trips into the high country.

In late September 1968, Rocky brought a freshly taken bear hide to school to show the kids. He and Lenora had packed up to Fisher Basin, one of their favorite places, for the High Hunt. During twilight hours, a large bear came down to the creek close by camp. Rocky lifted his old rifle and got off a good shot. While he knew it was a big 'un, he didn't see that it had a shoulder hump and frosted coat until he got to the kill. This was the last-known grizzly bear to be taken in the Cascades. Just days later the North Cascades National Park bill was signed, prohibiting hunting in that place and throughout the newly established Park.

This past summer I hiked from Highway 20 over Easy Pass into Fisher Basin, a much shorter trip now than it was for Rocky and Lenora when they visited that high, beautiful valley years ago. Mountain slopes were just coming into peak bloom, the weather was hot, and the melt ponds were cold—but a refreshing respite from a hungry hatch of bugs. My partner and I camped near Rocky's old camp and wondered if grizzlies would someday again be part of that place.

❖ Forest Service Seasonal ❖

In 1965, I began working seasonally for the United States Forest Service. Much of the Skagit District had recently been classified as Primary Recreation, and I was one of the first of a new breed—a recreational guard. I quickly learned that this meant taking care of toilets, tourists, and garbage, in whichever order they became a problem.

Some Forest Service hands were of the old school, possessing a philosophy of mountains, pack animals, and people born of long stints in the backcountry. From their point of view, horses and mules, although sometimes a mite cantankerous, were at least predictable. Now, people, especially flatlanders, were a different story.

Most visitors of that time were from nearby areas and accustomed to doing their own thing with little restriction. The code of the woods had to do with taking care of oneself and being careful with fire. Enforcement of the newly adopted, and more restrictive, Recreation Regulations had to be done with considerable diplomacy. In that role I met wonderful, usually independent, people and made numerous friends. My campground toilet and garbage runs were often interrupted by invitations for coffee and goodies.

One of the grand old Forest Service traditions was still in place. Each evening, fire lookouts would go on the air with open mikes. Talk ranged from recipes, views, and sightings of the day, to deep, and often far out, philosophical questions. Sometimes there was live entertainment. One denizen of lofty places could play a guitar and a mouth organ at the same time. "Lookout Hour" was sacred. No matter how provocative the discussion, we lowlanders did not intrude.

I came to understand that working those mountaintop stations was more than a summer job—it was a place and time to come to know oneself and one's place in the universe. A lookout friend related, "Those summers on Sourdough and Copper Ridge have changed my life forever." I visited a young woman lookout on Desolation, a Native American graduate student in biology who was seeking to communicate with cougars. There were those who were not ready for such encounters. One young man pleaded to be assigned to Lookout Mountain late one dry summer. Within days he was concocting stories to come down. We laughed off his story of a bear trying to get into the lookout with him. His next call, in a very faint voice, was that he had fallen from the tower and was badly injured. An hour later, I watched him run from the rescue helicopter when it landed at Marblemount—a miraculous recovery.

Forest Service programs were centered around fire. Pre-suppression money was allocated to build and maintain trails, phone lines, lookouts, and guard stations. With fire suppression money, fires were fought and caches resupplied. The joke was if there were no fires there wouldn't be surplus coffee to supply the ranger station for the winter. In the 1960s, fire was still an icon of the USFS.

The original Forest Reserves were established to exempt some public forest land from the great land grabs of the nineteenth century. By the 1940s private timberlands had been mostly stripped and public forests stood as ripe plums. In my memory, each landowner was "entitled" to an amount of free public timber, usually cedar fence posts and shake bolts. Then came the small, unbid, local "Ranger Sales" of commercial timber. These sales were soon found to be illegal. That set the stage for competitive bidding, favoring large timber companies. Sales were now laid out in huge blocks. The Forest Service and the United States Treasury reaped new money from this "harvest."

When I shifted to the Baker River District, my jobs were timber related. In the fall of 1970 we surveyed a road into the Lucky Burn, up Kindy Creek near the boundary of the recently established Glacier Peak Wilderness. I was relieved when it was determined that road building costs would outweigh revenue from salvaged timber. Logging in upper Kindy was put on hold. Creeping into such decisions was the idea that there was inherent value in wilderness. There were forest managers and loggers who didn't understand "letting those trees rot and go to waste."

Another dilemma for the Forest Service was how to meet harvest quotas set by Congress while staying out of legislated Roadless Study Areas. Consequently, roaded areas were horribly overcut. The Finney drainage became a scalped land of large clearcuts, ribbon-thin leave strips, and a maze of logging roads. Most managers still espoused the concept that clearcutting and burning were the means to rid the land of "decadent" old stands and to get young, high-value trees growing. I was to work in Finney, laying out roads, doing controlled burns, fighting escaped fires, planting trees, and doing road-cut stabilization.

I worked on reforesting a number of clearcuts in the Baker Lake area near where I had logged a few years earlier. Planting midelevation slopes to Douglas-fir made sense. But we were directed to grub out naturally returning mixed stands of true fir, hemlock, cedar, and hardwoods in an attempt to replace them with Douglas-fir—a futile effort to create a monoculture crop with no consideration for natural processes.

While torching a slash burn one fall on Finney, we saw fire running up a logging unit on an adjacent slope. I have never experienced hotter fires in the Western Cascades than in those heavy, dry-slash areas. We pulled back onto a logging road that night as the fire screamed up the mountain, crowning through leave strips. I covered my face with my hard hat for protection from intense heat and rocks being swirled up in the draft. What was meant to be sound timber-management strategy, replicating nature with fire-treated seedbeds for Douglas-fir culture, was out of control, well beyond the inherent balancing processes and mediation of nature.

The debate about establishing a national park in the North Cascades was a difficult issue for me. Changes had been made in Forest Service management in proposed park areas that I liked. The North Cascades Primitive Area, an administrative classification, had provided some protection for the high country. With the Wilderness Act of 1964, the heart of the mountains was to be legally protected. A moratorium had been placed on logging in the high mountain hemlock zone, and management for recreational values was in place.

While I supported the national park idea of preserving special features and places for future generations, I also knew that park status would bring many visitors and related pressures to our little-known North Cascades. My father, who loved the mountains, often said, "Someday people will come from all over the world to see these mountains." This was soon to be, and my career would be intertwined with those visitors and the mountains.

❖ National Park Ranger ❖

The North Cascades National Park bill was signed on my birthday: October 2, 1968. I became a seasonal park ranger in the spring of 1969 and permanently left the classroom soon after. For the next several years I worked summer in the Park and fall and spring with the Forest Service. These were exciting times in the North Cascades, times of environmental awakening and many questions. Federal legislation to protect air, water, wildlife, and wilderness spawned many differences in philosophy and tactics on how the laws should be applied. North Cascades National Park was a testing ground for wilderness management. Fires were not always fought,

Falls above Holden Lake

camping was eliminated from subalpine meadows, campfires were limited to for-ested areas, backcountry permits were required for overnight stays, road and trail camping were restricted to designated sites. Throughout this time we had to re-spond to the often-asked question, "Are national parks for people or for bears?"

One hot September afternoon I hiked up Little Jack Mountain on High Hunt patrol. (That area, within the Ross Lake National Recreation Area, remained open for hunting.) The next morning I was on the highest point waiting for daylight and watching for hunting activity. I checked in with Sourdough Lookout and compared views of the sunrise just coloring the high peaks. I was joined by a hunter, he, too, evidently waiting the legal opening hour and enjoying the incredible scenery. He displayed buck and bear tags and carried a powerful rifle with a long-range scope. As daylight entered the headwaters of Crater Creek below us, three bears—probably a mother and yearling cubs—made their way into an open area and began browsing. We watched, and as the sun warmed the slope the youngsters began wrestling and rolling toward us. I expected the hunter to take aim, but he sat quietly on a rock scoping the bears and whispered, "What a treat. Who could spoil such a sight?"

The summer after the North Cascades Highway opened, I led nature walks along Ruby Creek, a place rich with natural beauty and mining history. A family from California who seemed to be delighted with the experience joined me on one hike. The father asked several questions concerning ownership of mining claims. As we were returning to the trailhead, I became more aware of his interests. He identified himself as a real estate person and exclaimed, "With this new highway, with no developments or services in miles, do you realize that we are standing on a potential gold mine?" My interpretive expectations and his mind set were far apart.

A very worried man contacted me one night after my campfire program at Colonial Amphitheater. He and a woman friend and his two children had hiked to Fourth of July Pass that day. The woman and boy wanted to go on and come out at Panther Creek trailhead on Highway 20. It was decided that the father and daughter would return to Colonial and pick up the woman and boy at the trailhead late in the day. The hikers had not made it out by dark. They had no flashlight or extra gear and were very lightly dressed.

I headed up the long ridge from Panther trailhead. I knew of a place where the creek often washed out and could be confusing to follow, especially at night. I dropped down the steep switchbacks and followed the creek up valley. Crossing the log bridge, I hoped to find the couple at Panther Camp. They weren't there. I worked up Panther through brushy avalanche tracks. As I approached a timbered area I heard the woman's shout. I was a welcome figure in their long, scary, cold night. They had become confused along the creek and decided to return through Fourth of July Pass. It was getting late. As they hurried along they were startled to find a cougar standing in the trail. The woman had extensive hiking experience and had taught hiking/survival skills in the Sierras. They made loud noises, and the cougar moved into the woods. A ways further there was the cougar again, this time coming toward them. The woman led the boy into the creek where they perched on a rock. The cougar reappeared several times above and below them. It was getting dark and they were cold and wet. The woman decided hypothermia was a greater threat than the cat. She made a bough bed in the cradle of tree roots and huddled in with the boy. The boy fell asleep—she watched for shadowy movements.

I gave them my extra food and clothes, and we started up the trail toward the pass. As the couple warmed they became quite animated in telling their story. The woman was very concerned we might destroy the cat. I assured her that was not our intent. It was a beautiful night—a full moon slid over Snowfield Peak and Neve Glacier as we descended into Thunder Valley.

A few days later, I received a thank you note from the woman. She pleaded again for us not to take action against the cat and said, that after the scare was gone, she remembered vividly the beauty of the "panther" that would make their night on its namesake creek so memorable.

As the North Cascades National Park Complex matured, my job evolved. I became a permanent park ranger in 1974. With my background in natural history and my connection with local human history, I fell easily into interpretation. Along with interpretive activities, I worked with bears, fires, emergency medicine, law enforcement, campground maintenance, trail projects, and evaluating and cutting hazard trees. One park manager described me as a "logging naturalist." I trust my range of duties and experiences gave me a broader insight into the North Cascades than could be acquired in a more specialized role.

Many park visitors are from far away, with limited time or abilities to experience the greater park. Interpreters often use vicarious methods to bring park experiences to visitors. Through interpreters' eyes, visitors can see the beauty and wonder of a glacial basin or a cougar stalking its prey. Through stories they can know some of the trials and adventures of those who came here before. I often call upon my personal experiences and recall stories from old-timers to bring people–mountain connections alive.

❖ Connections from the Past ❖

One spring day, while exploring the pools on upper Ruby Creek, I found a rusted gold pan protruding from the gravel. I later asked my long-time friend and Upper Skagit pioneer son, Glee Davis, who it might have belonged to. He laughed and said, "Well, you know, that could have belonged to any number of those old-timers, including me." (The gold pan is now on display in the North Cascades Visitor Center near Newhalem.) Glee used that occasion and many others to pass on delightfully vivid stories of the characters and events of the Upper Skagit. Through Glee and other storytellers, I have come to know those "spirits of the past" and their special haunts. When I walk where they walked, I share their excitement, their loneliness, the beauty of a meadow or stream, my experiences connecting with theirs.

❖ Custer's Pen ❖

The Northwest Boundary Commission began a survey across the North Cascades in 1857. Cartographer Henry Custer was hired to explore that formidable route. In Custer's journals, along with notes and maps, were scribed eloquent verses. On a late summer day in 1859, Custer sat on a high divide and wrote:

> No mortal pen could be found to describe this grand and glorious scenery properly and justly. This endless variety of shapes and forms, these thousands

of different shades and colors—here the green and blacks of the endless forest, and the lovely mountain meadow, here the gray in all its endless nuances, the blue, the red, the dazzling white of the snow and ice masses, reflecting and breaking the steady rays of the midday sun, and the whole landscape covered by a light mist, which chastens down the color and gives the whole matchless view an almost fairy like aspect.

Custer's impressions were recorded a short distance from where I experienced the sunrise with my logging crew ninety-nine years later. As I remember that scene, as striking as it was, our view had been altered by a reservoir covering a once-meandering, broad river valley. I wonder what that scene might be in another hundred years. Will there be forest cuts and waterfront developments? Will vegetation be paled from acid fallout? Will glaciers have succumbed to global warming? Custer went on to say, "Whoever wishes to see Nature in all its primitive glory and grandeur, in its almost feroci[o]us wildness, must go and visit these Mountain regions."

❖ Upriver Lure ❖

In 1872 Jack Rowley and his partners, from the Lower Skagit, took up Custer's invitation and challenge—they set out to prospect the Skagit to its headwaters. Panning each river bar, they found scattered flecks of gold, enough to keep them going. At the head of canoe navigation, now Newhalem, they were still seeking that elusive mother lode. Native guides were hired to lead them high above and around the river's narrow canyon. It was tough going and very hot. Sourdough starter began to work in a prospector's pack, messing up his gear. The place was christened Sourdough Mountain. The Indian guides would not descend into the widening river basin below, a place of unfriendly spirits, probably those of their ancient enemies from the north. A side canyon entering from a far drainage to the east lured the prospectors into the gorge. There, in waters containing ruby-red rocks, they found fine streaks of placer gold flushing from that impassable chasm.

Rowley returned five years later. He had dreamed of a hand pointing the way around the steep rock walls. Rowley followed his vision through Hidden Hand Pass, at the base of towering Jack Mountain, and traversed into the creek dubbed Ruby. Enough color was found to keep his dream alive.

In 1879, about 10 miles upstream in a narrow side canyon, Rowley struck rich placer and staked his Original Discovery claim. A few days later Albert Bacon and partners, working the stream below, were about to starve out. It was nip and tuck if they could hold on another day. In a final effort they rolled over a rock, and there, as sediments cleared, were golden nuggets shimmering through the clear waters of Ruby Creek. Rowley's Original Discovery and Bacon's Nip and Tuck claims kicked off the first Ruby Rush.

❖ McMillan's Place ❖

John McMillan responded to the Ruby excitement in 1883. He brought in pack animals and ran a pack line from Fort Hope, Canada. For years John was a partner of Tommy Roland. They built a cabin on the river and cleared a horse pasture above Big Beaver Creek Falls. After Tommy became a bit strange (he thought he was a religious prophet), John split, settling on the Big Beaver homestead.

On a trip north to Fort Hope, John came upon an ugly scene, a trapper beating a young Indian woman with a club. When John jumped off his horse to intercede, the trapper stuck a rifle in John's face. This made John mad. He knocked the gun away and "beat the living hell out of the man." According to hearsay, John was awakened that night in his camp by the woman moving in with her meager possessions. Being a kind man, John took her home.

John and his common-law wife had one child. They named her May. One story reports that, several years later, John became unhappy with his in-laws, who kept moving in on him, and sent the whole family packing. A kinder account said that when May was of school age, John sent mother and child north to be near family and school. May is remembered by her namesake, May Creek, a merry little stream which drops into the valley near Roland Point on Ross Lake.

In time, John journeyed to Seattle to seek citizenship. While there, he fell in love with a young woman named Emma Love. Part of John's proposal was that Emma return with him to Big Beaver. Emma agreed to marry John and go to the Upper Skagit for the summer. They stayed a lifetime. John and Emma were to live a hard but wonderful life in that remote land. John prospected, trapped, and packed supplies for gold miners along Ruby and Canyon Creeks. In later years the couple ran a small hotel, the Ruby Inn, in the mining village of Ruby City.

As mining activity waned, John and Emma settled in on their Beaver homestead. In 1922 John became very ill. Emma packed him out to the doctor in Concrete. Old Doc Mertz gave John little chance of recovery. John's final request was to return to Big Beaver. Emma led John's horse over the long, rough trail up the Skagit.

Friends from far mountain reaches gathered to bid John farewell. One man made a quick trip to Marblemount to acquire some of that most potent Scottish medicine. The story is told of how John's grave was dug behind the cabin and his coffin made from hand-split planks as he passed his last hours in the company of Emma and friends. Undoubtedly, some sipped from that bottle of pure mountain spirits, and some passed it by. George Holmes led prayers as the coffin was covered by the soil of Big Beaver Valley.

Emma spent winters in a little cabin near friends at the present site of Diablo. Each spring she returned to Big Beaver. Early-day trail men told stories of the kindly "Old Bread Lady" who for many years invited them into her aging cabin above Big Beaver Falls to share baked goodies and wild berry jams.

It was a beautiful October day when I found the McMillan Place. The cabin and outbuildings were tumbled down and overgrown. Huge old stumps marked the place where John's horses once pastured. Behind the cabin, I found John's grave. The wooden head marker was nearly rotted away, but the great rock face of McMillan Mountain stood watch over that peaceful place.

I carved John a new marker and every few years return to clear growth from his grave and visit awhile. I have never learned of Emma's final resting place, but I sense that both John and Emma are at home in their beloved Big Beaver Valley.

❖ The Black Prospector of Ruby Creek ❖

George Holmes arrived on Ruby Creek in 1895 after much of the excitement had died down. A quiet man, George revealed very little of his past. He had reportedly been born in Virginia to slave parents and had traveled the country looking for freedom and a home. George was devoutly religious and possessed exceptional strengths in body, character, and patience.

Holmes first came to the Upper Skagit as a stable hand for the Skagit Queen Mining Company. It was rumored that after a pay day and a trip to Seattle's Skid Road, he became infected with a venereal disease. In his penitence, he made a pledge that if he were cured he would return to the Upper Skagit and be a Christian example to the sinful miners of that wild country. George was that example for the next thirty years.

Holmes worked up and down Ruby Creek, but eventually settled in and built his cabin in an isolated place between a steep mountainside and a deep, swift section of that beautiful stream. Although a loner, George was known to be a kindly person, always ready to lend a hand when anyone needed help.

I had heard many stories about the "Old Black Miner of Ruby Creek," but never knew where his diggings were. One night on a late patrol, I saw a fire down the mountainside on Ruby Creek and went to investigate. A noisy party was under way in the remains of an old cabin. I calmed the participants and cooled the fire. The next day I went to check out the site and found a remarkable collection of rusting, cobbled-together mining paraphernalia. Mining records showed that it was the Himlock II, filed by George Holmes.

George built crude hydraulic systems to wash stream sediments through sluices. He also dug deep holes along the creek and washed ancient deposits. It was hard and lonely work, but George Holmes had found his place. George traveled to Seattle every couple of years to peddle his gold to jewelers who paid top dollar for the precious Ruby Creek metal, but he was quick to return to Ruby.

George was very upset when he heard of a railroad being built up the Skagit. He didn't want to see the changes in his mountain wilderness that he knew a railroad would bring. A friend wrote, "Holmes preferred the solitude, the contentment of his lonely existence, to anything else the world had to offer."

In 1925, friends carefully carried the dying old prospector in a litter, made from a dugout canoe, on his final trip down the Skagit Trail. Holmes passed away two days later in Mount Vernon. A few years ago, I led a drive to place a monument on his unmarked grave. The epitaph reads, "George Holmes found a freedom in the wilds of the North Cascades which few attain."

❖ A Pioneer in Petticoats ❖

Lucinda Davis was born in Boston in 1848 and reared with considerable refinement. She dreamed of going West. In 1884 her two brothers came to Washington Territory to take up homestead claims. Lucinda, now married with three children, managed to get her husband to Denver, Colorado, but no further.

In 1890, Will Leach wrote to his sister that their brother had drowned and pleaded with her to come and take up his claim. Lucinda left her husband and set out with her children—Frank, thirteen; Glee, nine; and Dessa, five—for the Cascade River near Marblemount. Glee told me of their exciting trip by train, riverboat, and stagecoach, climaxing in an Indian dugout canoe ride up the Skagit. Glee said his mother, at that time, was deathly afraid of Indians and water.

Lucinda and children settled into homestead life. In the summers of 1893 and 1895, she ran a small trading post at Goodell's Landing, where she heard stories of the wild and wonderful lands beyond the Skagit Gorge. Lucinda was intrigued. She took her family over rough miners' trails to explore the upper river, and they became enthralled with that wild country.

In the fall of 1897, after early snows and heavy rains, a great flood washed away most of Lucinda's land and possessions. She reclaimed what she could and moved her family to Sedro Woolley for the winter. Twelve-year-old Glee herded the family cows 45 miles down valley over muddy trails. Lucinda worked very hard to provide for her family and keep their spirits bright. Frank, now twenty years old, returned up river to hold claim to a creek bar they had found deep in the Skagit Gorge.

The next summer Lucinda moved her family over the developing Goat Trail to Cedar Bar where she was to establish a home, a roadhouse, and a legend. Many years later Glee told me, "It wasn't an easy life, but we worked hard and made a go of it. It was a good life."

The Davises hand-built a large house from the forest, cleared land, raised gardens, and gathered precious wild hay. In time, the Davis Ranch was to become a place of food and rest for an array of mountain travelers, from miners and trappers to recreationists and foreign mining investors. The boys also trapped, packed, prospected, and worked for the miners and the newly created Forest Service. Lucinda loved to explore and fish. They climbed mountains, found the best berry and fishing spots, and guided guests on mountain trips.

A party arrived at Davis Ranch late one evening, requesting board and room. Lucinda asked if they preferred fish or pork for dinner. They decided on fish. Lucinda picked up her fishing pole and headed for the river. This impressed the young boy in the party and years later, when he told me this story, he wondered what might have happened had they chosen pork.

Lucinda believed in hard work, social graces, education, and a "clean" life. Not only was there no drinking at her place, but she soundly scolded men who were known to imbibe. She saw that each of her children spent time in the lower valley attending school. Glee laughingly recalled that no excuses of floods, snow slides, or wild animals kept them from going to school.

While at school Glee met Hazel Campbell. They were married and, in time, added two daughters to the close-knit family at Cedar Bar. Glee filed for homestead rights and, after a legal battle with the Forest Service, was awarded part of their claim.

Others were interested in Cedar Bar. Seattle City Light had gained a permit to build a large dam in the canyon above the Davis Ranch. They needed Cedar Bar as a gravel source and campsite for the project. The City of Seattle forced the Davis family to vacate and sell their home.

Lucinda, by then in her seventies, saw the tremendous change coming to her wilderness canyon. She stayed as long as she could, renting rooms and makeshift cabins to the men who were building Diablo Dam. When the dam was completed in 1930, Lucinda packed her belongings, said goodbye to her home and life on the Upper Skagit, and rode the train down the mountain canyon she had ventured up many years before.

❖ We Belong to the Land ❖

Since the last great ice flows were melting from valley bottoms, people have inhabited this land—some for many thousands of years, some for decades, and some very briefly. Today, in remote valleys, I find hints of human presence—a healed-over tree blaze, signs of a marten trap, a moss-covered stump, a flattened place with humps of rotted sills and blackened rocks. High on beautiful ridges, I find rock flakes of ancient times. In other places I find artifacts of bold intrusion—caved-in adits and rusting equipment.

I have found wonderful settings where I would have loved to have lived, and places where I wonder how a person could have survived a short while. In historic times many came to seek their "El Dorado"—few survived long. These mountains, as stunningly beautiful as they can be, were a horrible barrier to those who sought easy rewards. Those who came to know this land in all its moods and seasons found rewards in lifestyle and place which far overshadowed riches to be taken from the land.

Place names in the North Cascades often speak to human interaction with the land. Names such as Terror, Nightmare, Eldorado, Formidable, and Challenger reflect strong human feelings. Never could the Cascades be taken lightly. Native place names often speak to a spiritual connection. The name Sahale—"high, heavenly" from the Native Trade Jargon—suits well that high setting above Cascade Pass. Native people went there to hunt and gather roots and berries, and to speak with the powerful spirits of that place. Anyone who goes there today surely, too, must feel a special communion with that grand alpine scape, still molding in nature's hands.

People of our century have recognized special places of natural wonder and national treasure by establishing park and wilderness areas to be enjoyed in their natural state and, in the language of the 1964 Wilderness Act, "untrammeled by man." While this is a grand idea, is it truly possible? We know that there can be no protected islands. Outfall from our human-impacted world knows no such bounds.

Recently I spent a day along the Skagit River with people who shared concerns for the health of the valley. We looked at threats to the land and water. We also talked of possibilities. What would it take to care for this land in the best possible way? Could the resources again be whole and healthy? At the close of the day, an Upper Skagit person, a leader in overseeing natural resources under tribal treaties, gave us these words: "We must remember that the land does not belong to us—we belong to the land." This profound understanding comes from generations of people who know that human beings must respect the spirits of the land if they expect to receive gifts from it. This wisdom was passed on to us by the great-granddaughter of the old river man, Frank Tom.

There is no question in my mind that we must hold dearly to our remaining wild lands. Wilderness and park lands can give us inspiration and hope, and provide an ongoing working laboratory for our understanding of natural processes. But we must look to a much bigger picture. Until we allow healthy ecosystems to occur in nonprotected lands near and far, the treasures of the North Cascades and our world's resources will disappear.

I also know there must be places highly managed for human beings. I believe that the key to survival for us, and our fellow earthly beings, is in the way we interact in everyday life with our total environment. We must come to understand and respect all parts of our world. As trees alone are not a forest, we certainly are not able to stand alone on this planet.

The people whom I knew as a boy, and those who were here long before us, did not always respect and treat the land well. But they knew intimately a very important reality—that they were dependent upon the land for their survival. Do we, today, make that connection? It is scary when political and economic leaders show little regard for that most basic truth. We must remind them and ourselves that the land does not belong to us—we belong to the land.

Sometimes, in a moment of optimism, I look up the Skagit to the forests and high mountains beyond. I envision people of the past and the future receiving gifts from the river. I see forests growing and healing. I see soils fertile and productive under nurturing human hands, a model for others to follow. But too often I see and am saddened by decimated hillsides and gutted-out spawning streams. Sometimes I listen to the river and see an old Native leaning against the current and I wonder, what will our future be?

In a brief ceremony at the close of each North Cascade Institute's Mountain School Camp, each participant places a twig of cedar on the campfire and makes a personal wish. Around the dying fire, as each twig sparkles and ignites, I have heard wonderful words of hope, which are often phrased, "May this place, with its trees, animals, and river be here for others to enjoy forever." These words and these children give me hope. I sense that on that river's shore, under those great old cedars, dwell spirits of many children and elders from the past who smile and share those wishes.

A lifetime resident of the Skagit Valley, JIM HARRIS has been a logger, teacher, and National Park Service interpreter. He specializes in historical interpretation in his work with the park.

Part II

Landscapes
of Experience

Introduction to Part II

Probing the past, we find many North Cascades. So, too, when we travel there in the present. We go into these mountains to ski at Mount Baker, Stevens Pass, or Mission Ridge. We hike in summer to Cascade Pass, Monte Cristo, or Snow Lake. We find inspiration, adventure, solitude, and natural beauty. We may live around these mountains, the rhythms of our days governed by the forces of climate and weather and the constraints of remoteness. We may be merely visiting, and may come here to learn, to heal, to grow, or even to retreat. Whatever brings us, we feel the power of the place and are changed by it.

Our lives are fast-paced and stressful. We build a cabin in the mountains to which we withdraw to think and take stock and reconnect to nature. Or we travel light, taking all we need on our backs, and climb up the passes and peaks for the fun and sport of the trip. We come with sketchbook and journal, sit for hours trying to capture the essence of a scene. We botanize and watch birds and butterflies. We city dwellers find reconnection to some roots here. We are incurable romantics about wild places, imagining ourselves to be figures in adventures from an imaginary past.

Each year we encounter more fellow mountain travelers. Popular trails are crowded on fine summer days. We need permits to travel overnight in some areas. The prospect of permits for day hikes looms for heavily used trails. Our growing numbers threaten the freedom and solitude we seek on mountain trips. Waves of development lap up onto the western foothills.

A few of us live in and around these mountains. We work here, suffer the inconveniences and pain of isolation, and enjoy the rewards of solitude. Our roots may be deep in the land and the community, our consciousness of this place shared with many others. We tell stories of our lives here, and find humor and solace in the telling. These stories, often dominated by powerful nature, define our community. This is our place, we say, and we love it.

For some, the North Cascades is just scenery, a landscape of rock and snow, high meadow and deep-green mountainside, alpenglow and scarves of cloud. All who come here are struck by this scenery, but those who see only the scenery and travel quickly on experience only the surface of this land. Those who have the opportunity to look beneath the scenery find a rich and complex tapestry spun by the interaction of diverse communities.

Here, in the experiences of a few who have lingered and studied and reflected on this place, we find insights into these worlds.

Beaver Is Greedy

CHARLES LUCKMANN

The beaver, well known for altering the land, has changed the dynamics of many a watershed. As a boy I remember pulling my canoe over beaver dams of aspen and birch limbs, cursing some that were 6 feet high or more. I preferred the tumbling waters to the placid pond behind the dams, but I admired the beaver for his human-like achievements. The beaver also has a very attractive fur which, in the eighteenth and nineteenth centuries, was the fashion rage in Europe, especially for making hats. The desire for beaver fur lured independent men to the mountains of the American West to trap them which, in those years, fueled a competitive commerce between the British and Americans. In the early nineteenth century, the British fur posts trapped out all the beaver, especially in the Snake River country, to try to discourage Americans from coming to the area.

After the beaver were gone, gold enticed thousands of men into the mountains in the hopes of "striking it rich." The early Euro-American history of the upper Skagit River is chiefly a story of the gold rush during the 1870s, when thousands of miners made the arduous trek up river, negotiating rapids and precipitous trail through such places as Damnation Creek, Devil's Corner, and Nightmare Camp to reach Ruby and Thunder Creeks, where the gold was supposed to be. That the land's mineral resources could be exploited by the first who could claim it as theirs was the ethos precipitating the stampede of gold seekers.

Very little gold was mined, however, and during the first two decades of the twentieth century, after most of the miners had left, the Skagit River's hydroelectric potential began to dominate discussions about the development of the river. Competition between those interested in the river for hydroelectric development played itself out among several private companies, such as The Skagit Power Company, North Coast Mining and Milling Company, and the Thunder Creek Transportation and Smelting Company. The United States Forest Service did give The Skagit Power Company permission to build a dam in 1914, but because of the magnitude of the project and the financial and political capital needed to fund it— which proved beyond their means—they had to abandon the idea. By 1917 the other companies had lost interest or were out-maneuvered by James Delmage Ross, who obtained a permit that year from the Forest Service to build a series of hydroelectric dams on the river for Seattle City Light. Ross had great expectations that the "blank page" of the upper Skagit River could be transformed into a productive resource for the citizens of Seattle.

The Skagit is the second-largest river in Washington State, its watershed draining the western slope of the North Cascades. The Columbia River and its tributaries, however, drain Idaho and most of Oregon and Washington State, including the eastern slope of the North Cascades, as well as parts of Montana, Wyoming, British Columbia, and Alberta. The Columbia is one of the mighty rivers of the world—1,200 miles long—looming larger than the Skagit in our collective imaginations. The salmon run on the Columbia was once the largest in the world, but today more than 95 percent of the wild salmon are gone—blocked by more than 50 dams in the Columbia River Basin. My understanding of dams and their significance to interpreting the landscapes of the Northwest began one day several years ago on a bluff overlooking the Columbia River at Wishram, about 10 miles upstream of The Dalles Dam. I stood with two Columbia River Indian elders as we watched wind surfers skim across the lake that now covers Celilo Falls, once the largest Indian fishery in North America. The day was exceptionally clear, and to the southwest, glistening in the sun, was the 11,234-foot, snow-capped peak of Mount Hood, or "Patu" as Selam called it in his native Sahaptin. His long, silver hair blowing in the wind, James Selam told me that during his youth he used to fish at Celilo Falls every year until he went off to fight in World War II. Born a few miles upstream in a tule mat lodge in 1919, Selam spoke about the River Spirit, about how the Columbia River was created, how Coyote brought salmon to the River People, and shared stories that mirrored events of the twentieth century that have dramatically changed the river. As he talked, Selam pointed to landmarks and told me a little bit of the significance of each.

Below the train trestle spanning the river, Selam indicated where, on the Washington state side, he grew up in the Indian community of Skin. As a boy, during certain seasons when the river level fluctuated because of snowmelt or drought, he had to walk carefully across the narrow railroad trestle above the roaring falls to reach the Oregon shore and the fishing sites that were accessible. Selam pointed to sites, now under water, where he and his family would fish for salmon. The type of fishing done at each site would be determined by the time of year and water level. When the water was high and the salmon would attempt to bypass the falls along the Washington state shore, the Indians would gillnet; at other times of year they would catch the salmon in a dipnet dragged through the water or held to catch salmon as they tried to leap the torrent rushing over the precipitous drop; at certain water levels, the salmon were speared or gaffed as they waited in the eddies before attempting to leap the watery slides.

Selam pointed to the Oregon shore and indicated the Indian village of Celilo. I could see the new longhouse not far from the interstate highway. He spoke of the islands near there that were claimed as fishing sites by certain families, such as "Albert's Island" and "Chief Tommie Thompson's Island." Thompson was the Salmon Chief at Celilo Falls until it was flooded in 1957 by the waters backing up from The Dalles Dam. The larger islands were used communally by the River People for drying fish. Each of the places had an Indian name that Selam would say in his native language and then explain in English: *walawála* (high water fishing site near the sandy beach below the village of Skin); *Sapawilatatatpamá* (at the lip of the falls near the Washington state shore where the fishermen dipnet to catch the leaping salmon); *tayxaytpamá* (where shiny stones and clear water facilitate spearing the salmon); and near the Oregon shore were islands that had to be reached by canoe or swimming, *qíyakawas* (a good place to gaff salmon); *awaxanáycas* (where men would stand and sweep their dipnets through the current); and *swáycas* (could only be reached by swimming, where the dipnet poles had to be over 20 feet long to reach the current).[1]

When the first salmon arrived in early spring with the return of the swallows, Selam said that the people of Skin would have a ceremony celebrating the salmon's arrival and its journey from the ocean. In earlier times the village would have been out of food, Selam said, and the salmon's arrival would also indicate the coming months of plenty. A strong swimmer would swim well upstream above Celilo Falls and place, in the middle of the river as deep as he could dive, the remains of the first salmon taken.

During the heady days of summer fishing when a year's supply of food could be caught in a short period of time, Selam explained that the Salmon Chief, different from the village chief, would close the fishing, usually during the night and during times of mourning and religious ceremony, to allow the salmon to migrate past the falls to other fishing sites and to other native people farther up river—to Kettle Falls and the upper Columbia River extending into Canada and to the Snake River watershed in Idaho, a major tributary of the Columbia.

Also with me that day was Selam's nephew, Johnny Jackson, Chief of the Cascade Tribe, who told us that, based on the journals of Lewis and Clark and other early explorers and traders to the region, the Columbia River Indian fisheries had been estimated at over 20 million pounds of salmon a year. By 1995, on the other hand, the entire harvest had plummeted to just over 1 million pounds. If the dams on the Columbia River hadn't been built, the river's fishery would probably still be the largest in the world and worth billions of dollars. During the 1940s and 1950s, however, politicians often touted electricity over salmon, predicting that the revenue produced from electricity would far surpass that of salmon.

Today there are 14 hydroelectric dams on the Columbia River and another 14 dams on its major tributaries, most notably the upper, middle, and lower forks of the Snake River. Chief Jackson and many other Columbia River Indians cling to a way of life along the river that is little noticed by hundreds of wind surfers who now park their cars every weekend near his plywood shack. The River People, as they call themselves, never signed away their right to the land nor have they felt that the compensation—a few *in lieu* fishing sites—were adequate. By allowing the damming of the river and the destruction of the salmon runs, fishing sites, and communities like Skin, Jackson believes the government has violated their treaty rights.

Spending three days with Selam and Jackson listening to their stories of growing up on the Columbia River transported me back to 1974 when my interest in the impacts of hydroelectric dams innocently began. With five others, I canoed 500 miles of the Eastmain River, flowing from north-central Quebec westward into James Bay. Most of us were college students, and we spent that summer and fall exploring the Eastmain River before it was dammed and diverted 200 miles north to feed into a colossal series of dams destined to be the largest project of its kind in North America—the James Bay Hydroelectric Project. Engineers designed the James Bay Project to create a lake the combined size of Maine, Vermont and New Hampshire, to produce electricity for eastern Canada and for export to the urban areas of the Atlantic seaboard from Boston to Washington, D.C. Public utilities from these American cities supplied much of the funding for the project.

As young romantics with a love for adventure, we wanted to explore this pristine country before it was inundated, before the roaring canyons and cataracts—some more than 3 miles long—were silenced. We wanted to experience the feel of wilderness and what it takes to hunt and fish for your food. The Eastmain River country was home to trout, char and northern pike, ducks and geese, rabbits, beaver, moose, and herds of inland caribou. It was also home to more than 6,000 Cree Indians. During our three months of canoeing the river we occasionally passed

Snow patch along Sunrise Mine Trail

hunting camps where Cree subsisted almost exclusively on the wildlife. A "hidden" cost of the power project during the ten-year construction period was that most of the wildlife couldn't escape the rising waters; moreover, the project destroyed the anadromous fish runs and displaced the Cree from their land.

The Cree respected us for canoeing the river, and we were in awe of their bush and woodcraft skills. We would stop at their camps to say hello or to ask about what lay downstream. We liked to inspect the many skins of beaver, mink, caribou, and wolf that the Cree were drying and tanning. They taught us to respect the animals we hunted. Their rituals for honoring the taking of life, such as a bear's skull wrapped in birch bark or the long and sinuous vocal chords from geese placed in the top branches of a spruce tree (symbolically returning the voice of the geese to the sky from where they came, or so it seemed to me), captured my imagination.

We would ask questions of the Cree. Why did they pluck the down feathers from a duck's breast after they had shot it and place the feathers back in the water? Why did they wrap a bear's skull in birch bark? Or why did they hang those honker vocal chords in a tree? They would answer us enigmatically, "Because that's the way it's done." We talked mostly with the younger Cree who learned English from attending schools in southern Quebec and Ontario. The elders spoke a different language which we didn't know. I have been interested in the indigenous languages of North America ever since. I studied Athapaskan intensively when I was in college in the hopes of understanding, if only superficially, the social memories and natural history knowledge that these elders used to interpret the landscape. At the time of my visit in the mid-1970s, I was dumb to their land, an interested stranger passing through.

After three months we reached the mouth of the Eastmain River at James Bay, boarded a deHavilland prop plane, and left. In the years following, I often thought of the Eastmain River and the Cree, but I never was able to return. I followed in books and magazines the building of the dams and the consequences. I had trouble coping with my feelings of powerlessness, and I often wished I could just wave a wand and stop the destruction. Standing with Selam and Jackson, overlooking the inundated Celilo Falls, resurrected these submerged and discordant feelings. Why does my cultural tradition view the land differently than Selam and Jackson? I left Celilo thinking that I needed to use the dams as a window "to see" and to interpret the landscape.

Two hundred miles upstream from where I was standing with Selam and Jackson is the largest dam on the Columbia River and the biggest producer of electricity in the world—Grand Coulee Dam. Built in the 1930s, it is a marvel of monolithic construction, its architecture of a scale and design ahead of its time. I am moved by the sheer wonder of so much concrete piled so high. The base of the dam rests on the riverbed, and a network of over 20,000 steel trestles, 1,700 miles worth, give the concrete its strength. On May 25, 1939, 41,900 tons of concrete (still a world record) were poured in a single day!

One of the political reasons for building the dam during the Depression Era was for jobs to get the people of this country working again through public works projects. Other major considerations were flood control and irrigation. The latter has transformed the scablands of eastern Washington into a major producer of fruits and vegetables. The salmon runs were destroyed when the decision was made not to build ladders for the migrating fish. Today, with our increased ecological understanding, I doubt that such an obviously flawed decision could be made.

Grand Coulee Dam is run by the Bureau of Reclamation. When you enter the Bureau's Visitor Center in Coulee City, the first display that greets you begins: "In the Columbia River Basin man and nature work closely together to redistribute nature's gifts." Though the language seems dated, I wonder who spoke for nature and if nature can be consulted, as is implied by the phrase "man and nature work closely together." I doubt that the Bureau of Reclamation thinks the river has rights and interests. More likely it believes that to "work with nature" means analyzing a project according to cost-benefit perspectives. On the other hand, maybe the river does speak to us but we cannot hear or understand its language.

The mythological stories we have from the local Indians, who have lived along the Columbia River for 9,000 years, may be the best communication device we have for articulating and understanding nature's wishes. However, because the dam was built in a time of national emergency preceding World War II, the protests of the indigenous people went unheeded even though the land on the north and west sides of the river belonged to the Confederated Colville Tribes. These tribes are a collection of Salish- and Sahaptian-speaking peoples who, before the treaties of the 1850s, inhabited the land stretching from the North Cascades to the northern Rockies. One Coyote story of the Okanogan Salish relates how five sisters blocked the migrating salmon with a rock dam. Coyote turned himself into a baby and floated down the river on a cradle board which hung up at the dam and was discovered by the sisters who took Coyote in, believing he was a baby. The next day, when the sisters went off to dig camas and other roots, Coyote turned himself back to his real self and began working to tear down the dam. When the sisters returned each evening he would change himself back to a baby. This went on for four days, and on the fifth day, when the sisters were digging, one of their digging sticks broke and they took it as an omen that something was wrong with the baby. They rushed back to their homesite to find Coyote working feverishly to destroy the dam. The sisters attacked Coyote, but it was too late. He had freed enough of the dam that the force of the water surged through, destroying the rest of it and allowing the salmon to swim upriver. The sisters were turned into sandpipers and return each spring to announce the arrival of the salmon. Could this story from the distant past be a Salish interpretation of the river's wishes?

One day in summer 1995 while visiting Coulee City and Grand Coulee Dam, I met Andy Joseph, an Okanogan/Colville Indian and director of the Colville Tribal Museum. Joseph is a fluent speaker of interior Salish and has written a dictionary of the language. We took a drive up the western side of Lake Roosevelt, the body of water behind Grand Coulee Dam, to visit the national park at Kettle Falls. Before Coulee Dam was built, and 100 miles upstream of present-day Coulee City, Kettle Falls—*Shonotkwu* in the native Salish—was the second-largest fishery on the Columbia River. In the early nineteenth century, explorers like David Thompson wrote of a village at Kettle Falls crowded with over 1,000 Indians. Joseph told me that his family fished at the falls until 1941 when it was inundated by water backing up from Grand Coulee Dam. He also told me the story of Coyote and the sandpiper sisters. "My ancestral village is buried under the water. When the waters backed up, it threatened our school, churches, and other buildings. The government said they would relocate our village, but they never did; we had to save what we could at the last minute."

The upper Columbia River watershed, including what is now Lake Roosevelt, was land given to the Confederated Colville Tribes by executive order in April 1872. I asked Joseph what he thought about the future of the river, implying in my question how he had reconciled the loss of his village, fishing, and other cultural sites by the building of Grand Coulee Dam. After a pause he said, "The dam has been here for only fifty years. Our stories have been here for thousands. Maybe time's on our side."

Since 1972 and the completion of the North Cascades Highway (State Route 20), you can now approach the Skagit River Valley from the eastern side. Leaving Andy Joseph at Coulee City I drove through the Okanogan and Methow River Valleys, past the towns of Twisp, Winthrop, and Mazama to Rainy Pass, the east-west divide separating the Skagit watershed from the Columbia's. As I descended from Rainy, the highway followed Granite Creek, a tributary of Ruby Creek loudly pouring into the Skagit Basin.

In 1906, the first generator erected on Ruby Creek began supplying electricity to the gold mines in the Ruby Basin. Ruby Creek also caught the imagination of James Delmage Ross, Seattle City Light's superintendent and the person with the strongest political will to see the Skagit River developed for hydroelectricity. Ross first investigated Ruby Creek as a potential dam site in the early 1900s.

The glaciers that carved Ruby Creek and the Skagit River, and where Ross Dam now sits, stopped at Rip Raps—the lip of what used to be a thundering canyon—just downstream from where Ruby Creek joins the Skagit. Stopping my car at an overlook above Ross Dam, I saw to the east and immediately below me the flooded basin of Ruby Creek, and Ross Lake stretching to the north for many miles. The flooded Skagit Basin is also named after the superintendent. Another Ross, Alexander Ross, a British fur trader and explorer, first "discovered" this impassable canyon when he canoed down the Skagit River in the early 1800s. A few miles further west of this overlook is a trail to Ross Dam, a short, descending mile through hemlock, fir, and lodgepole pine. I hiked to the dam in less than an hour.

The journey to this spot at the turn of the century from LaConner and Mount Vernon, the way the miners and Ross had to come, was a dangerous and difficult trek that took many days, if not weeks. People frequently lost their lives crossing the river or negotiating many precipitous trails. Though Seattle City Light built a railroad from Rockport to Newhalem to facilitate the dam building, a road was not built to Newhalem, the town that housed and supported the construction workers, until

1939. The first dam was built at Gorge Creek, which began generating electricity to Seattle in September 1923. Initially, Seattle City Light planned to build a fish hatchery to compensate for the disrupted salmon runs, but the hatchery never materialized. The second dam, Diablo, named after the canyon where the Skagit rushed over steep drops between narrow stone walls, was dedicated in August 1930. At the time, Superintendent Ross crowed that soon the Skagit would be completely tamed.

Ross's prediction is now fact, and the place names coined by the miners—Devil's Corner, Diablo Canyon, and the like—conjure a culturally derived relationship with wilderness, labeling it as evil. The names imply that what got in their way—steep rock, fast rivers, big trees—was the work of the devil, to be tamed. It also implies that wilderness was an evil force that stood in the way of their desire: gold.

Twentieth-century America is a culture of inanimate things: concrete and steel, plastic and neon. On the Skagit and Columbia, and along other wild rivers of North America, we substitute nonliving objects for the living things of nature. I worry about the loss of this indigenous and natural language. These ancient languages, like Sanskrit, contain a vocabulary of our genetic, primordial, and mythological past, a knowledge worth saving. I worry that we force the fish and animals to abandon the land. Does the language of the river have to be sacrificed too, dumbing thousands of years of what was alive and singing? I have an emotional interest in this ancient speech; it reinforces my humility before the Creator. When we replace a river's voice with an object of steel and concrete, are we worshipping a golden calf and not the language of God?

These were some of my thoughts as I stood on top of Ross Dam and felt the wind and rain in my face. The last of the three dams on the Skagit River to be built, and finished in the late 1940s, Ross Dam provides flood protection for the lower valley as well as additional electricity for a growing Seattle. Visitors today can take a two-hour tour that visits both Diablo and Ross Dams, and on the *Alice Ross*, a boat named after Superintendent Ross's wife, cruise for fifteen minutes on the milky-green water of Diablo Lake over a canyon that seventy-five years ago roared with the heady speech of the river.

My friend Larry Campbell, who grew up in Concrete, met me recently at Diablo Lake Dam. Campbell has spent his entire life living near the river, and his Samish, Upper Skagit, Colville, and Swinomish bloodlines reveal that his ancestors have lived in either the Skagit or Columbia watersheds since the retreat of the glaciers 7,000 years ago. As we talked Campbell told me that his biological rhythms mirror the life cycle of the salmon. He fishes from May to December and at the end of the salmon cycle, when ceremonies take place in the smokehouse from December through April, his attention turns to spiritual concerns. The idea that we are genetically tied to our occupations and a particular landscape rings true to me. It was

Snags by the Nooksack River

not too long ago, just 5,000 years or so, that all our ancestors were hunters and gatherers and most likely our biological rhythms, even today, are tied genetically like an umbilical cord to the land.

As we leaned over the downstream side of Diablo Dam and remarked on the steepness and closeness of the canyon walls, a good place to build a dam, Campbell explained that the smokehouse ceremonies, in part, are for insuring the return of the salmon each spring. Campbell smiled and said, "During the first salmon ceremonies the elders would go down to the water and look at some of the salmon passing by and would indicate that such-and-such run of Chinook salmon should be allowed to swim upriver, unmolested, that these salmon were meant for Native people living farther upstream."

Like the salmon chief at Celilo Falls, Campbell's elders were teaching that the river's resources should be shared with everyone living on the river. Are the modern beavers who built the dams sharing the resource equitably? Or maybe Seattle City Light and Federal Energy Regulatory Commission are like the beaver in the Northwest Coast Indian myth as interpreted by Northwest poet David Wagoner in "How Raven Stole Beaver's Pond."

Raven said, "The Beaver is rich, he has many crayfish,
His pond is filled with trout, he has berries
Weighing their branches down into his mouth,
And frogs wait at his lodge door to be eaten."

So Raven dressed himself in his poorest feathers
And went to Beaver's lodge. He said, "I am poor,
I am your brother, we had the same father,
Show me your rich pond, we must eat together."

And Beaver took him to the water's edge
Where alder and cottonwood, maple and willow
Grew in young groves and peeled him the inner bark,
Bit off the pale-green shoots of waterlilies.

While Beaver gnawed at them, he said, "Good brother,
Why do you hide your hands under those feathers?
Your feet look crooked and sore. Your two black teeth
Look old and hollow. I must chew these for you."

When Raven saw those crayfish and trout and frogs
Swimming beyond him, the ripest berries hanging

Over the water where he could not reach them,
He scowled at the sticks and twigs heaped for his dinner.

He shouted, "Beaver is greedy! Beaver is no brother!
Yellow Teeth cannot fly! He is fat and muddy!"
He folded that pond together like a blanket
And carried it in his beak to a high fir tree.[2]

As a wild river the Skagit had a certain energy that the three dams have changed. How important is that change in the river's character? If, like Larry Campbell, we are genetically and spiritually programmed to regulate our lives according to certain natural energies and rhythms, how much turmoil in our inner life can be attributed to the changes in our natural landscapes? And since these changes have occurred quite recently, what genetic and spiritual changes in our relationship to the land are they precipitating?

Just a smooth sheen of water flows over the spillway at Diablo Dam, and the canyon downstream is quiet and empty, filled with boulders. Campbell told me that the spirit of the river is still there. "The dams and power stations have interrupted or made it more difficult for us to communicate with this spirit, and as the land has changed, our ceremonies have changed to reflect this. We no longer can go to the vision-questing spots near where the dams were built, or to the vision sites near the power stations—for one thing, the electrical current buzzing through the power lines interferes with our ability to hear what the river spirits are saying. Our elders say that the spirits are still there, but just harder to find. Some elders say, though, that the spirits are leaving like the salmon. I wonder," Campbell mused, "if I'll have to leave, too, when the salmon are gone."

CHARLES LUCKMANN has worked as an archaeologist, Outward Bound instructor and program director, high school and college teacher, naturalist, technical writer, and editor. Since 1992 he has developed educational programs for the North Cascades Institute. A resident of Bellingham, he is also the editor of the *Journal of Experiential Education*.

Cascade River: 1974–1996

Bob Keller

All our landscapes, from the city park to the mountain hike, are imprinted with our tenacious, inescapable obsessions.

Simon Schama, *Landscape and Memory*

Over the years, she had learned more from the river than from any one person, and what she'd been taught had always come with passion—intense pain or joy. It was the nature of the river to be both turbulent and gentle; to be abundant at times and lean at others; to be greedy and to yield pleasure.

Ursula Hegi, *Stones from the River*

On clear spring or summer mornings the sun appears south of Eldorado Peak to throw early light over the last 7 miles of the Cascade River Valley. The stream flows west to meet the Skagit at Marblemount, and a short distance above the confluence I watch daybreak slip down the slopes onto bottomland, dark trees that were invisible at night now taking on shape and color. As light reaches the valley floor, alder and cottonwood along the riverbanks transform themselves into flaming green. At such moments, as someone has remarked, it feels as though "no other day will ever attain the impossible splendor of this one." Silver mist hangs over a current which had its origin in the ice and snowfields of Eldorado, Hidden Lakes Peak, Razorback Mountain, Forbidden Peak, Snow King, the Triad, Johannesburg. The river flashes white when its water curls past a boulder or rushes against the bank. In every direction except where the Skagit carries it west, peaks and hills hem in the blue-green, free-flowing Cascade. Crisp and clear air, clean and cold water: this stream of mountain mornings is comparable only to daybreak in the desert or sunrise on isolated ocean beaches.

Our culture deems it unsatisfying merely to enjoy such places. The additional power, pride, and pleasure that come with land ownership thus led me to buy property on the Cascade River. But why *here*, when experiences of beauty and splendor inspire a long list of places equally compelling? My wife and I had lived and hiked in Arizona's Sonoran Desert; I have wandered for hundreds of miles in the Grand Canyon and Wind River Mountains, traversed the Olympics a number of times, stood at the snout of the Hoh Glacier 30 miles from a road, kayaked in Alaska, the Queen Charlotte Islands and along the west coast of Vancouver Island. In some ways I prefer Maine, still a hinterland compared to our new Northwest. My children loved Tucson, and I even liked living in Chicago. Puzzling over where to buy recreational land near Bellingham, we were torn between the North Cascades and the San Juan Islands. We first decided in favor of saltwater, set down earnest money on 150 feet of Eliza Island beachfront, then backed out at the last moment to choose the mountains instead. I don't know why, except I grew up in the shadow of Mount Rainier and helped my father build a lake cabin in the hills west of it. Forty years ago I took my first hike on Rainier's Wonderland Trail and slept beside its glacial streams. Maybe the Cascade Range is in my blood?

For whatever reasons, in 1974 we purchased land near Marblemount on the Cascade River: 1,300 feet of frontage, parallel to the river road, 50 miles inland from Skagit Bay toward the mountains, and 340 feet above sea level. The river, nearly 70 feet wide as it passes my property, still moves along briskly after having fallen several thousand feet during a 20-mile plunge from alpine basins. B&W Mountain, standing for Bartell and Weeden, rises 4,000 feet directly above us. The property includes three acres of meadow and about twenty-five acres of alder, fir, hemlock, maple, pine, cottonwood, and cedar. Total acreage in any given year depends on the mood of the river. A salmon stream threads through the meadow and a seasonal seepage channel in the woods provides more salmon lodging. Deer, beaver, coyote, weasels, and rabbits pass through. Bobcat and bear tracks appear on sandbars, but only two bear have visited in twenty years, giving some credence to rumors that another 1970s newcomer to the valley shot forty-three during his first year. Mergansers cruise the river in summer, bald eagles congregate during the fall runs.

Piliated woodpeckers disappeared at the same time as the drumming grouse, around 1978, perhaps retreating into the national park 5 miles away. We still see heron perched on stones or wading the shallows.

We owned a home in Bellingham, and did not need the land—and the land certainly did not need more city-dwellers dividing it into recreational retreats. The purchase represented an idea, or rather a set of ideas, some held at the start and others evolving over time: to live here more simply and differently than in the city, to quietly observe the river and mountains, to own a private base camp for climbing, and to restore abused land back to health while coming to know it intimately—an ambitious and somewhat immodest set of goals. As the rumor about the bear killings might have forewarned us, the place and our work here would turn out to be less idyllic than first anticipated.

No one invents their own values and attitudes, and few of us have a clear comprehension of all the people, events, books, places, parents, teachers, and philosophies that shape our view of the world. In this case the main concepts seemed to have come from Aldo Leopold, Wendell Berry, and Henry David Thoreau. *A Sand County Almanac* prescribed a property-owner ethic and offered a model for practicing it. "That land is a community is the basic concept of ecology," Leopold insisted, "but that land is to be loved and respected is an extension of ethics. . . . Land is not merely soil; it is a fountain of energy flowing through a circuit of soils, plants and animals . . . whoever owns land has assumed, whether he knows it or not, the divine functions of creating and destroying."[1] From Wendell Berry and from *Walden* one learns that knowing a single place well discloses more than seeing many places fleetingly. "I have travelled a good deal in Concord," Thoreau said, celebrating the particular over the general, the immediate and specific over the distant and abstract. Thoreau had a "conviction that the whole world can be revealed in our backyard if only we give it our proper attention."[2] Above all, as we took title to this raw land, we heard the voice of Wallace Stegner who, more than any other modern writer, taught us to value a sense of place and made clear how much that awareness has been lost to our culture.

Ideals, of course, are relatively easy to hold, not so easy to maintain, and difficult to realize. My climbing plans succumbed to the pleasures of building a cabin, splitting firewood, and just walking around in these woods. Actively restoring land, as against leaving it alone, proved complex and required more knowledge than we anticipated. Next, even on thirty acres of privacy, enjoyment of the river and its solitude depended on what happened nearby and beyond our control—logging and the river itself. Personal use of the property by friends and ourselves, on the other hand, proved easier to manage.

The one-room log cabin took six weeks to raise, then a few years to finish. Standing at the end of a quarter-mile-long dirt road, it has two bunks, an icebox, table, stools, and rocking chair; it heats with a Franklin fireplace, has no electricity, no running water or propane. On the coldest winter nights it warms to 10°F above freezing; during summer it is abandoned for a tent and firepit by the river. After three break-ins, we stopped locking the door, there not being much left to steal or harm. Like us, friends and relatives find it a comfortable retreat.

The land and its cabin do not signify rejection of urban values; rather, both embody contrast. Instead of an American second home or cottage that replicates the main household, we wanted weekends, weeks, or even months in the North Cascades to be different, which to us meant doing without lights, television, oven, freezer, refrigerator, computer, radio, bath, microwave, fax, and telephone. Not counting a concession to the chain saw, all tools run on muscle, except in emergencies when a neighbor arrives with his tractor. Kerosene, wood heat, and hauled water are not better ways to live: the kerosene stinks, the wood pollutes, and the water pail quickly runs dry or may carry giardia. But they are simpler and different. We remain in relative control; physical effort helps us to appreciate sophisticated luxuries often taken for granted in Bellingham. We become aware of how variously people can and have lived. Most of all, we gain perspective on our culture, as Leopold did fifty years ago: "Nothing could be more salutary at this stage," he wrote, "than a little healthy contempt for a plethora of material blessings."

Whereas weekend or monthly visits can minimize human impact on land, such limited residence also makes it impossible to know people. Thus, we consider and accept ourselves as outsiders, perhaps not even as welcome as summer visitors who leave much more cash in the community than we do. In the eyes of local merchants we may belong with "those backpackers with their sunflower seeds and dried fruit who don't spend a nickel for nothing." Other differences can be striking as well: we do not fish or hunt, do not own firearms or operate heavy equipment, seldom volunteer in the village, and we do like the National Park Service.

Save us from gale and storm, O Lord
And from the German traveling abroad!

And from prosperous hikers, cyclists, mountain climbers, birdwatchers, and hobby farmers who burst into the country planning to make it over in their own image. In the 1960s the Federal Republic of Germany issued passports with a set of "Golden Rules for Germans Traveling Abroad." Many of the cautions make good sense for urban/rural relations, whether in Moab, Mazama, or Marblemount:

- If you are of the foolish opinion that everything outside Germany is worse, stay at home.

- ◆ Whenever traveling in a foreign country, see to it that it echoes with your silence. The quieter *you* are, the louder *others* will talk.
- ◆ Dress to blend in with the natives.
- ◆ Don't try to shine when a foreigner knows more than you; when you know more, let yourself be defeated with a smile.
- ◆ Try to understand what seems strange; if you can't, look first for the reason in yourself.
- ◆ In a foreign country, lift your finger only to learn, never to teach.[3]

Despite or perhaps because of these rules, we became friends with our neighbors who once owned the land, Ralph and Helen Dexter. He had been an outfitter, logger, and electrician; she had handled trucks, buses, and pack horses. The Dexters raise most of their food, build what they need, and can repair nearly anything. They share meals, cash, tools, and time with people in need, stranger or friend.

A short, slight woman who at eighty can still outwork many teenagers, Helen Dexter came to Marblemount from Idaho with her first husband, Larry Winn, a mechanic for logging outfits in Alaska and Oregon; he died from cancer the day before Christmas, 1965. It is hard to believe that this quiet, demure lady has led mule trains loaded with dynamite to the Thunder Mountain mines, cooked and bossed camps for trail crews, and once stayed in the backcountry for forty-one straight days. During a fall evening she crossed the Skagit at dusk in a canoe to deliver a child, Aaron Bussier, and earlier she was the first woman to drive a school bus in the upper valley.

Ralph Dexter, now in his late sixties, grew up just south of the Stillaquamish east of Granite Falls. He topped and rigged his first tree a week before his fourteenth birthday and he left school at age fifteen to begin logging on the Upper Skagit. Short and wiry, he quickly became a high-rigger, in those days the highest-paid job in the woods. He was among the first men to use a chain saw for topping trees, some of them Douglas-firs over 200 feet tall. Later he led crews that cut through extensive stretches of North Cascade old growth. A life member of the National Rifle Association, Ralph has guided hunters for deer, goats, and bear. He is also a naturalist with a large personal library to supplement his phenomenal memory for insects, flora, fauna, and birds. With rain slanting against the house on winter nights, he sits by a window reading Richard Dawkins' *River Out of Eden: A Darwinian View of Life*, books by Stephen Jay Gould, or Brian M. Fagan's *Ancient North America: the Archaeology of a Continent*. His knowledge of local history is immense and detailed, once the basis for a weekly column in the *Concrete Herald*. Dexter does not admire the Park Service, considering it a federal bureaucracy that put him and his wife out of the packing business so it could mismanage a wilderness, yet in the 1960s, on

The Kellers' cabin

environmental grounds, he opposed the North Cross-State Highway as well as Seattle City Light's proposed Copper Creek dam. Knowing Helen and Ralph Dexter has become part of our relationship with the Cascade River.

Besides enjoying friendship with the Dexters, we have bought supplies from Gary Stewart, cedar shakes from Clarence Jones, and hired a bulldozer from Gene Graignic to move the cabin. Fritz Wenrich hauled rocks from his quarry, and Keith and Dawn Nushart raised the finest pork on the Skagit. Dan and Sara Huntington were always friendly at the Mountain Song Restaurant, a collective enterprise founded in the early 1970s but now gone. Like everyone in Marblemount, we know Merv Peterson and also had the good fortune to meet his father Otto, an early settler in the valley. And like everyone else, we visit the post office daily, looking for mail and chatting with the postmaster.

We owned our land for twenty years before any conflict with Marblemount neighbors occurred, and instead of involving the Dexters, Joneses, or Petersons, it happened with urban immigrants like ourselves. In 1994 an Everett couple purchased eighty nearby acres with hopes of realizing their dream, the creation of a private recreational-vehicle park to be called American Alps Resort. Their resort occupies land formerly owned by Golden Phoenix. The new owners bought their recently clearcut unit with intentions of replanting and rebuilding the habitat. Well suited to the county government's growth philosophy, the resort conformed to zoning requirements and glided through hearings and reviews to gain approval by summer, 1995.

One can ponder how Thoreau or Aldo Leopold might have reacted to a new neighbor with one hundred full-amenity RV sites, fifty tent platforms, five cabins, two bathhouses, a service center, playground, swimming pool, caretaker, and clubhouse. The developers, the Forest Service, and local officials all agreed that expanding the actual or planned 700 RV sites between Rockport, Newhalem, and Colonial Creek was consistent with the future of the North Cascades. They noted that Skagit County's comprehensive plan called for promotion of outdoor recreation and tourism, with the Forest Service endorsing the new resort as "consistent with the desired future condition of the Skagit Wild & Scenic River."[4]

The Forest Service notwithstanding, American Alps Resort seemed incompatible with a one-room, nonamenity log cabin on wildlife habitat-zoned open space. Not only did the project mean more traffic, noise, outdoor lighting, and potential stream pollution, it also, despite genuine environmental convictions held by its owners, embraced a different philosophy about how society should use the North Cascades. As part of the continuing mechanization of outdoor recreation, an RV resort imports urban leisure values of power and convenience into rural settings. Dirt bikes, personal watercraft, snowmobiles, outboards, jet boats, dune buggies and helipads, ski lifts and trams reach their climax with motorized homes, vehicles which bring families into the country to enjoy comforts of townhouse and suburb. Instead of land for sleeping outdoors, running rivers, hunting, packing, climbing, and exploring on foot or horseback, the North Cascades becomes a place to recline and relax. Instead of being different, it is more of the same.

Like the owners of American Alps Resort, in 1974 we arrived upriver with intentions of restoring our land. The person who had previously purchased the property from the Dexters had cut a fresh road above the riverbank, his first and last step toward a future trailer court before cancer intervened, forcing him to sell to us. Years earlier the forest here had been logged and never replanted, a few cedar and fir stumps five feet thick the only remnants of giant trees once occupying this land prior to our tangle of alder, cottonwood, devil's club, and vine maple. Ruins of a collapsed sawmill poked up through moss and deadfall on the Cascade Lumber and Shingle Company site where, in 1954, Ralph Dexter had milled 20,000 board feet of fir and hemlock a day. Twenty years later, in 1974, a dozen abandoned cars dotted the riverbank woods, surprising the unsuspecting hiker. Six or seven open pits also pockmarked the land.

One of the first unpleasant tasks involved the gravel pits—telling Fritz Wenrich that his previous supply of accessible river-run sand and gravel was closed. Then came three years of planting, pruning, thinning, and more planting in an effort to make the land once again resemble the thick forests that rose above it.

Transplanting young cedars met with some limited success and a few healthy firs set around the meadow have survived, but the Dexters and others must have shaken their heads when we placed 200 Weyerhaeuser fir seedlings (only a nickel each) on either soggy or rocky ground under a cottonwood canopy. They must have laughed aloud at the sight of city folk planting alder sprouts in the gravel pits. Fritz Wenrich, who had spent all but two of his sixty years near Marblemount, watched us fret over his excavations. "Nature always comes back," he said of the gravel pits, "no matter what humans may do."

Besides transplanting alders, our naïveté did not account for two forces beyond individual control, one geological and the other economic: floods and logging.

For millennia all of our land had been floodplain. Today eighty percent still is. When buying the property my urban eye did not observe that most of the forest "damage" had not been the work of humans but of a higher order, namely rapid, swirling water loaded with debris. The valley's crisscrossing, empty, and overgrown channels that appeared on the assessor's aerial photos in Mount Vernon seemed only remnants of ancient history, not a warning. The massive stumps, old standing maples, and ninety big cedars scattered over thirty acres testified that the Cascade had to remain within or near its present banks. It does not, and never has.

The North Cascades requires a special combination of weather to unleash major floods down its western slopes, random conditions which coincide every few years. By early November the soil must be either saturated or frozen before a storm drops a heavy layer of wet snow in the foothills down to 2,000 feet. Before the snow can consolidate, a fresh storm sweeps in out of the south on warm winds, carrying sheets of rain that drench the earth for 2 and 3 days. After the first 24 hours, a turbulent Cascade has filled its banks. After 48 hours it looks more like surging mud than water, bouncing along boulders, stones, roots, and tree trunks that include 150-foot hemlocks and cedars as well as everything else that grows in the mountains. Now 400 feet wide, pushing aside anything in its path, including its banks, the river is sheer, breathtaking power. By the third day it runs and spreads everywhere, braiding new channels, stripping and shattering large trees into splinters, turning frontage land from green cover into rock, sand and silt.

It always recedes, the new landscape turning out to be wild if not very scenic. Four hundred feet of riprap from Wenrich's quarry has disappeared from our bank. Weyerhaeuser's saplings are somewhere between Hamilton and Fir Island in the Skagit delta. Medium-sized fir and pine along the proposed trailer court driveway are gone, as is the drive itself. Parts of the cabin road are now trench.

This has happened not once but eight times: in 1975, 1979, 1980, 1989, 1990 (twice) and 1995 (twice). The cabin, originally set 300 feet away from the stream, presumed safe among cottonwoods mistakenly imagined to be at least seventy-five years old, enjoyed a classic river view. Downstream between cabin site and river stood a grove of mammoth maples, some with moss-covered lower limbs 50 feet long and 3 feet thick, almost equal in girth to their trunks. The oldest maples must have looked over the Cascade when Alexander Ross came down the river in 1814. But after the 1979 flood these maples disappeared, probably lodged in a fifteen-foot-high jam between us and the state fish hatchery, a facility itself nearly submerged by Jordan Creek after the 1980 flood. The river, which normally erodes or rebuilds its bank a foot or two a year, by 1985 had sliced off 300 feet to flow within two yards of the cabin. A classic view indeed.

With the help of Ralph Dexter, Gene Graignic, and others we retreated another 400 feet from the river, moving the cabin to higher ground (but still low enough for the 1990 and 1995 floods to reach its steps). New trees installed around the meadow survived: a 6-foot fir planted in 1976 now stands 75 feet tall and a 1974 sequoia Christmas tree, the very first act of renewal, reaches 55 feet. A cedar sprout on a nurse log in twenty years has grown into a 16-inch trunk that rises up over 50 feet. Transplanted from near Lake Whatcom and flourishing in our meadow stands the offspring of a century-old butternut. Otherwise, land restoration, or perhaps we should say *rearrangement*, is left to the river. Dogwoods disappear on their own. Fir and hemlock do not like a floodplain of stones instead of soil. Cedar and maple do better, except that silt-caused rot around the base of maples will eventually bring them down as effectively as a chain saw. In the midst of this, we have learned to respect the tough virility and persistence of cottonwood and alder which require no human help with their sex life.

A more recent factor in the frequent deluges has been large-scale logging in the Cascade River watershed. Assuming that the Cascade parallels timber harvest rates in Skagit County, the greatest cuts in history occurred in 1977, 1983, 1985, 1986, 1987, 1990, 1991, and 1992. The record harvest happened in 1986 when almost eighty percent more timber left the mountains than a decade earlier.[5] Nevertheless, extensive removal of forests did not cause or start the floods. A November torrent swept away the Lucinda Davis homestead a mile downstream from us in 1897 after

Davis had barely survived high water in 1894 and 1896. The Skagit, coming up 23 feet in 8 hours in 1897, also took out Sauk City below Marblemount. In 1909 the waters rose 2 feet higher.[6] Early reports of the Lower Skagit describe one immense logjam 5 miles wide, and local folklore recounts an old Indian advising early settlers on where to put their homesteads: "See mud on tree. Build higher." Major floods racked the Skagit drainage in 1917, 1921, 1932, 1935, 1949, and 1951, well before the large-scale clearcuts of the past thirty years.[7]

Still, laying bare entire mountainsides no doubt increases runoff and produces heavy erosion, such as the Lookout Mountain and Boulder Creek mud slides into Cascade River Park. The former killed four people 5 miles above us on November 1, 1985, and was caused by logging on steep slopes, a 4-inch downpour in 24 hours, clearcutting, and faulty road construction.[8] Logging most likely contributed to an increased general flooding between 1974 and 1995; exactly how much is difficult to determine.

The most negative environmental impact on our land, however, has not been high water, which quickly recedes to reveal an interesting if altered landscape, but, instead, the ugliness of clearcut logging. The views across and upriver are no longer forested; they resemble the vistas of southern Arizona as fresh clearcuts shine like so many orange gashes under the morning sun. In a few months these 240-acre tracts will become gray-brown swaths that will remain for a half-dozen years or more until new growth takes over. The extent and magnitude of altered landscape is inescapable.[9]

I own a chain saw, am not opposed to logging, and have cut down perhaps 200 trees on my land in twenty years, including a number of large ones. I can even understand the logging error in 1995 that burned 225 acres of timber on the northwest slope of B&W Mountain behind my property. But shaving entire hillsides and stripping rock faces seems foolish, as do short harvest cycles, logging above 4,000 feet, and cutting on steep slopes or along creeks and streams. Today, trucks that work on lower Lookout Mountain carry loads that resemble the matchstick bundles extracted from Maine's exhausted woods.

The aesthetic and spiritual costs are clear. New forest growth at various stages, section by section, can never replace mile after magnificent mile of fir, hemlock, and cedar as far as the eye can see. Tree farms evoke no mystery, patriotism, or awe. A forest does. For Americans like William O. Douglas, Albert Bierstadt, James Fenimore Cooper, William Cullen Bryant, Thomas Cole, and Frederick Edwin Church, "the Promised Land is a dense woodland, not forbidding or packed with heathen terror, but a sanctuary in the literal sense of holy asylum. Its foliage trickles with sunlight; its waters run sweet and clear. It is the tabernacle of liberty, ventilated by the breeze of holy freedom and suffused with the golden radiance of providential benediction."[10] In 1974 the hills flanking the Cascade River still seemed to possess these qualities and a life of their own. Seeing them, one felt that "I matter but little" as when looking at stars that burn over the cabin on clear winter nights. A panorama of clearcuts sends no such message. It more resembles Seattle or Everett, where the glare of lights means people can no longer wonder at the stars.

Industrial-scale logging is visually and philosophically disturbing, but cutting on small, privately owned woodlots of a few acres is more annoying. During the so-called Spotted Owl crisis of the 1990s, timber prices rose, benefiting individual owners with small sections of forested land not blocked by cutting freezes.[11] In 1995 local mills paid an average of $400 per 1,000 board feet; export logs brought over $950. In the middle of Marblemount twenty acres of large trees came down because, people said, a widow "didn't want her kids to get it." Above us, an elderly couple cut their property in 1990 for $15,000 needed to supplement a token pension. To the west a younger man had spent ten years building a home in the woods, then moved to the San Juan Islands and sold his house and thirteen acres for $160,000 to a new owner who immediately collected $40,000 by just cutting the trees. Our neighbor Ralph Dexter, a sixty-seven-year-old retired logger working alone in drizzle and mud, could selectively cut four of his acres in 100 hours for a net profit of $8,000.

Eighty dollars an hour inspires a lot of loggers, including some who, unlike Dexter, are not especially good at it. The laughing men who logged the land directly north of my cabin were not selective or careful. A buzz of equipment shattered the morning solitude. Then, heedless of a salmon stream in their path, they splintered and destroyed alders and maples as they pulled out fir and hemlock; at one point they dropped two trees into a third. Cutting of immature stands on a few acres along the Cascade dissolves any illusion that the Northwest is still forested, an illusion lost years ago by those who climb or fly.

Logging and clearcuts are now part of the North Cascades and thus part of our modern memory—owning river frontage is no return to nature or escape from society. In our time any line between wild and domestic has blurred, perhaps never having been as distinct a line as we like to believe. Nor is the line between us and the past firmly fixed. If it seems today that "our impatient appetite for produce has ground the earth to thin and shifting dust," nevertheless humans always remember much more than what appears.[12] As Simon Schama has shown, all landscapes evoke a past, "generation laid over generation," to create meanings for us today and for those who come after us. Just as future generations will remember and no doubt better understand the RV resorts and clearcuts that so disturb me, occupying river land offers various levels of memory even now. With inquiry and effort we learn of the Skagit and Cascade Rivers' many-layered history and culture—of natives, of whom Annie Dillard writes in *The Living*; of miners pushing over Cascade Pass into Horseshoe Basin; of some other prospectors, or maybe just promoters, 660 feet deep in an adit above Skagit Queen Creek; of eternal summers, such as those Gary Synder and Jack Kerouac spent at places like Lookout Mountain, when lookouts were still lookouts. The names of peaks also tell of natives, miners, explorers, and climbers—Sauk, Sahale, Trapper, Tee Bone Ridge, Helen Buttes, Diobsud, Eldorado, Triconi Peak, Ripsaw Ridge, Sharkfin Tower, Mount Torment.

On our land beside the Cascade River lie the remains of a sawmill where a ten-man crew once cut 20,000 board feet of old growth a day. Above it rises the southwest gully of B&W where on July 15, 1952, logger Shirley Cook and his son Charley died in a roaring funnel of fire. What we now call our meadow was once someone's pasture bordered by prune trees and with water piped across it. My children first came here at ages ten and thirteen and they later brought along a Springer spaniel named Charlie who for fifteen years sniffed through the undergrowth and raced into any possible puddle. He lies buried beneath the sequoia, a grave that Ralph and Helen Dexter honored with flowers. Friends have used the land as a fishing and climbing camp, a rendezvous, a Big Brothers campout, a place to be joined in marriage, a site for meditation, or simply a place with clean air.

Land, river, cabin, and Marblemount carry these meanings and more. We camp next to the river after hot summer days and watch the sun settle behind Sauk Mountain as hills turn from violet to purple. In winter we stargaze under one of the best night skies left in Western Washington. Awakening into the Cascade's shining mornings, I like to imagine Alexander Ross 180 years ago with his Indian guides marching from Fort Okanogan across the crest, then over Cascade Pass, dropping down between Sahale and Johannesburg to stumble across the headwaters of my river. "We fell upon a small creek so meandering that we had to cross and recross it upwards of forty times," he later recalled.

> The water was clear and cold and soon increased so much that we had to avoid it and steer our course from point to point on the north side. . . . We were among the rugged cliffs and deep groves of the mountain, where we seldom experienced the cheerful sight of the sun; nor could we get to any elevated spot clear enough to have a view of the surrounding country . . . for we could seldom see to any distance, so covered was all around us with a thick and almost impenetrable forest.[13]

Familiar questions with no easy answers often come to mind for sojourners like Ross. The same questions came to Thoreau, Aldo Leopold, and Wendell Berry, and after buying the land they also arose in my mind. Who was here before us? What lessons can this place teach? Where do we truly belong in the world? In a lifetime, how many of the earth's places can a single individual know and love with steady, unremitting passion?

Writing this in Buchenbach, Germany, I know the river and land are still there, 9,000 miles away. I know, having been born in the Northwest, that I belong in

Washington and especially in its mountains, however fascinating the rest of the world may be. Owning one-twentieth of a square mile in the North Cascades for twenty-two years has brought me floods and gentle meandering, satisfaction and sorrow, joy and frustration. Not much has been achieved in trying to restore this land. Even when we own private forest tracts and streams, we end up feebly confronting our powerful society—feeling a cold fear for the future while finding personal pleasure in the present. Yet despite anger over neglect of rivers and abuse of land, much remains constant when I stand above the Cascade, a place of crisp mornings and spacious days:

> And what is grief beside it?
> What is anger beside it?
> It is unfinished. It will not
> be finished . . .
> The seasonless river
> lays hand and handiwork
> upon the world, obedient
> to a greater mind.[14]

A lifetime resident of the Pacific Northwest, BOB KELLER has taught history and mountaineering at Olympic College in Bremerton and Western Washington University's Fairhaven College in Bellingham. An historian, he has published extensively on U.S. Indian policy and is currently completing a book about national parks.

Finding My Way Home

WENDY WALKER

The Stehekin Valley is tucked away in the North Cascades at the wild north end of Lake Chelan. No roads run to the valley from the outside world. The only way to get there is by boat, plane, or long hikes through the mountains.

Less than a hundred people live in this mountain valley. It takes planning, effort, and time to leave Stehekin: a full day's hike, a four-hour boat trip, or an expensive flight in a float plane. Members of the Stehekin community are committed by isolation to intimacy with each other and to the place.

Is it possible to be intimate with a mountain valley? *Intimacy* seems too human a word to wrap around rock cliffs, waterfalls, and winter storms. And yet I experienced intimacy with the Stehekin Valley during the two years I lived there. Intimacy taught me how to love a place and how to find my way home.

I first visited Stehekin in 1976 on my days off from my wilderness ranger job in the Glacier Peak Wilderness. I was eager to see the place I had heard so much about, this isolated and mountainous valley with just a few, hardy people. So I hiked over Cascade Pass into the Stehekin Valley, took the Park Service shuttle bus down the Stehekin Road, and spent one night camped by Lake Chelan.

❖ Journal, *August 1976* ❖

I'm sitting in front of my tent in the late afternoon sun. A fresh wind off the lake rustles the branches of pines overhead. It would be hard to ever tire of this view.

Across the lake, rock fortress mountains rise vertically from the blue water. To the right, the Stehekin River Valley yawns green, hemmed in by ragged rock ridges. Far away, at the head of the valley, I can see the snow-capped peaks of the high Cascades. I was up there this morning.

Cascade Pass! I hiked up the trail at a see-how-fast-I-can-make-it speed, red-faced and sweating, feeling strong, exhilaration mounting. A few last strides and I crested the pass. I dropped my pack and felt like I could fly.

Sweet, heady smells rose from meadows warmed by the sun. Cool winds bathed my hot face. The glacier-hung crags of Johannesburg soared above on one side, Sahale Peak's meadowed shoulders rolled upwards on the other. And below, beckoning me east: the Stehekin Valley.

I followed the trail down through the headwaters of the Stehekin River. The stream trickled through mountain meadows, past wind-twisted clumps of subalpine trees, and then plummeted into a forest of hemlock and fir.

I rested for lunch beside a deep pool beneath a waterfall. The water was a clear lens magnifying pebbles on the bottom of the pool. I reached in for a speckled egg of granite. But the water was much deeper than it looked and my hand came up dripping and empty.

Hours later, I stumbled into Cottonwood Camp, the end of the trail. The river fans out there and flows slowly through the sunlit flat. I sat on the riverbank, my sore feet in the water, watching cutthroat trout shimmer in the shallows.

The Park Service shuttle rumbled up in a cloud of dust. I climbed in and we lurched slowly down the rutted dirt road. Out the dusty windows I saw Park and Agnes Creeks pour their milky glacier water into the river. Bridge Creek added clear snowmelt. The river grew into a raging turmoil of rapids and waterfalls. The roar of the water was louder than the roar of the old van.

The steep granite walls of the valley opened wider as we descended. The forest thinned and orange-barked ponderosa pine replaced fir and cedar. We rounded a curve to a sweeping view of green fields and grazing horses, with a large log cabin in the background. The driver told us this was the Courtney Ranch, belonging to one of the early homesteading families.

As we descended further, the river slowed and meandered away from the road and then back again. More houses peeked through the trees. We passed a 1950s car and a pickup truck that looked as if it had been built before World War II. Residents barge cars and trucks up the lake so they can drive up and down the one-lane bumpy road that goes nowhere at either end.

In the last few miles we could see Rainbow Falls, cascading for 300 feet off a valley wall, and we passed the little log cabin that houses the one-room school. The sunflowers and vegetable gardens of the Honey Bear Bakery seemed too orderly in such a wild place. Finally we glimpsed the blue expanse of Lake Chelan through the trees.

Our bus trip ended at the town of Stehekin which hugs the shore near where the Stehekin River flows into the lake. It consists of boat docks, a cluster of houses, a lodge and visitor center for North Cascades National Park, and some lakeside campsites.

After I made camp, I walked back up the road to the bakery and then strolled to the school, cinnamon roll in hand. The door was unlocked. Ten old-fashioned desks and a huge, old woodstove filled the room. I sat in one of the desks and ate my roll while I looked through student papers that had been left out for visitors to read.

I'd like to teach in that school someday. I long to live in a place like Stehekin. It almost seems as if I could go back in time here, to a simpler, safer era, where I might belong to a real community and live more in touch with myself and my surroundings.

The next day I asked about the school and found out that the teacher was well liked and planned to stay there for the rest of his life. I left my lakeshore campsite, took the shuttle to the Agnes Creek trailhead, and hiked the forested 20 miles to return to work patrolling the Glacier Peak Wilderness.

By 1982, five years later, I had acquired a teaching certificate, a husband, a daughter, and a job at a tribal school in northwest Washington. When funding was cut at the school, my principal suggested I start searching for another teaching position. There was only one job posted at the college placement office—at the Stehekin School.

So I applied, with my husband Carey, and we were hired as a teaching team. In August we barged an old pickup full of household gear up the lake, and moved into a Park Service house with our two-year-old daughter Erin. A week later we began teaching nine children, from kindergarten to eighth grade, in the same little log school I had found so enchanting years before.

Many of my memories of Stehekin have to do with travel—walking to school each day, biking the 5 miles home at night from my Park Service evening program, toiling up endless switchbacks to the valley rim, cross-country skiing with a new baby riding behind, bundled into a sled. I think I first got to know the place by traveling through it in the course of my daily living.

The Stehekin River became almost a sentient being for me. The river ran near

Magic Mountain
from Cascade Pass

our house; it ran near everybody's house. The river created the valley and we were living in its course. I never felt it begrudged us a flat spot, but then, I never lived through a flood. Old-timers told stories of the river pouring through houses, sweeping away bridges, and tearing up much of the roadbed, carrying it miles down-stream. During my time in Stehekin the river stayed pretty much in its banks.

But the river talked to us. Day and night we listened to its voices.

❖ Journal, *September 1982* ❖

I'm sitting by the woodstove at the school in the early morning. The students won't be here for over an hour. I built a fire so the school will be warm by the time they arrive. It felt good to split wood; now my arms are as awake as my legs.

I walked to school this morning along the one-lane road wedged be-tween dark rock cliffs and the clear, green river. I walked before sunrise. In the darkness, the sounds of the river guided me—so many different voices in the moving water—like watery conversation. I marvel that I only really seem to hear the river when my eyes aren't working.

Smells rose from the water, smells with no words to quite fit them—cold, fresh river smells. Morning breezes tossed around the sweet scent of ponderosa pine. A sudden gust of cold wind down from the cliffs brought the smell of snow.

I was breathing hard, coming up the hill before the school. My eyes registered a large, dark shape ahead. It moved. I sucked in my breath. A bear—a very large cinnamon black bear was lumbering across the road in the dawn light. Thick fur bunched and relaxed with each stride. Small eyes peered in my direction but the bear didn't slow down, just padded off into the trees, heading for the apple orchard.

I ran the rest of the way to school, adrenaline pumping. What a way to start the day!

The fire is crackling in the stove. I need to look over my lesson plans so I will feel centered and ready for the kids when they come through the door.

The Stehekin Valley changed the way I taught. The log school building was very different from the modern structures down lake. The woodstove provided the only heat and outhouses were the only bathrooms. The school had no bells, telephones, or computers, and the electricity was erratic. We kept kerosene lanterns on hand so classes could continue whenever the power went out.

But the changes involved more than adjusting to a rustic school building. The valley itself influenced the educational process. Stehekin was safe enough that many children walked or rode their bikes to school each day. Even first graders walked several miles to school and back. The kids arrived awake, alert, and often full of stories about what they had seen on their way to school.

School field trips were easy in Stehekin. We studied stream ecology right out our back door in Rainbow Creek. We found inspiration for creative writing and drawing by walking a quarter mile to sit in the roar and mist of Rainbow Falls. In the fall we hiked up into the mountains to study timberline ecology and abandoned gold mines.

One sunny October morning, we walked the half mile to the historic Buckner Orchard and pressed apple cider.

❖ Journal, *October 1982* ❖

We went to the Buckner Orchard today. The kids played tag as they ran down the trail along the irrigation ditch. We left the woods and entered the orchard to see McGregor Mountain rising skyward behind the rows of apple trees. Its summit was white-tipped with new snow. I wonder how long before snow falls down here in the valley.

The cold air smelled of wood smoke and rotting apples. There are windfall apples all over the ground under the trees. I'd like to come back at night to see bear and deer feeding. An old horse-drawn plow was leaning against a rusting steam tractor at the edge of the orchard, as if the farmer just stopped in the middle of a workday and walked away.

Carey met us in the orchard with our old white pickup truck. The kids chose a tree laden heavily with red apples gleaming amidst clusters of green leaves. We backed the truck under the tree and everyone started shaking the branches. Down thumped the fruit, filling the bed of the truck.

We drove the apples to the cider press and the younger kids began washing them and shoving them into the press. The older ones took turns turning the crank. Amber juice gushed out. What a tangy smell. We couldn't wait and slurped long drinks from the first jug. Ahhh! Each of us took home a gallon of cider from school today. I don't know if I'll ever be able to drink store-bought apple juice again.

In winter, the kids cross-country skied for physical education, built snow forts at recess, and produced an elaborate Christmas play. Half a dozen adults volunteered to help with the play and every person in the valley came on the snowy night of our performance.

When the snow melted in the spring we hiked along the lakeshore to study limnology and rattlesnake life cycles. We studied the history of the valley and created an exhibit for the Park Service visitor center, with photographs and student writings about the history of the school. In May, when tourists began to visit the national park, students gave guided tours through the school each afternoon.

Sometimes I felt the Stehekin Valley did more of the teaching than I did. The valley certainly amplified, illustrated, and made memorable many of the lessons.

There were unspoken requirements for staying year-round in Stehekin. The human community let us know in many subtle ways that we needed to learn how to take care of ourselves. I knew it would take a lifetime to really learn to be self-sufficient, but we began to be aware of what our responsibilities might entail.

Most of our food was delivered by boat, from the grocery store in Chelan, 50 watery miles away. We tried to grow food in our garden and gather it from the wild. But gardens were meager in the rocks and sand of the mountain valley, and our palates, accustomed to romaine lettuce from California, had trouble adjusting to steamed stinging nettles.

But each fall we picked as many apples as we could use from the old Buckner

Orchard. This historic site, now managed by the Park Service, had once been a commercial orchard, the only profitable farming ever done in the valley. The old trees were still producing common delicious apples, a tasty ancestor of red and golden delicious. We stored apples for the winter in a cool shed and made gallons and gallons of cider.

Our house was heated by wood, like most houses in the valley. After we learned early on from friends that getting our own firewood was one of the requirements for acceptance into the Stehekin community, we bought a chain saw and learned how to cut down dead, standing trees.

Firewood was rare and valuable because most of the valley was within the national park where no woodcutting was allowed. I soon found myself eyeing any dead tree as potential winter heat, as did all other valley residents. People applied to the Park Service for woodcutting permits for particular trees. If you noticed a dead tree, you rushed to the park office to lay claim to it before someone else did.

❖ Journal, *November 1982* ❖

This morning, we picked up the permit for a big, dead pine next to the road near our house. Then we headed out to cut our first firewood. Carey fired up our new Stihl chain saw and started cutting. Erin and I stood behind him at a safe distance and gave silent moral support.

He had cut the tree almost all the way through when the wind blew it back toward us and it started falling in the wrong direction. We all ran for dear life. The chain saw stalled as the weight of the tree pinched the cut closed. But the tree didn't fall. It just stood there, swaying in the wind.

The tree swayed back and forth, held upright only by a few inches of wood. The stalled saw stuck horizontally out of the tree trunk, looking like a bow tie. A stray gust from the wrong direction could have toppled the tree down onto an unsuspecting passing car or truck.

Erin and I stayed with the tree, ready to flag down any vehicles that tried to drive past. Carey drove to a neighbor's and sheepishly asked him to come help us free the saw. The neighbor thought it was hilarious that we green-horns had gotten ourselves in such a fix.

He showed us how to use a wedge to remove the saw and stayed to help buck up the tree once it was down. We learned today that helping your neighbor is also highly prized in this valley. But I suspect that it will take a long time before we outlive the stalled chain saw jokes.

The seasons mattered in Stehekin. The weather was more extreme than down lake, and we were less buffered from it than people who lived near shopping malls, movie theaters, and bus lines. When it snowed the drifts piled up enough to bury the picture window in our living room. The electrical lines from the little valley hydro-electric plant would sag and short out, leaving us living by candlelight.

When freezing rain fell, we couldn't drive to the landing for the mail. When it rained the river swelled, the roar of river growing louder, and sometimes we thought the bridge would wash out. Sun, heat, and wind all made a difference in our daily patterns. We had to adjust, adapt, to pay attention.

Weather was unpredictable and powerful, and human contrivances couldn't always protect us from it. Walking to school helped me notice the weather and the seasons as they turned. And I learned that sometimes it is better to let the weather dictate my actions, to go with it instead of trying to stand up against it.

❖ Journal, *January 1983* ❖

I woke up today to discover that more than 3 feet of new snow had fallen in the night. Snow nearly buried our old pickup. The truck looked organic, as if it grew where it stood. There was no choice about transportation. The weather had decreed that I would walk to school. I didn't even consider staying home. The teacher I'm replacing never missed a day during his seven-year tenure.

It was dark when I walked out the door. There was no wind. It was very quiet. All I could hear was the muffled hiss of snowflakes falling through the air. The snow poured down like a powdery curtain, parting to let me through and then closing, seamless, behind me.

I plowed my way through the soft, wet snow, leaving a wide furrow. My legs began to ache. I felt no cold, only the weary heat of deep, gasping breaths and burning muscles. My feet felt very heavy, each step lifting clumps of wet snow.

The going was slow. It took me half an hour to travel the forested half mile from home to the stretch along the base of the cliffs, usually a ten-minute journey. At the cliffs, I lost track of time and just focused on short-term destination. "I can rest at the big boulder up ahead" or "count 150 steps and then stop."

Soon I was floundering in hip-deep snow, oddly chunked and icy. Forward motion was nearly impossible; my legs felt imprisoned. The only way to move was to lurch forward, flinging myself up, bellyflat on the snow, and then crawling over the lumps for fifty feet until reaching smoother snow.

I stood up as soon as I could and stumbled over to a tree where I could lean and rest. I looked up in the half-light of dawn to see that the snow had stopped falling.

After I caught my breath, I looked back at my tracks and realized, with horror, that I had just crossed the path of a fresh avalanche. It must have roared down from the cliffs above sometime during the night. Tons of snow had smashed into the roadbed and spread into a thick apron of snowy chunks, ice, and broken trees.

An urgent question swept over me: "What if it happens again?" Without wasting time for thought, I ran clumsily through the snow toward the school, my legs powered by fear.

Two more fresh avalanche piles blocked the final half mile. But turning back was just as dangerous as going forward. So I clambered over the lumpy surface of each, looking upward, listening for an ominous roar.

When I finally reached the porch of the school, I fell through the front door and collapsed into a chair with exhaustion. What a commute to work!

It is now midmorning. The snowblower just came by, clearing the road. The kids should be able to get here by lunchtime. The driver slowed down and yelled to me, "Are those your tracks in the snow up the road?" I shouted back, "Yes!" He bellowed, "Were you trying to kill yourself? An avalanche came down and covered your tracks."

Experiences like this taught me it is impossible to ignore geography when you live in a place like Stehekin. Weather and avalanches and rivers and mountains force themselves into your life. People make their livings within and because of the place. It has daily, hourly significance. It is part of the way the valley defines who you are and how you will live.

It was hard to leave Stehekin for a weekend, so we rarely went down lake. We committed ourselves to staying in one place for most of the year. And there was not much room to move around in that place, at least compared to the 100-mile jaunts to Seattle I had thought of as day trips. We traveled up and down the 20-mile road, mostly within the lower 5 miles, and explored a mile or so on either side of the road before hitting impassable cliffs.

When we did leave to visit family in Seattle I found it hard to readjust to the frenetic pace and gray walls of the city. The noise and stimuli were overwhelming. I could not wait to get back home to Stehekin.

❖ Journal, *April 1983* ❖

The Lady of the Lake just passed Moore Point and the Stehekin Valley came into view. I heaved a great sigh of relief. The familiar shoreline, trees, and mountains give me a powerful sense of contentment and safety. I am coming home.

We've changed houses twice since coming to live in Stehekin, but I find that houses don't matter too much to me here. The whole river valley is my home, not just the four walls of a house. I have never felt this way before about a piece of geography.

I wonder if my sense of the whole valley as my home is similar to how Native Americans used to feel when they returned to a regular place on their seasonal round. I imagine them paddling up this lake in their canoes, coming within sight of the valley and knowing that this place offered food, shelter, and safety, that this place would take care of them, that they were coming home.

The pace of life slowed during our sojourn in Stehekin, maybe because we lived close to organic rhythms and there was not a lot of urban "noise," like freeway traffic, shopping malls, and television ads, to drown the rhythms out. On some days I spent hours writing long letters to friends and family or reading books. Other days were spent wandering the lakeshore, building mud castles with Erin by the river, or weeding the garden. I do not remember ever being in a hurry.

We spent much of our time out-of-doors. There were fewer distractions than in the outside world. I became more aware and responsive to subtle meanings and events. I noticed when a tree lost its leaves in the fall. I woke at night when rock slides clattered off nearby cliffs. I learned to tell winter temperature by the sound of the river. When it was warm up high, snow melted, swelling the river and making it roar more loudly.

Stehekin had no phones and no television during our time there. Well, that is not quite true. Two families had installed satellite dishes, but most of us survived quite well without Perry Mason reruns and Super Bowls. No phones meant messages had to be delivered in person or by mail. People showed up at each other's doors without warning, and dropping in on your neighbor was a welcomed and well-practiced art.

No television meant we had to entertain ourselves. It was a big event just to go get the mail and it was very exciting to play bridge on Tuesdays. And . . . wow! What a heart-stopper to see a rented, 16mm movie once a month at the old fish-hatchery building. We held a square dance once or twice a winter, and even those who hated each other or were on opposite ends of an argument would do-si-do and *allemande* together.

We had a second child during our time in Stehekin and the place gave us precious time to get to know our newborn son. I did not work at the school the second year. I stayed home and enjoyed being a mother animal.

I have felt my animal connections most powerfully during pregnancy, childbirth, and the first few months of my babies' lives. Instincts kicked in and overrode all the cerebral chatter about humans being logical, superior, independent beings.

❖ Journal, *November 1983* ❖

The cool fall sunshine is filtering through the tangle of brownish-red maple leaves that are left on the tree in our yard. I just spent a blissful hour lying in the leaves with one-month-old Alden sleeping on my stomach. I could look up and see the rock teeth of Sisi Ridge chewing on an iridescent blue sky.

I felt euphoric and content lying there. I didn't need to go anywhere, I didn't need to do anything. My task was to let go—to lie there and breathe, to feel my baby's heartbeat, to feel my breasts swell with milk, and to wrap my arms around my soft, yielding bundle of baby to protect him from tumbling into the fallen leaves.

I am enough. My animal self is enough. Time stands still. I am at peace.

Children lived outside much of the time in Stehekin and were free in a way most children never experience. Parents might not have even known where their offspring were playing during the day, but it did not matter. Because if a child was old enough to stay away from rattlesnakes and out of the river, there was nothing else likely to hurt them. Kids who lived in Stehekin developed a strong sense of

Border Peaks, sunset

personal freedom which allowed them to feel comfortable exploring their place.

Our daughter was two when we moved to Stehekin. She came to awareness in a place where she knew everyone by name, where every truck that went by had a driver who waved. When we attended community meetings she went too, and played hide-and-seek with the other kids outside while the adults deliberated. When we had a square dance, the kids danced too. Children were expected at every community event; they were welcomed and celebrated.

❖ Journal, *June 1984* ❖

Erin wanted to walk to her friend Corey's house by herself today. She is four years old and he lives a quarter mile away via dirt road. If we lived anywhere else, I wouldn't even consider letting her go. But what can hurt her here? She has a chance to try out her fierce new sense of independence. I wonder if kids were physically independent this early in the olden days?

I watched her heading off down the dusty road wearing her little backpack. I kept my eyes on her until she turned into the wooded driveway to Corey's house. I ran to the turn in time to see her knocking proudly on his front door.

I treasured the friendships we made while living in Stehekin. It took months, even years, before some people accepted us as part of the community. But when it happened we felt honored. I had not experienced a real community before then, at least not at the level of intensity offered by Stehekin.

Those of us who lived there had chosen to share the same small, contained piece of the Earth. We had to pay attention to each other and we could not run away from conflict. Most valley residents planned to stay for their whole life, so relationships were, by definition, long-term. But that didn't mean we always got along.

Only eighty people lived in Stehekin year-round while we were there. It was an explosive mix of varying values: Park Service employees, resort workers, middle-aged hippies, property-rights activists, and the descendants of the original homesteaders. Valley residents rarely agreed on any issue, and tempers flared regularly, with greater frequency in midwinter when cabin fever made all of us more irritable.

Our first winter there erased any illusions I had held about people living in harmony in this mountain paradise. What I found instead was a microcosm of the same problems and conflicts played out in larger scale in the outside world. But problems in Stehekin took on greater intensity due to the intimacy forced on us by the walls of the valley.

Controversy swirled around issues like trapping animals, hunting, land ownership, and water rights. Most of the arguments had to do with whether the valley's future should be decided by the National Park Service or the local residents.

Locals felt they ought to be trusted to develop a community that would not spoil the character of the place. The Park Service argued that outside developers could come in and turn the valley into a commercial nightmare. Neither side trusted the other.

While we were in Stehekin, Park Service wildlife experts began pointing out that dead trees in the lower valley should be left standing for wildlife habitat. Environmentalists from outside the valley demanded that residents in Stehekin barge firewood up the lake instead of cutting dead trees.

Most people who lived in the valley thought it was ridiculous to barge wood up to a valley that was covered with forest. A huge debate raged, and I think still rages, over who has the rights to dead trees. And this is just a mild example of environmental debates in Stehekin.

Carey and I often were caught in the middle of valley controversy. At first, since neither of us worked for the Park Service, locals would talk to us. We were environmentalists and did not own land and Park Service families invited us to dinner. For awhile, we were perceived by both sides as being somewhat neutral. As a result we had friends with widely divergent opinions on valley politics.

By the end of our second year in Stehekin, I had begun to understand some of what it meant to live there. It was no Shangri-la, no place to escape the harsh realities of life. The valley was a home for our small clan of the human species. We were all very different, but we shared a common bond: we had chosen to live here. And that was enough of a connection to make community possible.

I discovered *community* did not mean a group of happy-go-lucky friends living together in harmony, but rather a group of animals who shared the same habitat. We all derived our livelihood from the same place, which also gave us our shelter, food, water, and safety. And we shared responsibilities toward each other and toward the place, even if we did not like it.

❖ Journal, *July 1984* ❖

Intimacy with this mountain valley has taught me how to live close to the ground, to pay attention to the details, and to respond to natural rhythms. I am learning to love this place.

Everywhere I've lived has changed me, but Stehekin is working a major revision on my soul. I'm at peace here in a way I have never been before. My place defines me and gives me value. I have meaning because of where I live, not because of anything I have done or will do. This place has slowed me down, turned up my senses, and helped me to stop striving. I feel content just to be, to live, and to let events happen instead of having to control what happens.

I am taken by the giant processes so obviously at work in Stehekin. Rock slides and avalanches and slow erosion have put me in my place. I am hungry for experiences that belittle me. I crave the epiphany that comes with the realization that I don't really matter very much in the big scheme of things. Why do I find this reassuring? It baffles me, but I do. Maybe because I am in charge too much and need the balance of being overwhelmed by things bigger and more powerful than myself.

Like all animals, I am molding myself to the wild habitat in which I flourish. My body, personality, and soul are adapting to this place. My children are being poured into this valley while they are still young enough to be fluid. I know they will wear the imprint of Stehekin for years to come.

I wonder who we will become if we spend the rest of our lives here?

But we didn't spend the rest of our lives in Stehekin. One July day we got word that a family was moving away, taking three children out of the school. The regular teacher had returned from his leave of absence and had first rights to the head teacher job. There were not enough children left to justify two teachers.

Carey was ready to leave anyway. He was uncomfortable with valley politics—especially when he and I took different sides on an issue—and he wanted to go to graduate school in Seattle. But most importantly, neither of us was willing or able to make the commitment to stay without a full-time professional salary. Staying would have meant earning a meager living doing odd jobs and seasonal work.

That fall we moved from Stehekin, with eighty people, to Seattle, with half a million.

❖ Journal, *September 1984* ❖

We left Stehekin by floatplane today. I had trouble holding back tears as we climbed from the dock into the plane. The engine roared and the plane skimmed up the lake, taking off into the wind. I took one last look up the valley that has been my home. The plane banked and turned down lake, toward civilization. I felt part of myself being ripped away. I felt pulled up by the roots. I couldn't bear to look back. It hurt too much.

That evening we sat in the living room of our new house in Seattle. Four-year-old Erin looked out the window at a pickup truck roaring by on the busy street. She asked, innocently, *"Who was that, Mama?"*

WENDY WALKER teaches environmental education at Western Washington University's Huxley College of Environmental Studies in Bellingham. She has published two books and numerous articles. She has lived in the shadow of the North Cascades for over thirty years and attributes what sanity she retains in mid-life to time spent hiking and camping in these mountains.

The Biggest Fence in the West

JEANNE HARDY & JEFF HARDY

Fence: " . . . a barrier intended to prevent escape or intrusion . . . "
—dog-eared *Webster's Seventh New Collegiate Dictionary*

We live just out back of the biggest fence in the West—the North Cascade Mountains. Tucked into a 60-mile-long valley, surrounded by millions of acres of national forest and wilderness, we are connected to the outside world in winter by a couple of two-lane, winding country roads. In summer when the North Cascades Highway opens, there are three.

No stoplights, lines of headlights, or rows of porch lights intrude here. Out back of the Cascade fence we are cut off and in the dark, spellbound under the stars. "Intrusion" through the fence comes in the form of a lively tourist trade, with some seasonal and other limitations. And "escape"?

"We'd have left the valley a long time ago, but we never could get enough

---

Community sections of this chapter are written by Jeanne Hardy. *Wilderness* sections are written by Jeff Hardy, her son.

money together for bus fare out," locals are fond of saying. This is tongue-in-cheek, of course. There are no public buses in the valley.—Jeanne

❖ *Community:* Five Towns ❖

Over 100 years ago, writer Owen Wister called the Methow Valley "a smiling country." Local librarian Sally Portman, who also teaches skiing at Sun Mountain Lodge, wrote a book of local history and named it after his descriptive phrase, *The Smiling Country*.

It's a good name—but the fact is, if you look at a map you will see the valley is shaped more like a question mark than a smile. That seems appropriate. Making a living here has always been questionable. Getting through the winters is difficult. The growing season, often short on one end or the other, or both, has always been questionable.

About 4,000 people—1,500 or so living in our five little towns and the rest strewn all across hills and side valleys—take pride in being part of a small community, in knowing each other, in getting through tough times.

Fed by three rivers—the Methow, the Chewuch, and the Twisp—the valley winds its way down the length of the question mark. Directly north sits the mighty half-million-acre Pasayten Wilderness. East lies the rest of the 1,700,000-acre Okanogan National Forest. The Sawtooth/Chelan Wilderness is west of the valley. At the south end, the Columbia River rolls on by. The Methow is cut off physically and morally from any hint of urbanization.

The Cascades, visible from many valley vantage points, help define who we are. Even at its widest point—about a mile across—the valley is small enough that we know what is going on in our little world. At its narrowest, the valley is one road plus one river wide. It could easily become a cocoon, this little wrinkle scraped out by a passing, long-ago glacier. It could be all comforting views and narrow as a shoe box. However, the challenges of isolation, extreme weather, and lack of certain amenities shake us out of our comfort zones. The high Cascades looming just beyond—in all their beautiful, awesome ferocity—keep us informed of the size and power of the world beyond our mountain home.

Hu Blonk, late managing editor of the *Wenatchee World*, once explained why he spent so much time writing stories about Methow Valley people: "It's full of friends . . . and characters. I think it draws people who are independent individuals; who want a certain lifestyle." Part of that lifestyle for many residents is holding down three jobs in the summer and none in winter.

"You've got to be like the squirrels," Ted Hallowell, a Winthrop log truck driver and valley native explained. "Pack it away for the winter. Soon as a person figures that out, they've got it made. They can stay in the valley forever or until they decide to leave."

Jim Gerlach, an architect from California who settled here twenty years ago, put it this way: "It's a place of reckoning. It forces the best and worst out of people. The valley is such an incredibly difficult place to make a living; it's hard not to respect someone who's been here any amount of time. I'm not talking about people with independent incomes. Although they contribute stability to the economy, most have no understanding of what we have-nots have to deal with. What most who come here have to face is that there is no real security in life."

In accepting that fact, and finding strength in community, we find more safety than in bigger, more anonymous towns.

❖ *Wilderness:* The King's Forest ❖

Many years ago I stood on Slate Peak for the first time. Like the bow of a ship, the rocky top cuts into the Pasayten Wilderness heading toward the west and middle forks of the Pasayten River. These two drainages are at the heart of this landscape. Unable to take these huge U-shaped valleys in one glance, people come every day of the field season by carload and truckload, and stare. It may take several minutes for them to get to a point where mind and body together comprehend the scale of this immense scene and their hearts skip a beat. I've seen children throw their arms wildly about. I've seen well-dressed people sit down on a rock and forget their busy schedules. They're seeing the corridors of the gods, the entrance to the King's Forest. And like the King's Forest of mythology, magic awaits within. I knew, upon seeing this place, that I would have to go into the wilderness, too.

Unlike most wilderness, a trip from the Harts Pass area into the Pasayten is downhill. Eight-thousand-foot Slate Peak is host to trails leading into the North Cascade Crest north and south, Buckskin Ridge, and the Pasayten drainages. It is a wind-blasted point of rock, around which it often rains and snows uphill, the wind tearing off even the best-fitting cowboy hats, and pulling curses out of the most patient men. To begin and end journeys in such a place, journeys which venture into the ever milder climate of the Pasayten, where just the smell of the lupines can lull you to sleep on your horse, requires a shift in thinking. Often the most challenging part of the tour is your arrival and eventual return to the trailhead. Yet sometimes you'll rise up over the rocky backbone of Slate Pass and amidst the craggy peaks of the North Cascades the setting sun will be framed by the ears of your horse.

❖ *Wilderness:* Pasayten ❖

The Winthrop Forest Service trail crew maintains all the trails in our district of the Okanogan National Forest. Most of our time was spent within the borders of the Pasayten Wilderness. As a new member, I hadn't walked many miles with this crew before I realized that the stories I heard day in and day out were a continuous thread back to the frontier and beyond. The way we sat around the campfire in the evening, where the most intricate social grace might have been the way we threw another stick of wood on the coals, made me feel as if I had been there for generations. As soon as the glaciers retreated and the forests returned, I was there at the campfire warming myself, looking up at noises around me, listening to the stories of my ancestors. Even then I might have looked up at my favorite mule and wondered who might last longer. I might mourn the passing of this way of life or I might mourn the passing of the human race. Out in the wilderness there seemed to be little difference.

So I tried to open my eyes wider, laugh a little louder, drink a little deeper, and attempt to take in as much as my mind would hold for some purpose yet unknown. To put the ship in the bottle maybe, to preserve an entire wilderness, a large space into a small one. To continue the thread and keep us all connected to the world.

❖ *Community:* Chickens for Eggs ❖

People native to our valley display a deep sense of self-sufficiency. Local seamstress and historian Shirley Schade said, "The valley will provide. When I was a girl here, everyone had a cow for milk, cream, and butter; chickens for eggs and meat; and grew a cash crop for what few things we couldn't make ourselves. My dad grew potatoes. People have to learn to make their own way."

The beauty of the place attracts a variety of modern settlers. Included in the population are a retired university president, a physics professor, a nationally known sculptor, a psychologist who worked in the penal system with serial killers, former seamen, a boatbuilder, a ship's cook, a New York ballerina, a cowboy poet, a retired railroad man, a well-known television weatherman, a retired college dean, a composer, an origami expert, a tae kwon do teacher, an Olympic skier—and the list goes on. A onetime employee for the Twisp Water Department remarked, "The best thing about the Methow is the people. There's a higher proportion of interesting and loving people here than anywhere else I've lived."

It's anybody's guess whether that is a fact or if it just seems so because we're seriously involved in each other's stories. Results are the same in either case. We are sold on the spirit of neighborly concern that helped the settlers here get through the steep and rocky times.

❖ *Wilderness:* Flat Ground ❖

Years from now, some linguist will translate the word *wilderness* to mean "no flat ground." Outside the wilderness, members of the Pasayten trail crew live in houses with smooth floors surrounded by flat yards and roadways. Their tables are level. Coffee doesn't spill. Every summer, the crew lives in a land of slopes and pitfalls, a Buster Keaton land of plenty. Sometimes it was so steep inside the cook tent that the pack boxes tipped and spilled cans out over the ground. Usually, a short bush or tree in the middle of the floor kept people tripping until it became so fixed in everyone's navigational database that they automatically negotiated around it. During bad rains, water ran across the floor in muddy streams. After a week, we automatically walked around stobs, points of rock, tent pegs, and guy wires. At night, groggy from sleep, directions to fixed points had to be said aloud to avoid tripping and falling. I remember many times talking my way to the outhouse: "OK, now step over this log and watch out for the branch coming up and the big step onto the rock and make the turn in the trail—" We fell all the time. After numerous spills you give in to the terrain and stop fighting it. Injuries to both person and pride come in trying too hard to avoid the inevitable. We would really beat out a camp after a couple of ten-day tours but never did the ground become flat, only more visible.

Ten days in and four days out. Interesting how the word *wilderness* changed our perspective. People in our valley community go *out* to the woods or the National Forest but they go *in*to the wilderness or *in*to the hills and back out to town. Over the summer, the Pasayten was our home and excursions took us out to the valley every two weeks. It always took us a day or two of our four-day weekend to get our civilization legs again. After 10 days walking in the hills, flat ground took some getting used to.

❖ *Community:* Necessities ❖

Settle in the Methow and forget the past. These mountains don't want to hear about your Ph.D. They want to know if you have basic winter survival skills. Methow Valley people joke about the folks with doctorates driving school buses—and happy to find the work—and physicists flipping burgers. Life gets down to essentials. As Joe Kitzman who works at the rental shop in Twisp put it, "A chain saw and a pickup truck are pretty much the necessities here."

"There should be places like this," another resident remarked. "I like the way the weather forces you to deal with your environment."

People understand the joy of testing their spirit for endurance. Having endured, they find they are at home in the world.

Nativeborn valleyites take a fierce pride in their roots. They own the history here—the history, that is, after the first white settlers arrived looking for good grazing land. Their parents and grandparents were in on the beginnings.

"Newcomers"—residents not born here—build their own histories, and give birth to new generations of valley natives.

Most-repeated stories of earlier days tend to center around weather, fires, local characters, rodeos, and other daring feats. People like the Kikendall brothers—who ran a dogsled supply route to the Azurite Mine in winter; Frances Lufkin and George Honey, America's first smokejumpers; and early mail carrier, U.E. Fries, who rode through deep snows and floodwaters to deliver mail between Malott and Winthrop for $6.60, round trip: these come to mind. It took unusual daring to constitute an adventure here when average citizens were dealing with snows that buried fence posts and drought that ate rivers dry.

One winter in the 1930s, Ed "Kike" Kikendall was taking a man to the Azurite when slides and "soft weather" forced them to hole up at Horse Heaven, halfway between base camp at Robinson Creek and the mine. Their major problem was food. As the story goes, Kike got a bent pin, pulled a bit of red yarn from his sock for bait and caught enough fish through a hole in the ice on the Methow River to keep them eating until they could move on.

Just as remarkable are the "short stories." A fellow who grew up in the valley described riding a mule over the hills on a full-moon night through deep, fresh powder snow. In every direction the mountains were visible; the temperature hung around zero. Powder snow parted like water at the bow of a ship, sending sparkling white waves off on either side of the trotting mule.

In a small community set among big mountains, the immediate is more noticeable by people who are attuned to the outdoors. The outdoors here is bigger than the indoors but is composed of a great many little things.

One spring not long ago, two men were hiking in the hills. It was a good year for the yellow balsamroot sunflowers, and the men encountered a natural bowl in the hills full of them. A small ravine ran down the mountain, out of the bowl, and it, too, was splattered with sunflowers. "It looked just like someone had filled that place with yellow paint and it had overflowed at that place and spilled down the hill," Dick Chavey said later—in one of several tellings of that story.

❖ *Wilderness:* Camp ❖

I can smell the mixture of sweat and leather and hear the "boys" stomp and blow, impatient for the trail and the pasture at the end of the day. I can see them round the corner and come into sight.

When the string came along, in the midst of a wilderness reverie, it was as if a three-ring circus had just planted itself in front of me. Moments before I was enjoying the subtle sights and sounds of the wilderness, the sensations that take time and patience to appreciate and understand. Then I was confronted with a hollering packer named Ellis, on a tall horse, regarding me with a carefully fashioned conservatism, hoping to offend. He was followed by six mules. Some were lions and some clowns: Dan was mad at Benny, Benny was mad at Betsy, Ellis was mad at Dan and everyone else was trying to stay out of the way. Mules dominated the view and, at a 1200-pound-apiece average, they commanded respect. They filled the air with smells, ground their teeth, chewed on trailside grass. When stopped, all the kinetic energy of forward movement now had to go somewhere, so they fidgeted, got revenge, scratched, and blew. Chains clinked back and forth and the boxes on their backs creaked. Everything was moving, smelling, and making noise.

When we arrived in camp, this time the abandoned Pasayten airstrip, there was no time to sit. The string was on our heels, but we stood for a few seconds and admired the strip and cabin, Tatoosh Buttes and Dot Mountain, while quietly saying to ourselves, "Man, it is good to be here again." Someone went to the corral and closed the bars to keep the stock in once we let them go for the evening. Others would break the string down while Ellis climbed down, stretched his legs, and said a few kind curses to Shane while he took the bridle off. The cursing began in earnest when we started removing top packs, boxes, mantie packs, coolers, and tools, as the boys fidgeted to get to the grass. After we put up their ropes, hanging them in neat coils on the saddles, they usually spent a short time at the hitch rail while the last were unpacked. The saddles came off. The mules, out of their halters first, would immediately roll in the dirt, stirring up clouds of dust. Horses got belled and hobbled and were also let go. We always took a short breather to watch them run for the pasture, tossing their heads back and galloping into a well-earned open space.

Then we turned to our camp, and hauled boxes into the cabin, undid mantie packs, and organized the tools under a tree. The cabin door scraped heavily open and closed across the floor. As we worked we opened a box or two to see if we happened on the candy bars, cookies, or crackers. Generally someone would ask about something specific like the radio batteries and the answer always came back the same: "It's in one of them boxes." There was no way then to get around rummaging through eight boxes to find what you needed.

Someone would start a fire in the cookstove and begin heating stuff on the Coleman stove, our "mountain microwave." People sneaked off to go set up a tent, lay out personal gear, swim, or watch the "cowboy TV"—stock and deer grazing in the pasture. There were always chores, too: fixing the water system, chopping kindling, feeding pellets and grain, but most of us just put a tape in the tape deck and sat around keeping the cook and each other company. There would be accounts of the day, the weather, problems that arose, and how much work was done. We might move on to the job at hand, or the tasks for the next day. Then we would start into the best part. Stories. Harassment. Laughing and bragging. There were the tellers and the listeners. I was an avid listener. Some of the more vindictive tellers would take advantage of my gullible nature and tell me a real whopper and I would take it all in. True or not, it was all great. Sometimes dinner was an intermission—only because the tellers might have too much of a mouthful on board to speak. The telling went on into the night. Sometimes it would move out by the fire. Sometimes it stayed around the dinner table. We would take breaks to check the boys or coax Shane, Ellis's tall horse, through the cabin with a pan of grain just to show he could do it. I rarely tired of the stories.

One well-meaning but committed bureaucrat once asked me why we worked so hard to make all those above us look good and I told him we did it for the glory.

The glory, I explained, was the thrill of victory we felt at the completion of some task, something we felt transcended the common worries of promotion and wage. I showed him a picture of Ellis and me standing in a he-man pose on a huge stump we had rolled out of the trail. We could be heroes every day and get paid for it.

The experiences I had in seven years on the trail crew happened within this framework. We told stories in the evening, slept soundly, and awoke before dawn to catch the boys and saddle them. Mornings were all business as we turned our attention to the day ahead. We would have breakfast and hit the trail.

❖ *Wilderness:* Cabin ❖

I awoke under the dark square of canvas to a heavy thud. I peeked out, squinting in the morning sun, to see a huge mule standing over me. The boys were all around me as it had been snowing and they had taken shelter under the trees. I knocked the snow off my tarp before the sun started melting it. It wasn't quite warm enough to make me want to get out of my bag, but I did anyway and from the direction of the cabin I heard "Good morning, squire!" Ellis already had the fire going, the bacon and coffee started.

In the cabin the rest of the trail crew were still groaning in their bunks. I stopped sleeping in the cabin because the rats and mice were too noisy for me to get a good night's sleep. They lived in the attic and we would bait them once in a while. I was nervous about looking up for fear that one really big one lived up there and was looking for revenge. Once, while I was eating spaghetti, a wilderness ranger pulled a revolver out of his duffel and blew a rat on top of the food cupboard almost in half with a buckshot load. I was still choking on my food when he carried its remains, still twitching, out the door. On another night, a rat got into the Coleman stove and was chewing on the spilled sauce and other leftovers inside. The sound of its teeth against the metal was annoying and eventually a guy off the crew got up, slammed the top shut and put the stove outside. I could still hear the rat trying to get out, so this wasn't much of an improvement.

❖ *Community:* Porch Deer ❖

"Only fools and newcomers predict Methow Valley weather," is probably the most often heard bit of local lore.

Methow Valley weather is like everyone else's. We just have more of it. Seven-year drought cycles, heavy snows, flooding, temperatures that vary from 110 above to 30 below zero occur in other places—but here all of this is stuffed into a tight area and so it's more intense. Or so it seems to us.

Roy Kumm of Winthrop has been keeping track of valley weather for sixty years now, having recorded its ups and downs for the United States Department of Commerce. It was Roy who discovered the pattern of Methow weather after long

Backbone Ridge above
Doubtful Lake

and careful study: there *is* no pattern. People ask him what an upcoming winter will be like. He grins and says, "I'll tell you next spring."

The only thing here as popular as a people story is a weather story.

Does Roy remember the big snow of 1935? Fifty-two inches of fine snow fell at Winthrop in about 27 hours. It was -5°F. "Fred Dammann over here," Roy said, "got up and found his back porch and shed full of deer." Full of deer?? "The snow was so powdery they couldn't get above it," he explained, "and they couldn't go through it without suffocating. So they took refuge on his porch."

Jay Stokes had a new automobile in 1968 when record-setting cold hit the valley. It was over fifty below in some places. Livestock died where they stood. Machinery froze. Orchards bit the dust. Jay, who owns a ranch on Beaver Creek, was working at the school back then. A fellow worker called and said his car wouldn't start. Jay offered to give him a ride. Hardly anyone made it to work that day, but Jay did. Shortly after that, several people talked about purchasing the same make of car. "What I didn't mention," Jay teased, "was that I got up every hour during that cold night and started it up to keep it from freezing!"

Out in what they used to call "back country" and now call "wilderness," there is a lot of weather, too. Back country packers tell about icicles hanging from bushes along the trail, ringing like glass chimes when they passed by on their way from somewhere to nowhere and back again.

❖ *Wilderness:* Pasayten Weather ❖

Probably the most interesting subject to people who live outdoors is the weather. In town, it starts conversations, then moves from this "small talk" on to the more important topic of your neighbors. But in the wilderness, the weather is big talk. There are few windows out of which you can watch the snowstorm develop and fall. No comfortable hearth will shelter you. But on the other hand, no wall will stand between you and the full celebration of a sunny day.

Humans, brain and body, resist working outside in the rain and snow. I have often heard farmers in the valley say, "He didn't have enough sense to come in out of the rain." I have never heard anyone in the woods say this. It's generally not an option. What we did instead was get wet and get used to it. The process of getting wet is like the process of dying (that is, denial, anger, grief, acceptance). On the back of a horse this is intensified. There is little else to think about while staring at the back of your horse's head. When the storm clouds boil you tell yourself it isn't going to rain and keep this story up even after the first drops hit the ground. Once, when the crew was coming out of Robinson Creek, I told myself this. When it began to pour, the rest of the string disappeared in the rain. My horse Skipper and I became isolated lifeforms in big country, wishing we were somewhere closer to the ranch, wishing the clouds had decided to open up at any other hour but this one. I cursed Earl* for his cruel behavior as the first drop of water worked its way through the seam in my cowboy hat and ran down the back of my neck. I continued cursing him as my chaps soaked through and my boots started filling with water. I grieved as each square inch of my body became soaked with cold water, fresh from 8,000 feet. But once completely soaked, a strange transformation took place. I felt peace, accepted this fate, and began to sing, succumbing, I suppose, to the shower effect. Skipper's ears turned back to listen and he blew the rain off his nose.

The mood was completely different in Andrews Creek, clearing deadfall from the right-of-way. It began to snow hard. We got on our horses and headed back to the Spanish Camp Cabin. As the miles ticked off we got wetter and wetter and no one felt like singing. My then-wife Laura eventually gave in—but not to singing. She

---

Earl is the commonly used name in the wilderness for the god who oversees the weather. Ironically, John Miles is the first one I heard refer to Earl, and he claims that the National Outdoor Leadership School used it. But the trail crew adopted the term independently of John or me, probably out in the woods somewhere.

had grown increasingly quiet and soon hunched over in her saddle a mile or so to the cabin. Duffy and I got on either side of her and after talking to her, determined we could make it to the cabin and get her warmed up. It was an intense mile back as both Duffy and I worked through in our minds the procedure of getting a fire. We made it to the cabin, got Laura into a sleeping bag with a cup of hot tea, and soon were all telling stories over dinner.

Duffy and I once rode up over Topaz Mountain where it started snowing so hard I could barely see him a horse-length away. In the midst of this, the radio cracked to life and a new wilderness ranger, one ridge over, called into the office:

"Winthrop, this is 60 Hoffman."

"This is Winthrop."

"Winthrop, I'm on Coleman Ridge and it appears to be snowing here."

Winthrop didn't know quite what to say to that but through the snow out in front of me I heard Duffy mutter, "It does have that appearance, doesn't it?"

There's an outhouse at Hart's Pass that has a tall ventilation chimney on it with a steeple point, like a church. We call it St. Earl's. And before heading into the woods we would often worship there. We would pray for better weather than on the last trip we had. Once, at the Pasayten airstrip, I heard Ellis say into a snowstorm, "It's going to clear up." To which Duffy replied, "Yep. Clear up to our ass and still snowing." "Clear and still" became our preferred way to describe the current conditions over the radio.

Good weather for the crew was when it was blowing and cold or maybe raining like a cow peeing on a flat rock. *Bad* weather was when the sky was blue. We used to curse the big, blue clouds. I think this is the same psychology the French use when they say it is good luck to step in a pile of dog poop on the sidewalk. You might as well make the bad good, because a fair dose of the bad is coming your way. It's a little deception we put ourselves through which seems to work. Much of what we did in the woods was uncomfortable, but we developed our abilities to make the bad into good—spinning gold out of straw—and made it worth the effort.

❖ Community: The Robbery ❖

There was a bank robbery once in our little valley. It took place in the 1950s and was written up in the newspapers. The robber came to town wearing a Hawaiian shirt and stood on the street corner drinking beer before robbing the tiny Twisp bank. Everyone noticed him and knew he wasn't local. They also noticed when he drove up the Twisp River road waving a fistful of money: he'd forgotten to bring a sack to the crime.

People thought it was a joke.

When the thief got to the end of the road, he set the car on fire and then proceeded into the Sawtooth Range wearing tennis shoes and light clothing. He headed in the general direction of Lake Chelan. No one could figure out how he survived—but they were waiting for him when he stumbled out, half dead, on the other side. He was arrested and went to jail—which was something of a relief after what he'd been through. He told Hu Blonk he'd wanted enough money to buy a sailboat.

There are really *no good escape routes* out of the valley out back of the biggest fence in the West.

❖ *Wilderness:* Traplines ❖

As the day faded, I followed an old trapline along the middle fork of the Pasayten River. The valley bottom was already in the shadows of the ridges and the air was cooling fast. Nothing stirred in the lodgepole pine and spruce except the *beep-beep* of a nuthatch. I began by walking out from camp in concentric circles looking for signs of the old trail. An older worker, Jim, explained that the trapline followed the west side of the river to where a trapper's cabin sat. I clambered over downed spruce, jumped across old creek beds, and skirted around an occasional doghair lodgepole thicket so dense I had to squeeze between the trees. But I found no sign of the trail.

Traplines generally followed practical routes along streams and rivers where the wildlife was most abundant. Often overgrown and invisible, the lines can be traced by watching for blazes in trees, logs cut to clear the right-of-way, and an occasional tin can nailed to a tree, in which bait was once stored. I eventually found the old trail by walking along the route I would have taken to go along the river. I found a blaze first and then a tread. After three decades of neglect, the trail was in surprisingly good shape and soon I was able to walk along easily and reflect on the people who once had followed it.

The middle fork of the Pasayten River was territory for a family named Tuttle. Two of the cabins they'd built and used in their trapping business were still standing: Three Forks Cabin, now home to a large white rat, named Moby by one of the rangers, and Silver Creek Cabin which I hoped to find on this day. The trail connected the cabins, one near each end of the middle fork, and then went south to civilization. The last trapping the Tuttle family did here was in the late 1940s, probably 1948 or 1949 according to a reliable packer. They brought in their gear during the summer and then wintered over in the cabins. They brought two horses along in October or November: one was slaughtered for food and the other for trap bait when the weather turned cold. They trapped up and down the river. They would go out for one resupply during a hard freeze or after snow swept out the slide chutes. I once saw an old black-and-white photo of a couple—Tuttles, perhaps, or McKinneys—the woman dressed in a man's clothing and hat, looking rough, framed by a backdrop of fur.

The main trail was moved long ago to the east side of the river, probably because it melted out earlier in the spring. Many trails were moved or abandoned due to snow. But this trail I was following in the late fall evening appeared to have maintained itself. It followed a bench of evenly spaced lodgepole pine, subalpine fir, and grass, very similar to an area up north called the Enchanted Forest where we expect, at any time, to hear the quiet laughter of little people among the lupines.

Just when I thought I must have passed it, the cabin appeared in an opening above the trail with a carved sign near it: "Silver Creek Cabin." The ridge beam had partially collapsed from a heavy snow but otherwise held old lines. It was a one-house ghost town far from any railroad. What does a room in the wilderness do once its occupants have left for good? It melts into the ground, log by log, for spiders and mice.

Inscribed on the door is a sketchy journal of its visitors dating from the Depression to the late 1970s. I recognized one of the later authors and read the inscription:

Sheela McLean, September 17, 1977.
5 years wilderness ranger
Tough

Other names were penciled in the weathered door, mostly McKinneys and Tuttles, dated in the 1940s. Inside were three low bunks with dirt below them to conserve floor material. For decades a raised earth hearth quietly supported an old, rusting sheepherder's stove, a "mountain microwave," as the trail crew called them. The only light came from a small, four-paned window, and the dark-cave quality which must have been comforting when the northern storms blew down feet of snow and deeper cold now gave it a crawling-skin, get-out-of-here feeling. I stayed in only long enough to survey the situation. The fire had been out too long now and only imagination could bring some life back to the little place.

On the return trip, I thought about the people who had occupied the cabin, whose existence must have been much closer to the realities from which we have so brilliantly insulated ourselves with brick, glass, and cement. How close to the bone life must have been lived, and how clear a body's decisions, living in a 16-by-20-foot space, 12 miles of snowshoeing away from another person living under the same conditions. Similar thoughts followed me back until I began hearing my own lively trail camp and melted back into its everyday life.

❖ *Community:* Sheela ❖

Sheela McLean was the first woman wilderness ranger here. She worked alone for five years in the Pasayten. One of the things that was amazing to her, she said, was how attuned you became to what was out there. "Your ears grow extremely sensitive," she recalled. "Once a friend went with me on a trip. Two things happened. I could hear a horse party coming four or five minutes before she could. The other thing is there would be tracks in a trail I could see, but I'd have to outline them before my friend could pick them out of the mishmosh on the trail."

There were experiences with wildlife: the delight in seeing a line of little ducks following their mama, diving under a half-submerged log and popping up, one by one, on the other side—and the fascination of locking gazes with a cougar.

"There was a presence there," she said. "There's a presence there when I look into your eyes. It was exactly the same with the cougar."

The strangest experience she had out there was after she'd spent a long time in the wilderness, then headed back to school without a break to readjust to civilization. The next day she went to class, sat down, looked at the professor—and couldn't understand a word he was saying! He may as well have been speaking Greek.

"It took a couple of days to get my gears shifted," she said, laughing.

❖ *Community:* Vicki's Cougar ❖

There are people who move to the valley who want to change it to suit their needs. There are more people who come here who want to keep it from changing. There are people whose families have lived in the valley all the generations it's been settled, like Sheela. We are all thrown together into a pretty small space and expected to behave ourselves.

Generally, people do.

Even those with widely differing viewpoints can sit down together at the Winthrop Barn for a benefit dinner and enjoy friendly conversation. The reason for this is simple: we all know each other, and are connected by marriage, or work, or a bit of history shared, or membership in the same organizations. Living in close proximity we know the person we are rude to this week is going to be the one who pulls us out of a ditch next week. It works better, being courteous.

Vicki Nordness, a home health care nurse, lives way to heck and gone up a mountain road that eats four-wheel-drive rigs for breakfast in February. A couple of winters ago, she was out walking with her dogs and heard a commotion. A pack of dogs with radio collars had treed a cougar a short distance off her property. Soon hunters roared up on snowmobiles and there ensued a polite but heartfelt conversation regarding the fate of the cougar.

They were a local family who'd been hunting here for generations. At the time, Vicki had lived in the valley about ten years. The men began walking up toward the treed cat, and Vicki, desperate, blurted out, "I'll give you 500 dollars for that cougar!" The men stopped. There was a muttered "Oh, lady . . . " and a bit of mumbling as these mountain men considered this passionate, delicate-looking but strong-willed woman. They took some video shots of the cat, finally, and left. They refused to take any money.

In talking about the incident later, Vicki made it clear she respected those men; they just saw things differently than she did. The incident illustrates the presence of wide contrasts among valley people—where old traditions and new ways meet.

They all went their separate ways, unchanged perhaps—even the cougar that Vicki nearly bought. But something unusual had taken place.

❖ *Wilderness:* Ellis ❖

When Ellis was a kid, the wilderness packers of those days would bring him into the woods and, wide-eyed, he would take it all in. The wilderness made him feel big while, with a twist of perspective, it made the adults in the group feel small. The packers told Ellis they were going to Soda Creek where he could expect to get a soda or milkshake at the Soda Creek Fountain. Of course, he was disappointed to find that his leg was being pulled—the closest soda fountain was probably 30 miles away. It's hard to picture Ellis as a kid.

I've never seen him scared, even when the mules were all tangled on a steep rock face and threatening to jump. He calmly jumped into the middle of them and untangled the mess. I would have my pocketknife in my hand but he wouldn't even cut a rope. He untied each animal in turn, spoke calmly to them, and soothed us all. He told me once that he hid behind the couch when the flying monkeys appears in *The Wizard of Oz*. It's hard to put it all together sometimes.

Ellis's hands were beaten up from countless ropes jerked to an acceptable tightness. When the ropes were right, the packs didn't just stay on the animal, they balanced, causing a minimum of friction on the mule's back. That was important because if the mule wasn't comfortable, the packer wasn't either. He could tell if something was wrong even from the back of his horse. He watched their ears. When all is well, the long mule ears flop back and forth in a rhythm matching the string's pace. They keep tabs on all the sounds around them in a lazy, rambling way. If something is bothering them, one or two ears will remain stationary or, if it's really nasty, stay pinned back. There could be a fight in progress, a threat like a bear or a bees' nest, or a pack not riding right. In these latter cases I would often see Ellis, from my vantage point at the rear of the string, fidget in his seat and never get quite comfortable. He would turn as much as he could, his horse would cant to the side while walking down the trail, so he could watch the packs—or, more aptly, the rings on the decker saddles to see if they were riding dead center. We'd stop and adjust when necessary and when all the packs were riding right and all the fights were fought, we'd settle in for a long, comfortable ride.

Having grown up on a farm, Ellis knew to take care of the animals first. It didn't matter how hungry he was, or how tired. They must be fed and unsaddled before we could think of our meal. Sometimes if we were really aching we would tear through a pack box as it came off an animal and eat a found candy bar while we worked.

We mostly enjoyed the work, even in the worst situations, something we learned from him. One terrible, rainy day, he made a big deal of his fine new hat soaking through before mine. We laughed at the storm. We told the story in the evening after dinner by the fire. He laughed and laughed. I once asked him if anyone had broken his heart and he replied, "No, but I've broken my own a time or two."

❖ *Community:* Small Happenings ❖

In our communities, events are something we *do*. Depending on the nature of what's happening, we generally split roles, fifty-fifty. Half put it on, and the other half go watch. Or half play and the other fifty percent cheer them on.

In winter, when the pace settles down after the North Cascades Highway is closed by decree of Earl, the weather god, our entertainment is truly homegrown. Highway crews put up the sign, "Highway 20 closed 17 miles west of Winthrop," south of Twisp. The irrigation ditches are shut off and we all start promising each other we'll have lunch together soon. Most of the tourists have gone; things are quiet. Someone will start a new club, or a new project, or an annual event.

The Priscilla Club, whose stated aim is to not have an aim, has been meeting for several generations of valley women. The music association puts on their annual Keyboard Confections—a piano concert plus desserts. Some of us take advantage of the cross-country ski trails or downhill skiing up on the Loup Loup Pass. There are Grange potlucks, dances, shows at the art gallery, lectures at the high school. Usually each of these is a labor of love of one determined individual.

The yearly "Freeze Yer Buns Run" in Twisp in January was the inspiration of Howard Day, who noticed there weren't any races regionally in the dead of winter. Howard kept the run going long enough that it became an institution, with five or six hundred participants doing pre-race calisthenics to keep from freezing in place and wearing long johns under their Hawaiian shirts and hula skirts. It is the most color we see from November through March.

First prize is always a trip to Hawaii for two. Pearl Clark walks the 2-miler every year. Pearl is ninety-something now and still going for a ticket out of here for a mid-winter gander at palm-lined golden beaches. "I have a feeling I might win this year!" she cackles.

There are events and memories connected to the weather.

The night of dress rehearsal for "The Music Man," put on by our local theater group, it was snowing heavily. Halfway through, the power went out. Within a short time, dozens of candles were produced from somewhere, and the show went on. It was magical. Somehow the candlelight raised a spirit of joy that made the dress rehearsal more memorable than the actual play. Ten years later, people still refer to it as a highlight in recent valley history.

The difference between watching a Broadway play and seeing one put on by our community theater is the difference between eating corn on the cob you bought at Safeway and having it right from the garden you planted, nurtured, and are now—by the grace of the corn goddess—harvesting. Both are good, but there is something about an exchange of winks and hugs between cast and audience that adds to the flavor of theater.

When the Washington State Cattlemen's Association had their annual meeting in Okanogan, in the next valley over where the association was born long, long ago, they decided to ride into town—like old times.

"Dad always had a good saddle horse," said Morrie Stokes, "and we'd prefer that to the automobiles in those days."

The Stokes family has been ranching here for almost 100 years. Vic Stokes, Morrie's brother, is active in the association—as their father, Jay, was years back. "A horse didn't get stuck on an unpaved, muddy road," Morrie pointed out, "and if you met up with someone you could ride along together and visit. Can't do that in a car!"

Okanogan, the county seat, was a natural choice for a cattlemen's ride-in. It's pretty near the only place left where you can do that. "Can't ride into Everett," Vic noted, "or Spokane."

Human and natural events occur in closer proximity in mountain country. An avalanche seals off the highway for another two weeks in spring—causing merchants to echo the trail crew's philosophical cursing of old Earl. The last big flood, in 1948, tore out a riverbank at Carlton and toppled the new Methodist Church into the Methow River and carried it off. There are people who are still upset about it, too. Drought earlier in the century drove people off their dry-land farms, changing the course of family histories.

Outside events have limited effect here. It is a matter of local pride that the Great Depression didn't change life in the valley a great deal. People never had much cash before, and they didn't have much then. Since everyone was in the same situation, they didn't consider themselves poor. So they weren't. Today the communities are still largely free of social expectations. A former Twisp business owner put it this way: "The Methow is freedom from conforming trends. People tend to do that in a city. Here we don't fall in line with that—the 'in' fashions, the 'in' places to go. Our values are more functional than frivolous."

The biggest events are memorable. It is memorable to be participating in an activity with 600 people you know, including the performers and organizers. It is a way of belonging that is unique to a small valley in an immense mountain range, far from worldly distractions.

May Ann Yakabi, who works at the Winthrop Post Office, echoed our feelings a few years back when she said, "I'm not a religious person, but going outside here is a religious experience for me. Looking at the trees, the clouds, the mountains—

you can't lie to them. They know what is true. You can't get that connection to the land in a city. It's so beautiful you stand there with your jaw open!"

"It makes you want to be a better person," she concluded.

The gym at the Twisp community center was dark and crowded the night they handed out awards for the young people's book review contest. On stage, children performed between each prize being handed out. The crowd, as usual, was made up of people of all ages. A very small person was doing a fast crawl through a forest of standing-room-only legs.

People were keeping an eye on the little ones. Children are a priority in our little valley.

Beginning music students one-noted their way through Christmas songs on the piano, while proud parents, grandparents, neighbors, teachers, friends, and cousins watched. Many of us had come from cities where children are not as cherished—and have only a few people looking out for them.

Finally, the music teacher began to play Bach's *Ave Maria*. At the back of the gym, a young mother started to waltz holding her baby. The two pirouetted, dipped, stepped to the music. People turned to look, and smiled. "Ave Maria . . . full of grace." Mother and child, laughing, at perfect ease in a friendly place. Our place. Dancing.

Suddenly, my eyes were full of tears.

❖ *Wilderness:* The Bells ❖

Years from now, I see myself back in the Pasayten Wilderness standing in a high meadow on Tatoosh Buttes. In sight are all the peaks of the western Pasayten Wilderness and beyond—from Jack Mountain to Mount Baker. A warm breeze blows and the scent of the flowers makes me sleepy, and in the quietness, I am brought back by a faint sound which at first seems to be a far-off songbird or cicada. Thinking I must have dreamed it, my attention wanes and drifts again but as it does, the wind changes and there it is again, this time very clear: the sound of the Swiss bell and the string.

Three miles an hour is the average speed for a horse, packer, and six head of mules loaded with an eight-person camp. We sat at Oregon Creek on the west fork one day and made some calculations while eating from our sack lunches. "Any time now," someone said. We listened and, as sure as trees make a sound when they fall, we heard the faint *dinga* of the Swiss bell on the tail mule of Ellis's string. We packed up and headed down the trail.

Walking at a good clip a person can travel about 4 miles an hour, and this is what we did. But nothing is as steady as a packer and his mule string in the second half of its day. All the packs are adjusted and the animals have settled into the pace that will get them to the grass at the end of the trip. The packer listens to the bell, occasionally checks the loads, and watches the scenery go by. He might sing a few bars of "God Must Be a Cowboy at Heart." He might doze a little.

Ahead of the string, we cleared the trail. There were rocks to kick and logs to cut and clear. We worked leapfrog fashion: two cut a log while two others went ahead to the next one. We threw another log out and when it settled into the brush beside the trail, we listened, our hearts pounding in our ears. Pretending to be angry, a squirrel chattered and squeaked. Then the quiet but steady ring of the bell filtered through the lodgepole pine. There would be no time to pause for a drink.

Ellis would invariably stop to chat with us "hippie backpackers" while we adjusted loads, ate sandwiches, predicted the weather. Then he would give the command, "Boys?"—a warning to the mules that they were going. As the bell faded into the distance, the whole experience would linger like the tracks in the trail.

This was how, dressed in work jeans, flannel shirts, and boots, we spent our days. With sweat-soaked red bandannas tied around our foreheads, we were range hardened and often covered with dirt and pitch. I would look down at my gloved hands in wonder and be seized by a sudden urge to jump up on a log and make the hills echo. I became, as we all did, one of the trail crew. Within the boundaries of this wilderness, no job was too big.

When we were far enough ahead of the string, the crew members became individuals again.

"What'd you do over the weekend?"

"I went to Seattle. I was scared to death the whole time. I had to call Gretchen in Bothell to come and save me."

"Have you been there before?"

"Nope. Closest I'd been was Wenatchee a couple of times. Otherwise, haven't been out of the county."

"What classes you taking in school?"

"Conversational German and statistics."

"All feet are the same. It's the only German I know."

"Want some gum?"

"No thanks, I always forget to chew."

"How'd you get across the creek without getting your boots wet?"

"Jack laid down in it and I walked on him."

The college students would talk over ideas, explorations into subjects one notch below the meaning of life. One person on the crew knew nearly all there was to know about the state of Delaware (the highest point in the state: 442 feet). Another crew member liked to rock snags back and forth until they fell to the ground. Once part of the crew split off and sang "Sentimental Journey" in three-part harmony. I sometimes walked alone and settled into a pace. With my body occupied by travel, my mind roamed freely. Time disappeared. I wouldn't become aware of my surroundings until I rounded the first of the last three bends to the airstrip. Surprised at where life had brought me, I would feel intensely alive.

The bells are fading from the wilderness as the mules, one by one, are being sold. I work at the ranger station now, mapping the areas I once walked or rode. From time to time, I manage to get out into backcountry.

One day I will be alone again in a high meadow on Tatoosh Buttes remembering the bells. If I listen carefully enough, anywhere within the Pasayten, I can hear their steady ring fade into the distance. The sound and the place—sometime during those years—became a part of the same memory.

JEANNE HARDY is a humorist and writer whose essays appear in local, state, and national publications. She is contributing editor, cartoonist, and feature writer for *Crone Chronicles;* feature writer for *Ruralite Magazine;* and publisher of three monthly newsletters full of warmth and humor: *The Spotted Chicken Report, Methow Valley People,* and *Birdy's Circle.* She lives in Twisp, next door to her son Jeff.

JEFF HARDY works for the Forest Service, grows garlic on his farm in Twisp, and looks for opportunities to teach an environmental ethic.

Vignettes from a
Field Journal

LIBBY MILLS

The contribution by Libby Mills to this collection is unique. Libby is an artist and a naturalist; she records her encounters with the North Cascades in a combination of words and images. In these selections from her field journals, art and natural history come together to reveal the richness hidden in this landscape.

Libby teaches, studies, and travels extensively in this region and is never without her sketchbook. While most of us may occasionally stop briefly to compose a picture through the lens of our camera, Libby stops, looks, sketches—and looks again. Her art requires her to study the textures and details of this place with greater care and intensity than those of us who do not see it through the artist's eye. Sometimes she sets out to portray a scene or detail with painstaking completeness. At other times she simply wanders the mountains, casually recording her encounters in her field journal. These journal entries are not completed works but impressions that she uses later to reflect upon and deepen her understanding of her experience. They also remind her of qualities of specific places that might deserve a longer look on a future trip.

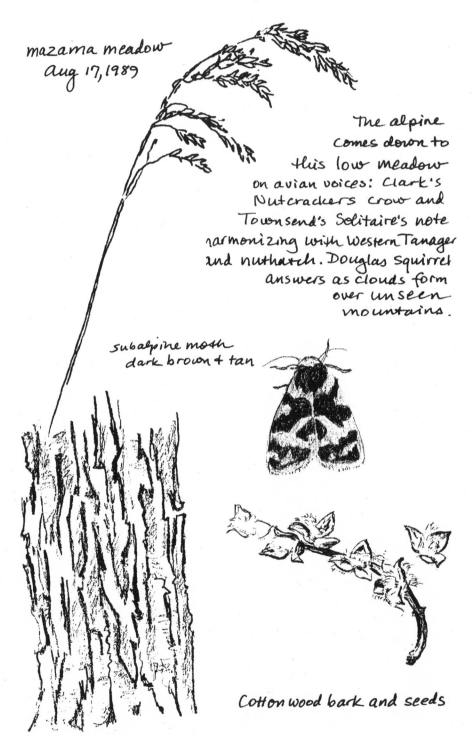

mazama meadow
Aug 17, 1989

The alpine
comes down to
this low meadow
on avian voices: Clark's
Nutcrackers crow and
Townsend's Solitaire's note
harmonizing with Western Tanager
and nuthatch. Douglas squirrel
answers as clouds form
over unseen
mountains.

subalpine moth
dark brown & tan

Cottonwood bark and seeds

Field Journal Class
Mazama meadow—
7-21-90

Any number of ants here making it impossible
to feel alone in the universe with this
young pine. Shoes and socks after lunch.
It is so hot and dry; but a breeze helps.
Mazama meadow, buzzed by a hummer or
very large insect. Does the ant bite me to
remind me I am never alone here, there is
always animal company? or to remind me
to be in the moment, and not drifting
back 20 minutes or so....

ponderosa
pine

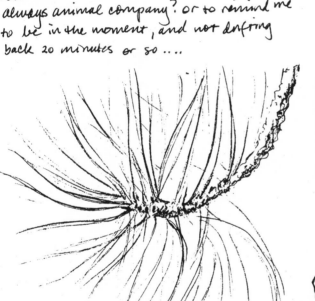

This piece
of the
puzzle bark
fell onto
my shoulder
as I sat quietly drawing

The meadow is hushed at noon, just a light breeze
sounds rubbing needle against needle on the soft
ponderosas. If butterflies sang there would be
a chorus of swallowtails, cabbages and others I've
barely discovered today, because I'm looking at a page,
not the air they live in. So nice to be back!

a twig of poplar
the sweet scent aged out
now in august

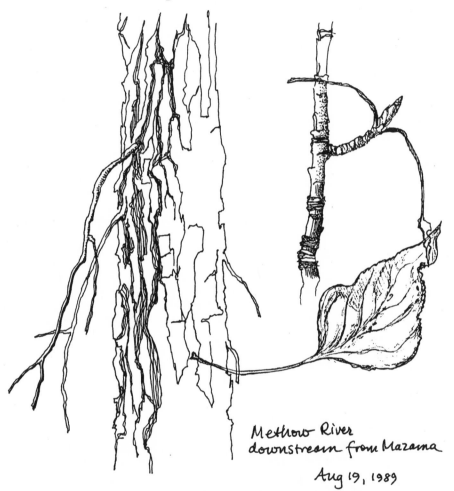

Methow River
downstream from Mazama

Aug 19, 1989

Wind in the cottonwoods and
the quiet rush of water... sounds
that melt together, mix and sort out.
Having exchanged their messages
the tree leaves ripple and the river blows...

How do you draw the way
the aspens sound when the
breeze blows through them?

Bright
Western
Tanager
calling...

I thought we'd
heard
the last from you
on your journey
southbound.

intermittent warm evening light
blazes onto the meadow
and rock walls...
shadows suddenly
bring the beauty to life!

8.22.92
Mazama
meadow

How do we draw water? Good question

Lost River
8-19-88

By the river
a tributary to the
Methow. Overcast and
threatening, restful
to the eye.

Road to Harts Pass
July 24, 1993

Finally the day to sit and gaze
into this superb view of the
Methow Valley. Listening to
Robinson Creek in its rush to
converge with the Methow,
and Western Tanagers perching
in all their colorful glory,
feeding young before our dazzled
eyes, this stormy unstable day.
For now, we have more than
enough sun, having chased away
the clouds with our sheer
gathered will power.

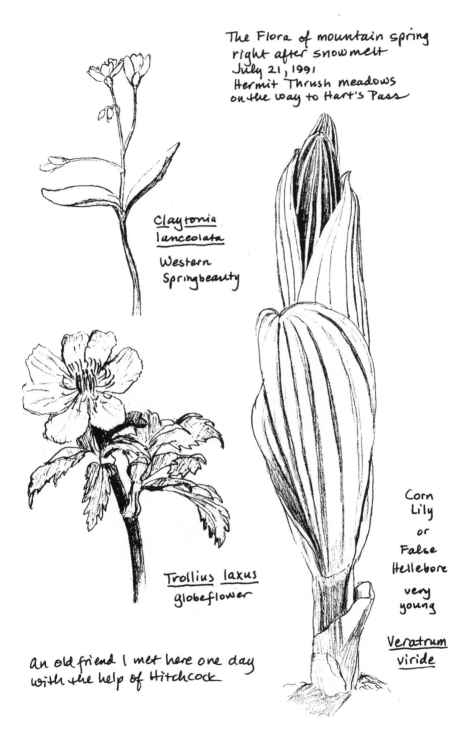

The Flora of mountain spring
right after snowmelt
July 21, 1991
Hermit Thrush meadows
on the way to Hart's Pass

Claytonia
lanceolata

Western
Springbeauty

Corn
Lily
or
False
Hellebore

very
young

Veratrum
viride

Trollius laxus
globeflower

an old friend I met here one day
with the help of Hitchcock

" A bee-loud glade... "
— Yeats

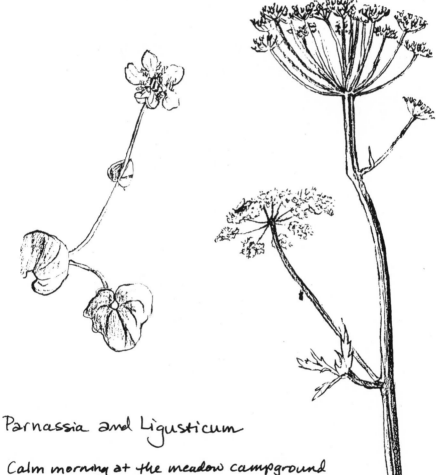

Parnassia and Ligusticum

Calm morning at the meadow campground
by Hart's Pass. Sun dodging in and out
of quickly growing clouds. A marmot whistles,
gray jay & Clark's nutcracker, juncos make
their calls. So MANY flowers in bloom.
Gentian dots the meadow blue,
red paintbrush, yellow arnica.

Crater Mountain
Pasayten Country

what a joy it has been
spending this afternoon
caressing your stones and snowfields
with my simple pencils
and hearing nothing
but butterfly wings
and melting snow.

Slate Peak
July 22nd, 1991

Mountain days
I could never have enough
of these sweet breezy
brain-toasting hot sunny days,
of these ridges riding off into
a distant sea of more montane ridges...
birds caressing the soft singing branches
of ancient nutcracker pine and fir

Sunday – July 17, 1988
Not so early morning
the birds have been up.
Hermit thrush
generous of flutey song
Hummingbird exploring
each color red.
Pine siskins chittering,
flocking, landing impatiently
on limbs, and moving on.
Fox sparrow, the jazzy
swooping song of sunny
subalpine fir and brush.
Junco rolls its call out
over tree tops, the same
yet sweet. Quiet creek,
more like a constant breeze
the high whisper spills
down meadowside.
Clicking sound, mostly
heard at dusk, sounds
again from fir branch...
a bat? A cricket.
The breeze rushes,
not yet sunny and
warm as the day that
has created it.
Sky of deep blue has
covered the night stars,
even more sparkling
than my fantasy dreams.
The night deer,
odd thumps and
scrapes in the dirt
invited my weak eyes
to stare into the
brilliant Milky Way.
Now sunlight tries
to warm us on our
borrowed meadow
recently freed from
snow, punctuated
with pika "peek".
Morning comes
again.

Subalpine Fir
Near Windy Pass

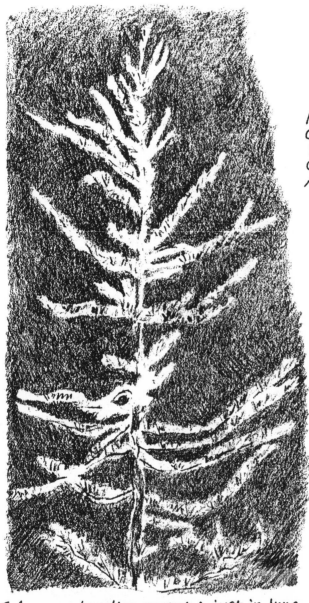

Harts Pass
Cold, sunny
3-5" snow
Oct. 17, 1989
Among the
Lyall's
Larch

Soft green bundles sprouted just in June
now sprinkled, seasoning the snow gold and tawny brown
You couldn't wait just one more week for us,
you couldn't risk the raging dessication of autumn's initial blast,
You let go.... why can't I?

Aug. 14, 1991

What a fine place to eat a peach!
Hill topping with the checkerspots and swallowtails,
the raptors and siskins. Only their sounds, marmot
whistles and the music of snow melting down
ragged craggy mountains. What a perch I've found,
all the finery of August dribbling on my chin as I try
to take in Mountains in all directions, and clouds lifting
to show swell after tumbled swell of glacial landscape.

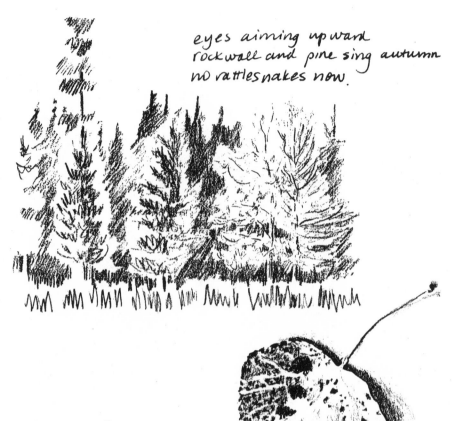

eyes aiming upward
rockwall and pine sing autumn
no rattlesnakes now.

yearning for sunlight
drawn to meadow overtime
aspen rustles, "Stay"

first bite in crunchy flesh
of autumn's sweet red fruit
Nuthatch chatters back

Back in the
mazama meadow
haikus
oct. 14, 1983

August 20, 1995
Wolf Creek Road, Methow River

Warm August afternoon
nearing six, we consider leaving
          this bend in the river
where cedar waxwings flycatch
                    over the rocks
Their trills turn the head in the evening light
to assess and discover

     beauty all around us.

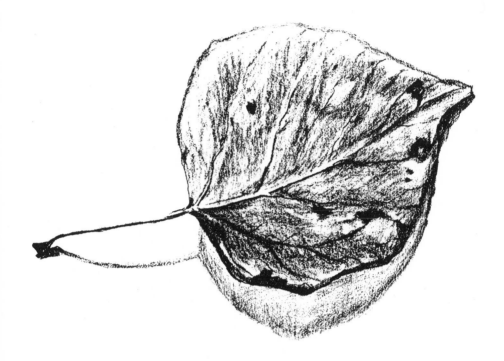

Methow River, Oct 15, 1989
Cottonwood leaf— gold

Tales are told of monarchs too numerous to imagine, and I long to lie below branches bending under their orange weight. But here are my swallowtails, sailing out from branches burning in their yellow brilliance, on each rustle of breeze. One minute they fill the air, and like butterflies draw my attention to follow their twisted trails. Here they lodge between boulders ... a dragonfly hovers over the scene of ochre wings, some dotted black. It darts away, avoiding autumn, as river stones are buried in blankets of gold. And then, too soon, the snow.

Window in the Storm:
A North Cascades Memoir

Tim McNulty

A clap of thunder jolts me awake and a blue-white flash lights the tent like a flare. Another clap peals and rumbles against the peaks and seems to shake the ground beneath me. Wide awake, I burrow into my bag and huddle even tighter on my foam pad. In the silence between strikes I can hear the sound of my heart.

I'm camped with two friends in a shallow snow basin just below the crest of the Cascade range. Our tents are perched on a rocky outcrop—an island in a sea of snow—as the storm blasts away at ice-streaked summits less than a thousand feet above us. I hear the zipper on my partner's bag jerked tight as he too retreats into a nylon cocoon, shuts his eyes to the lightning bolts, and tries for a bit more sleep.

Earlier, as we descended the broken summit of Mount Formidable, wending our way in and out of slanting, rocky gullies, we stopped to watch small, high puffs of cloud waft gently in from the east. My friend and longtime climbing partner Chuck Easton, who grew up in the Skagit Valley and had been traipsing these mountains since he was a boy, joked offhandedly. "Something about those high, puffy clouds from the east," he said. "I remember they mean something—but I forget just what."

Now, I can barely count 2 seconds between flash and thunderclap. As if reading my mind, Chuck whistles from his bag, "That's close!" "Maybe Le Conte," I suggest, but it doesn't matter, really. We both know there is nowhere to go—we are days from the nearest road, or trail. There's nothing to do but hunker down in our bags as the first wind-driven raindrops thwack against the tent fly like shots.

Though I'm loathe to admit it, experiences like these, as much as those stunningly sunlit days spent strolling the high meadows, are what lure me to the North Cascades. The range's volatile mix of coastal and continental weather, its varied, rugged topography, massive ice fields, and cascading streams have given birth to a complex wilderness ecosystem unique to North America. Here, the rumble and clash of forces that have shaped the earth remain vivid, and the collision of climate and geologic process is immediate and profound. In the wildlands of the North Cascades, the archaic gods of creation and destruction whirl together on a knife-edge ridge.

Too often in the lowlands I'm lulled by the scrim of blacktop and concrete into thinking the earth lies still for us, a passive tableau for any human ambition or design. The high mountains allow no such illusion. Traveling in alpine country, a necessary attentiveness and respect sharpen my awareness of the earth we live on and nurture an understanding as old as thought—that the earth is vast, dynamic, and long lived and we are small and momentary on its face. It's an awareness that heightens my appreciation of these wild mountains and rivers and deepens my sense of who I am.

I live and work in the foothills of a sister range to the Cascades, the Olympic Mountains. On clear winter days I can look out from the foothills across the glacier-carved trough of the Puget Basin and mark the snowbound summits of the North Cascades, sharp as cut glass against the deep blue of the winter sky. The Olympics themselves are a remarkably diverse and complete ecosystem and my work as a poet, writer, and conservation activist has been deeply nourished by them. I know that in my lifetime I'll never exhaust their possibilities, yet several times each year I'm pulled across the inland waters to join old friends in exploring those mountains of the mainland. To me the North Cascades represent a wilderness at once harsher and more rugged than my home mountains, a range hewn in granite, gneiss, and schist, studded with active volcanoes, and scored with steep northern walls. The North Cascades is not a contained, islandlike ecosystem like the Olympics, but a wilderness tied to vast stretches of wild country to the north and east, a region where wolves and grizzlies still haunt the landscape. Though its valleys have been more heavily roaded, logged, and mined than the Olympics, its mountains remain rougher-edged, more difficult of access, and vastly grander in scale.

Twenty-five years ago, it was wildness that first brought me to the Pacific Northwest—forests reaching back from rocky shorelines, rivers alive with music and light, and nearness of mountains wearing their ice like tattered robes of the past. I found in the mountains a chance to scuff off the patina of late twentieth-century life and let something of my deeper self breathe through.

I was lucky. Within a year or so of coming to live here, I got to know a few of Chuck Easton's old boyhood friends. They had stayed close through high school and college largely due to a common passion for their home mountains. Several had worked trails and fire crews, were accomplished climbers, and knew the North Cascades well. Tagging along on frequent high-country trips, I picked up the basics of mountaineering and began to discover firsthand the rugged and pristine beauty that is the North Cascades.

There were moments of epiphany in those years of discovery, moments that I can conjure vividly today: my first close-up look at the northern Picket Range from the top of Mount Challenger; a snowy bivouac below Buckindy Peak; a moonlight climb of Eldorado. There were long hikes through misty valley forests, hurried fords across roiling streams, and countless late-night cups of tea as the stars wheeled over snowy peaks. Returning to my favorite places over the years, I've developed a relationship with these wilderness mountains, and learned a quiet reverence for the community of beings that live here.

As my friends and I extended our explorations of the North Cascades high country, one remote area of rugged, glacier-shrouded peaks continued to hold our imaginations. The crest of the range between Cascade Pass and Dome Peak struck us as the very heart of the wilderness mountains. Isolated from roads and empty of maintained trails, the mountains crested into sheer ridges and peaks cloaked in ice and cut by steep hanging valleys and cirques. Traversing the area from either end put climbers within striking distance of some of the least frequently visited summits in the range, and travel across upper glaciers and narrow, windy passes took hikers through some of the most spectacular alpine country in the Northwest. Each spring, when we got together to plan summer trips, the Ptarmigan Traverse ranked high on our wish lists.

The route is named for an adventurous group of young climbers from Seattle who dubbed themselves the Ptarmigan Climbing Club. In the summer of 1938, Calder Bressler, Ray Clough, Bill Cox, and Tim Myers parked their Model A in forest shade at the end of the Suiattle River road and struck out for the unexplored high country north of Sulphur Creek. The four had been climbing together since their scouting years, and for the next 13 days they put their combined mountain skills to the test. The weather held for them during that summer of runaway wildfires, and the four traversed the crest as far north as Mount Buckner before dropping back to the lowland forests. Along the way they reached the summits of all the major peaks, sometimes scaling three in a single day. Six were first ascents; another four, seconds. Only a small circle of mountain enthusiasts followed such exploits in those days, but by the time a second party completed the traverse fourteen years later, the name "Ptarmigan Traverse" became synonymous with the route. Since then, climbers and alpine travelers have been drawn to this wild stretch of mountains as if to a wilderness mecca.

After a few years of juggling schedules and weather, and at least one false start, three of us climbed the trail to Cascade Pass, jubilant beneath the weight of ten-day packs. We camped that night on a bench above the pass and cooked dinner in a cluster of subalpine fir. Thick fog rolled in from the west, sifted through fir boughs, and dripped like rain on the packed snow around us. "We crawled into our bags with more than a little foreboding," I noted in my journal (we'd been weathered off the

Mount Formidable

traverse the year before), "and pulled our hats down over our ears." But sometime in the middle of the night, I heard Jeff Langlow *"whoop"* from his tent. The near-full moon had risen wide and luminous, floating over the eastern peaks "like a misty pearl."

Early the next morning we climbed through late June snow and crossed the small glaciers that clung to the north-facing slope below Cache Col. Easing our packs off, we gazed toward the magnificent array of peaks, ridges, snowfields, and glaciers that comprised the traverse and thumped each other on the back. Somewhere south of all this lay the Suiattle River road, less than 18 miles as the raven flies. But to us, the vast, steep, and broken country that lay between was as full of wonder as an unexplored pole.

There's a sense of freshness and discovery in the Cascades in late spring and early summer. Snow lends an impression of untracked wilderness. Weather is often unstable but the dawns seem to gather themselves from both earth and sky. Days are punctuated by the shrill calls of marmot, the hoarse clucks of ptarmigan, the *cronks* of passing ravens. Sunsets reflected in snowy basins can be stunning, and nights freeze hard under windy stars. The rhythm that comes of matching breaths to kicked steps up long snow slopes yields to an almost meditative calm, and the cool rush of wind at a pass is invigorating.

It was our general consensus then that the first few days of a trip were necessary to shake out the wrinkles and burrs of what we jokingly referred to as "real life." Typically, by the third night out, even the most broke, lovesick, or work-harried among us had slipped the ties of the world below and become fully alert to the moment, to what Buddhists might call the *suchness* of the mountain world. It was a state we lived for, but the problem of juggling work and schedules made stretching trips past long weekends difficult and taking off for more than a week, rare. A full 10 days in spectacular, unexplored country was a gift that might well have brought us to our knees in gratitude.

I worked in the woods in those years, planting trees on cutover lands in the Olympic and Cascade foothills. It was an occupation that dovetailed perfectly with my passion for the mountains. The work was deeply satisfying, the conditioning rigorous, and the higher peaks were nearly always in view for daydreaming. By the time conditions became too dry for planting, usually in early June, the mountains were just opening up. Chuck, a jazz guitarist, pursued a fairly late-night workweek in Seattle. When the summer mountain season arrived his schedule snapped wonderfully into reverse. Chuck kept his fingers limber in the mountains by packing along a small copper flute, and his evening improvisations rose and fell with the cadences of mountain streams. Jeff Langlow was a sculptor who kept body and soul together through carpentry. "Maurice," as we called him in the mountains (after his woolen beret and reverence for various French *alpinistes*), was ever alert for the right feather, stone, or weathered bit of wood that would become part of a future assemblage. With Chuck's music, Maurice's sculpts, and my continual jotting of images and scraps of poems in my journal, the mountains animated our creative lives and lent resonance to our daily lives as well.

Our third day was magic. We traversed the upper Middle Cascade Glacier, then ascended steep névé fields to the narrow notch of Spider-Formidable Col. The view to the south rose to meet us as we approached. Framed within the gatelike rock walls of the pass, it was strikingly beautiful. The alpine summits of Le Conte Mountain, Sentinel, and Old Guard peaks rose from broken glaciers and snowfields and raked the windy sky. The broad white flank of the massive Le Conte Glacier gleamed in afternoon sunlight and Dome Peak, Sinister, and Spire Point rippled off beyond it to the south. Glacier Peak floated in the distance, remote and hazy as a cloud. Streams and waterfalls plunged into the deep valley of Flat Creek, which wound through the spring green of avalanche meadows. We lingered longer than we should have amid the splendor that Fred Beckey called "the core of the North Cascades heartland." Before dropping down to camp, we promised ourselves that we'd save the next day for a climb of Mount Formidable, whose icebound northern face had loomed above us throughout most of the day.

We left camp at dawn the next day, and by late morning celebrated Chuck's thirty-first birthday on Formidable's blocky summit. The view in all directions was splendid, encompassing most of the country we had traveled through and much of what lay before us. We whiled away the afternoon and kicked back on our rocky perch while the sunlight warmed our toes. I tried to capture small bits of the scene in my journal:

> From the summit,
>   a mandala of peaks, etched white
>   against the empty sky,
> and a smoky haze down the Skagit.

That evening, as clouds built ominously along the ridges above camp, we joked that there were worse places to be weathered in, but measured out our cheese with a good bit of care.

The storm raged all night, and the next day rain and thick clouds kept us pinned in camp. With visibility less than 25 feet, and little hope of route-finding over cliffs and crevassed glaciers, we had no choice but to read, savor the cloudscapes, and warm ourselves with endless cups of tea. I had brought along Kenneth Rexroth's translations of poems from the classical Chinese. As the visible world emerged and receded into drifting clouds—a cluster of shaggy mountain trees, an outcrop of rock cliff and heather—the Buddhist sense of the transient, floating, "dewdrop world" seemed poignant. It's a sense that comes to me often in the mountains, and it attunes me to the present in a strangely liberating way.

We speculated there were few places left outside Alaska where you could get this lost, and what a shame that was. By now the wild mountains had worked their magic on our spirits and we found delight in the smallest occurrences. A marmot bounding down a snow slope, a pair of ptarmigan uttering their preposterous call *(begeek-GOCK)*, brought gales of laughter. With lots of time to take notes in my journal, I tried to catch the moment in a poem.

> Those thunderheads
> we watched drift in from the east,
> —high, billowy mounds
> that banked up over the crest,
> feathered and lovely—
>
> all broke loose past midnight,
> and we woke to bolts & flashes, a downpour,
> like the mountains were at war with themselves.
>
> Now, days from the nearest trail,
> we sip tea and wonder
> how we'll get our silly asses out of here,
> while low clouds & mist spill down
> over glaciers and cliffs
> like a Sung scroll . . .
> many cups.
>
> "The problem with transcendence—
> the higher you get,
> the longer it takes to cook your rice."

And another tree slips whimsically into the void.

The next day the void lifted just enough to navigate, and we climbed rock and snow to the crest north of Le Conte Mountain. Cloud and fog blew up out of the South Fork Cascade, and the peak drifted in and out of mist. The weather was clear east of the crest, and as clouds boiled over the divide they were torn to shreds and blown off in little puffs above us. The steep gneiss flanks of Mount Goode dominated the

northeastern horizon. Delighted with at least half a clear sky, we struck out across
Le Conte Glacier toward the summit of Old Guard Peak. Unlike Le Conte Mountain, which greeted us with a blanket of cloud, Old Guard yielded spectacular
views—a dizzying circle of snow-streaked summits adrift in swirling mists. That
night, from a camp on the shoulder of Sentinel Peak, I watched the ranges down
valleys to the west fade from pale blue to gray, then vanish in cloud-cover white. I
coiled the rope and hung it from my ice axe to dry. In the morning, if the weather
held, we'd climb Sentinel for a last view south toward the monolith of Dome Peak
rising above the broken ice of the Chickamin and Dana glaciers, and the serrated
ridge west to the turrets of Spire Point now shrouded in evening cloud.

Steeped this deep in the heart of the North Cascades, the mountains and
streams seemed endless. Wildlands rose around us like a stormy sea whose waves
crested above deep-green tides of forest. Traveling day after day we felt as though
we were carried along in their wake. From our windy perch there wasn't another sign
of human presence, yet we knew all too well that these wildlands were hedged by
roads and clearcuts on all sides, and each season the machines pressed closer.

"Too many people," was how Chuck put it, "and not enough mountains to go
around." Maurice was more circumspect, "Let them continue to muck up Tacoma,
Seattle, Bellingham, if it makes them happy," he intoned over his tea, beret
swapped for the warmth of a balaclava, "but give the mountains a break." In the
larger picture, we were certainly the odd lot out, huddled around the glow of a
small stove, our wet gear stiffening in the wind. We were all outspoken advocates
for wilderness: Chuck and Maurice had written letters and attended hearings in
defense of wildlands; I was doing grassroots work to secure federal protection for
wilderness lands throughout the state. We recognized wilderness was as much a
spiritual as a recreational concern, and our relationships with the wild, while
shared, were also deeply personal. But a deeper question underlay many of our
mountain discussions, one I've chewed over countless miles.

What is *wilderness* but another human artifact, "an invention" in historian
Roderick Nash's words, "of civilized man." Sure, legislated wilderness is a legal
mechanism by which we section off untrammeled landscapes and protect them from
what apologists for a paved earth euphemistically call *development*. That's fundamental. But in a sense, the term suggests a landscape valued as much for what *isn't* there
as for what is. In contrast, what infuses my soul in the North Cascades is not the
absence of roads, clearcuts, shopping malls, and pollution, but the immediate experience of the immense power, presence, and diverse natural beauty of the living
earth. The spontaneous eruption of joy my friends and I experience in the midst of
wild country is a natural human response. It transcends cultural biases and impera-
tives and issues straight from the heart.

"In wildness is the preservation of the world," Thoreau wrote. A century later, the poet William Everson equated Thoreau's "wildness" with the *mystery* of the natural world. Wildness, according to Everson, is the essential nature of an animal, a plant, or a landscape, and it is the wildness at the heart of our own human nature that responds. Wildness precedes human culture, but it informs the best of human aspiration—philosophy, music, literature, art—it is a quality of mind that makes us who we are.

To climb a trail, a pack on our back, step by step into the wild is to be one with wildness in an ancient and primary way. Kenneth Wyatt proposed an optimal rate of sensory stimulation for the human organism, the same rate one experiences in wilderness. Perhaps it's as simple as that, but I don't think so. The North Cascades, and all wild mountains, stand apart from the day-to-day world and have always captured the human imagination. The native people of the Skagit, Nooksack, and Chelan Valleys wove legends of the mountains that towered above them. As far back as ancient Mesopotamia and throughout the long traditions of India, China, and Japan, mountains were seen as places where the worlds of earth and sky merge, abodes of gods and goddesses. From our earliest history, mountains have been charged with religious meaning. Our modern temperament sees mountains as both the symbol and embodiment of natural process—makers of weather, sources of rivers, last bastions of primeval forest—but the old flavor lingers. We know now that the most ecologically significant parts of ecosystems are often found in more productive lowlands, beyond the boundaries of wilderness areas and parks; but mountains remain the human focus for those larger self-sustaining systems, dwelling places of the wild. Though I'm surrounded by the mystery of nature virtually everywhere, it's on foot in the mountains that I best awaken my capacity to see.

It was near the end of our traverse—actually during our last minutes in alpine country before we descended into Istwoot Lake basin and the trail out Bachelor and Downey Creeks to the Suiattle—that my friends and I stepped momentarily into the mystery at the heart of wildness. Nearly twenty years later, the memory remains as vivid and immediate as breath.

In retrospect, we had overextended ourselves that day, and we were fortunate events hadn't taken a different turn. Traversing south from the frozen basin of White Rock Lakes, we didn't begin to climb the long slope of the Dana Glacier below Spire Point until well into the afternoon; it was after 6:00 P.M. when we reached the 7,700-foot pass at the head of the glacier. The weather was deteriorating and we still had a couple of thousand feet to descend to camp. From there it was all downhill, 14 miles out to the road. But here were the splintered granite towers of Spire Point just a few hundred feet above us, and there went what was left of our good sense.

The route, as Beckey described it, was a short one, one moderate 60-foot pitch and a scramble to the summit. Had it been earlier in the day we might have made it up and back in an hour or so. But it was no longer early, and our fortunes were further compromised by a party we met earlier in the day. They advised us to avoid what *looked* like the crack Beckey described; it led off route into a dangerous cul-de-sac. Instead, they told us, bear farther right into the *true* crack. By the time we realized just how bad this friendly bit of advice was, we were far too committed to an utterly nonexistent route to down-climb. Maurice, the most dexterous rock climber among us, led a last, painfully slow, 75-foot pitch to the summit ridge while Chuck and I shivered on a belay ledge below. After what seemed an hour, a *"whoop!"* and some incomprehensible shouts in French told us he had made it. I followed and within minutes understood the long delay. Even with a secure upper belay it was fingernails and boot tips for forty feet as the wall went blank before me. I clawed my way to the ridge and was sputtering effusively at Maurice on his spectacular lead when he gestured with a thumb over his shoulder. To the west, the sky was an angry shroud of blue-black cloud swallowing nearby summits and bearing down on us with the malice of a runaway freight train. Here was the other side of the mystery of wildness. Now it wasn't reverence but a baser instinct that inspired me. I lost no time scrambling to the summit and rigging a windy rappel.

We descended quickly, intent on getting off the face before the storm reached us. We hit the true route then, as clean and straight-ahead as a staircase. As I gathered up the rope and worked down the last bit of rock to the upper snowfield, I could hear the wind rasp above me, and the rock was flecked with blowing rain. Glancing up, I saw the summit swallowed by clouds. Then, as we were about to step thankfully onto the snow and beat tracks back to the pass, the mountain world opened like a shell.

A flourish of setting sunlight underlit the storm cloud in a swirling pattern of salmon and smoke blue. Almost simultaneously, the snowfield and glacier became infused with a deep, almost liquid rose light. The rocks, our faces, even our clothes glowed in an almost otherworldly light. I had occasionally seen such intense alpenglow flare up momentarily on a distant peak, but never before or since have I stood in the center of such brilliance.

The storm held still as we stepped silent as acolytes onto the burning snow and stood as if blessed by the light. It was Maurice who first came to; "The camera!" he whispered, and dropped his pack to the snow to retrieve it. But that simple gesture broke the spell. The light switched off and dark clouds fell over us like a curtain. No cameras now but parkas, mittens, and wool hats were pulled from packs as sharp wind and stinging hail sent us hurtling down the snow slopes howling like blessed madmen. We made it by flashlight to a sheltered snow basin, where we had camped the year before, and piled wet and exhausted into a single tent. The storm raged throughout the night yet we remained exuberant, almost deliriously happy. When we woke to an impenetrable fog the next morning, we met it with a gladness worthy of the most promising of mountain dawns.

There are moments that stand out in memory like stars. When seen from a distance they form constellations around the places that have shaped our lives. When I think of the central place wild country holds for me—when I ponder my desire to speak for it through poetry and prose and to work for its protection—I understand this impulse is born of those rare encounters with the wild. I see my work as a writer is not necessarily to try to share those moments of clarity; words continually fall short of that. Rather, it is to render the wild corners of the earth I know as clearly and honestly as I can. With luck, a poem or essay might send others into their own wild neighborhoods to linger late and look more closely, might lead them through a window of granite or grass to their own moments of epiphany.

TIM MCNULTY is a poet, conservationist, and nature writer who has a long and intimate acquaintance with the North Cascades. His books include *Olympic National Park: A Natural History Guide* (Houghton Mifflin), *Washington Wild Rivers: The Unfinished Work* (The Mountaineers), *and Mount Rainier: Realm of the Sleeping Giant* (Woodlands Press). He is a contributor to *The Enduring Forests* (The Mountaineers) and *Our National Parks* (Reader's Digest Books). His poetry collections include *In Blue Mountain Dusk* (Broken Moon Press) and *Pawtracks* (Copper Canyon Press). Tim lives with his family in the foothills of Washington's Olympic Mountains.

Part III

Landscapes *of* Vision

Introduction to Part III

A little over two centuries ago the first European eyes gazed eastward from the deck of a ship in the Strait of Juan de Fuca. The white cone of the mountain George Vancouver named Baker rose prominently to the northeast, while southward stretched a horizon of serrated peaks. Here was a wild, untamed land ripe for the taking, a land of empire and opportunity. They claimed the place for the king of England and moved on.

The pace of change on this landscape was slow at first, then increased to a blur of settlement and development. The mountains that are the core of the North Cascades, because of their extremely rugged topography and discouraging climate, were on the margins of this process. Late in the nineteenth century, when thoughtful people began to worry that natural resources were being squandered without thought for the future, the hand of government reached out from Washington, D.C. and decreed that these mountain lands would be "reserved," placed off-limits to greedy entrepreneurs who were claiming land for logging and mining as fast as their schemes would allow. Subsequently these reserves were made national forests, wild and primitive wilderness areas, and parts of them became national park and national recreation areas.

The idea of *national park* is little more than a century old; of *wilderness*, less than a century. What seemed useless to those first Europeans—useless because it was wild and would only be useful when tamed—has now become useful *because* it is wild. Such an idea would only serve to bewilder the early pioneers who encountered this landscape.

We cannot predict what the future of the North Cascades will be, nor can we control that future, but we can and must consider it. How different this landscape would be today had people with foresight not promoted forest reserves late in the nineteenth century. Now, as the twentieth century comes to a close, many concerned people are thinking about what this particular landscape might be for future generations, and how these visions might be achieved. Time and again the grizzly bear appears in our thinking, a symbol of the nature that early settlers sought to conquer and which many of us today seek to restore. We have wilderness now, but is it really wild without the grizzly? As human populations grow in numbers and become ever more dominant all over the earth, some grow thoughtful and downright angry at the prospect of a world without deep wilderness, where a creature of the magnificence of a grizzly can go about its business.

Songs of Green Mountains:
A Naturalist's View of the North Cascades

SAUL WEISBERG

In the summer of 1983 my friend John Dittli and I climbed to the summits of ten peaks in two weeks. I remember their names like old friends: Sahale, Buckner, Sharkfin, Forbidden, Eldorado, Black, Mixup, Shuksan, Spickard, Redoubt. We were young. It had been a wet and stormy July. August broke with the promise of clearing. The southwest skies dawned with thin streaks of color instead of the leaden gray and black we had grown accustomed to. We were ready to move.

I remember it as a time of magic, surrounded by good friends, our bodies strong—we had a mission and dreams. I was newly in love that summer and wrote poems each night and played my pennywhistle to the clouds from every peak. Does everyone have a summer like that? I count myself blessed that I have had many, and most of them have been touched in some way by the green mountains of the North Cascades.

As a peak, Sahale is not very impressive. A high spire at 8,680 feet, it remains relatively inconspicuous in the company of the larger and more rugged peaks in the vicinity of Cascade Pass. As a climb it is not very difficult, either. But it was the first peak I climbed in the North Cascades seventeen years ago as a new backcountry ranger working for the National Park Service.

From Marblemount I had followed the Cascade River up through Department of Natural Resources (DNR) and Forest Service land into North Cascades National Park. At 3,600 feet the Cascade Pass trailhead lies shadowed beneath the rocky north face of Johannesburg Mountain. The trail to the pass is short, 3.7 miles of gentle switchbacks, and climbs gradually through forest before breaking free into small meadows and scattered clumps of mountain hemlock at timberline.

I was new to the North Cascades, new to the Park Service, and remember my elation at being set loose for a summer in the midst of such wild mountains. Kelly Bush, another seasonal ranger, and I hiked the sinuous trail up Sahale Arm from Cascade Pass one afternoon, climbing 3,000 feet to the small pocket glacier just below the summit rocks. We roped up for the short scramble to the top. It was a tiny place, barely big enough for two, with the world dropping off in all directions, an unknown landscape that filled my imagination. I stared out at the world of rocky crags and ice, green valleys and shadowed lakes that still fill my dreams.

Earlier in the season, on my first trip to Cascade Pass in June, I postholed steeply uphill through thigh-deep snow with Bill Lester, Backcountry Area Ranger for North Cascades National Park. The pass, and Pelton Basin lying just to the east, was to be my home for the next four months. As we slowly climbed through a silent forest of Pacific silver fir, Bill told me, "You have a unique opportunity to live in a wilderness. Get to know this place, learn it better than anyone else, take care of it." Bill taught me to touch the wilderness gently and showed me trails that now, years later, I discover again through the eyes of my daughters.

I was entering a new landscape and a new life. The job of a seasonal backcountry ranger was ideal for me: long days outside, hard work, solitude at the end of the day, remote crags to explore and climb, hidden plants to discover, new birds to learn. It was a welcome break from graduate school and the noise of the city. That summer I slept on rock ledges and glacier ice. I lay sheltered by clumps of subalpine fir and watched shooting stars dance overhead. At first I was drawn to the summits. It took longer to learn what the valleys offered. I camped along rushing creeks, the sky hidden by thousand-year-old cedars, and felt darkness flow like water. Surrounded by the calls of dark birds I began to listen to the mountains.

❖ Directions to a Place Called Home ❖

Home is the place to which I always return. Each time I walk into the mountains there is a moment when the place speaks to me and I say out loud, "Now, I'm back." Sometimes it happens when I'm walking through a light rain into green hills. Sometimes it comes when I'm sitting alongside the trail, back against a cedar buttress and

Stormy morning at Lake Sally Ann

feet bare to the breeze. The outside world slips away and I look around with the sudden realization—*I'm home.*

Sometimes that moment happens on the first day, in the first hour. Usually it takes much longer—days, nights, especially nights, with hours stretching themselves thin and the night cries of frogs and insects settling into place. It happens while hiking up Thunder Creek beneath the shadow of Pyramid Peak. And again under the cedar shadows of Big Beaver Valley as I walk toward the Picket Range. With each step I am coming home.

How can I give directions to a *time*, to a *place* where magic happens?

My home is bounded by shores and islands and a wall of mountains. Bounded by place and people and names that sound like falling water—Salish, Snohomish, Stillaguamish, Swinomish, Slesse, Sauk, Suiattle, Skagit, Sahale, Shuksan, Stetattle.

Each time I come back I slip into place a little more easily. I slide inside the pattern of green woods and dark forest trails as if I am entering my own bedroom, a room dark with eyes and the songs of unseen birds.

To know the future we must know the place we call home. The stories of common landscapes are as powerful as individual human histories—and as knowable. Some of us are drawn to live in dark river valleys on the west slope of the Cascades, others are called by the high open country east of the crest. Our understanding of a place expands as we learn the bioregion where we live and work and play. We learn to notice natural boundaries as well as human-made lines on the map. We see that watersheds are defined by ridges, that the places where we can easily travel are limited by large rivers, mountains, and oceans. We know without thought when the moon will be full. It is the beginning of recognition that cedar, hemlock, raven, and frog are also part of our culture.

Even today much of the North Cascades lies untouched and unknown. It is a landscape where green is the dominant color, where wind and storm provide counterpoints of gray and white. The essence of its wildness lies far away from roads and towns. It lives high in the cold mountain air where solitude and silence speak louder than the wind.

I think of many trails connecting me to this place. Some lead to high meadows just now breaking free from snow. Some follow green rivers toward an inland sea. The organic debris of centuries falls slowly around us. Maple leaves and fir needles sift down through the ages. This is an old place. Older than humans, old as the oldest rocks. I live on the narrow edge between sea and forest, river and ice. I can only travel for so long in any direction before dark trails call me home.

❖ A Naturalist's View ❖

Naturalists are people who know *home* in different ways. I love to look at patterns in nature, to know the names of birds and find out where and how they live. I follow the green songs of wild things down the trail.

Landscapes are made up of details—veins on a vine maple leaf, yellow and black scales on the wing of an anise swallowtail, striations in a piece of greenschist. Details show us where the magic hides. The ways things fit together—the interactions of living and nonliving things—all tell a story. To read the story, to recognize it in the first place, you have to see the details.

The poet William Carlos Williams said, "No ideas but in things." He was talking of specific objects, artifacts, details. Pieces of a landscape are the *things* a naturalist knows. A name is a bit of history you carry with you as you hike down a muddy trail ablaze with small pink flowers. Knowing the name means we can say "calypso orchid." Knowing a name is the beginning of respect. I believe it is harder to harm something once you have spoken its name.

Everyone should have an intimate knowledge of at least one group of organisms. It doesn't matter whether you are drawn to dragonflies, maples, or lizards. The ability to identify local species leads us to appreciate living things, and their relationships with each other, in new ways. Why alders like to live along the edge of trails, why hemlocks prefer to take root in decayed logs, are questions we can answer by looking closely into the face of the natural world.

Once when we were sitting on a log in a forest clearing, with small orange fritillaries flying all around us, lepidopterist Robert Michael Pyle placed a butterfly on the end of my nose. "For a naturalist intimacy is everything," he said with a laugh. A naturalist's business is this passionate paying attention, observing the details in things, places, and events. Paying attention brings us into intimate contact with the world and we immerse ourselves in small woodland bogs and alpine tarn pools with equal joy. Northwest botanist Art Kruckeberg once told me, "A naturalist is an ecologist in short pants." I would add that, after a day of scrambling after butterflies or kneeling by a patch of orchids deep in the forest, we are ecologists with scratched legs and scraped knees as well.

Aldo Leopold wrote that "the penalty of having an ecological education is to live in a world of wounds." One antidote to Leopold's dilemma is increased intimacy with the natural world. Pick a place and get to know it. From this knowledge and depth of experience come facts and feelings that call us to action. Naturalists have to be involved in the life of the world they study and celebrate. As we look to the future we have no other choice.

❖ Dreams of Roaring Mountain ❖

In the winter of 1983 a small group of us started a field school dedicated to natural history exploration. We began as Shuksan Institute named after Mount Shuksan, the "roaring mountain" that guards the northwest corner of the range. We were a group of dreamers, people who cared intensely about this place who wanted to create meaningful work in a land we loved. In 1986 we evolved into North Cascades Institute and began offering programs celebrating the natural and cultural history of the Pacific Northwest. From the beginning we were closely tied to this ecosystem, this region, and resisted calls for expansion throughout the state. "It is difficult enough," we said, "to learn one place well. Let this be our place."

From that small beginning, ten years ago, we have grown in spirit as well as size. The vision that brought us together continues to guide our steps and hearts. It must, for the work we do is needed. The Institute offers field-based environmental education for children and adults: natural history seminars, watershed education programs, teacher workshops, school programs, summer camps, Elderhostel. Our programs are nationally recognized for excellence and our staff include some of the best people with whom I have ever worked. It is a dream that grows each day. I often struggle with the conflicting demands of office and administration while my heart calls me back to the mountains.

As Executive Director of North Cascades Institute I am responsible for bringing many people to these mountains to learn for themselves the beauty of falling water and the color green. As an educator I know that small places in the landscape sometime tell us more than the big places. Big landscapes, especially mountain landscapes, often turn into scenery, backdrops for experience rather than the experience itself. As a teacher I look for powerful experiences to share with my students so that they remember the context of the place we are sharing as much as the content of the course itself.

Why, as naturalists and educators, do we feel it is important to share the North Cascades? For one, we love to teach outside. For another, it is the best way we know to assure that these mountains have a future as rich as their past. Why not keep special places hidden away for ourselves? We do keep some places hidden. There is a meadow that has seen me alone and at my wildest. There are dark valleys where I have howled and run naked through the huckleberries. They are still there. I will return when the time comes. But mostly I look for places I can share. Trails that can take the impact of a small group of learners walking quietly and carefully. Places where we can gather to marvel at the wing scales of a mourning cloak butterfly or sit and listen to the bubbling song of a dipper.

I go to these special places for myself and for others. I cannot imagine doing anything else. My students leave the mountains with a new view of wilderness and civilization. They know their home place in a new way. When it all works, when the mix of people and place and subject click together just right, it is magic and we all know it. Our new knowledge has power because we have experienced it with our bodies as well as our minds. It means something because it is ours.

The most important part is being outside—*inside* the natural world. A trip to the mountains immerses learners and teachers in nature. Make your next weekend hike a learning adventure to explore a new habitat. Go back to a favorite place determined to see ten new things. Take a new mind to a familiar place and see what you can discover. While looking at the hidden flower of wild ginger, take time to listen to the song of a winter wren warbling out of the forest. Get on your belly and look deep inside the flower. Listen to the forest. Teach yourself to hear the voice of a rotting log, the small songs of millions of insects clustered inside. Slow down and listen to the stories of tiny landscapes.

I want to share a naturalist's view of these green mountains and want you to look through my eyes toward the future of the North Cascades. For me, that future is wet and green. It is alive in mind and heart because of what I see each day on each trail I walk. I wonder, and worry, if what I see will always be here. I do not know. For me, the only way to look toward the future is to share the present, to celebrate what we have and to encourage others to walk gently into wild places with receptive and attentive minds.

I will let others sing the praises of grizzly and cougar and wolf, rare and unseen totems of the mountain world. I whisper the stories of common wildness: the songs of thrushes, small trails that lead to alpine gardens, and the soft breeze of gossamer wings.

Small Birds

You disappeared
into the dark silence
of green woods
and we are still
waiting for your song.

Forest birds are difficult to see but easy to hear. On the west slope of the Cascades four members of the thrush family share the montane forests. Their voices tell us much about habitat and ecology. As clear as a signpost in the forest, they announce their presence even if the singers are seldom seen. The American robin is our most common thrush, found in clearings from lowlands to midelevations. Our three other thrushes—varied, Swainson's and hermit—are similar in size but different in appearance, voice, and manner.

To know the thrushes takes patience, which is a naturalist's chief virtue. As I hike through the old-growth forests of Big Beaver Valley, the song of the varied thrush unfurls out of the moist, coniferous woods like a dark ribbon of sound. Its long, even, slightly dissonant, single-toned whistle floats out of the morning fog. After a brief pause the bird sings a second note at a slightly different pitch. The two notes alternate back and forth, mesmerizing in their simplicity. A friend calls it the telephone bird, although it seems rude to equate such an eerie song with something as mundane as the ringing of a phone.

As I climb higher into the mountains, the song of the varied thrush is replaced by the rapid, ascending spiral of Swainson's thrush. Its clear, flutelike notes seem to disappear into the tops of the Pacific silver fir and mountain hemlock forests that guard its domain. In coniferous forests at high elevations throughout the mountains, especially in areas surrounded by open meadows, the song of the hermit thrush provides the voice of timberline. Heralded by a single, high, flutelike note followed by a rapid series of rising and falling notes, its serene song continues with similar phrases repeated at different pitches.

Knowing the songs leads us to knowing the birds. I once hiked from summit to valley in one long day accompanied by a friend who said that knowing which thrush sang which song robbed the forest of its mystery and, therefore, its beauty. I was stunned, for I see the varied thrush inside my mind when its song calls out to me. Its grayish-blue back contrasts with orange eyebrows, wing bars, and underparts. Its breast is crossed with a single black band. "A robin that went to the circus" is how I once described it to a child. Swainson's thrush, on the other hand, is darker, reddish-brown above with a bold eye ring and buffy breast speckled with dark spots. And the hermit thrush's back is gray-brown, contrasting with its brick-red tail. A white eye ring and grayish flanks complete its costume.

The songs of small birds teach us about place, about their home and ours. We only have to listen. Their songs have the power to reach across time, to span years into the future. Today we mourn the passing of the grizzly. Will we someday weep as the last notes of the hermit thrush fade into the wind that sweeps up and over Sahale Arm?

Above Timberline

Climbing into a clear light
absence of sounds and birds
the hills falling below
On the crest of the ridge
one rock melted free of snow.

My passions take me to high places. In the mountains, in addition to the eight cardinal directions, there are two others: up and down. We do not have much that is flat around here. I love to wander unnamed ridges that snake upward toward unnamed peaks. Small waterfalls drop into valleys thousands of feet below and I have the illusion that no one has walked here before. Our rugged terrain and close proximity to the Pacific Ocean support a rich and varied landscape. Within a small geographic area the North Cascades offers an exceptional range of climatic, topographical, and biological diversity.

One of the first places I explored in the Cascades was Boston Basin, a steep, ice-sculpted cirque that hangs on the mountain slopes just below the jagged peaks of Forbidden, Torment, Sharkfin, Boston and Sahale. Northwest of Cascade Pass, the basin is a climber's paradise, with rock of Skagit gneiss and granodiorite forming the upper boundary of the cirque. The outer edges of the basin are dominated by long, narrow meadows; bare bedrock, flanked by lateral moraines, makes up the center. Eight creeks, fed by meltwater from the Quién Sabe and Taboo Glaciers, dissect the meadows, then fall steeply into the Cascade River Valley 2,700 feet below. When I worked as a climbing ranger for North Cascades National Park I set up my base camp in Boston Basin each summer. The peaks and the waterfalls became familiar friends. In 1982 my wife, Shelley, spent most of the growing season exploring the basin while studying subalpine plant communities for her master's thesis. It was then that I began to notice the flowers.

"Anybody can travel light; it takes a real effort to travel heavy." That's what we said to console ourselves as we packed for our climbing trips. We did go heavy. Climbing gear, beer, books of poetry, field guides. My climbing partner, John, had his camera gear in a second pack strapped on top of his already huge load and an extrawide fanny pack which he swung around and carried on his front for easy access. He is the only person I have ever seen use a wide-angle lens to self-arrest on a steep ice slope.

Shelley carried her botany tools, sampling frame, plant press, and twelve pounds of plant books, including Hitchcock's massive *Flora of the Pacific Northwest*. I, on the other hand, went a bit lighter: only my journal, a few books of poetry, a field guide or two, a hand lens, binoculars, a butterfly net, and a small bottle of sake—and, of course, a stove to heat it. Scrambling to the crest of the moraine which dissected the distant meadows of the basin, I looked down at John, engrossed with tripod and lenses, all attention focused on something too small for me to see. And Shelley, on her knees in some wet meadow, lupines crusted with dew, so wet that just by walking through you were soaked to the skin. A new flower before her nose, she was oblivious to rain, wind, and deerflies.

My stove sang a faint whistle to the marmots. A small pot of tea began to steam. Clouds rose out of the valley, sometimes covering the entire scene—which, over time, has been transformed—John's photographs made into wonderful images in magazines and books, Shelley's notes into the pages, graphs, and dendrograms of a thesis, and my own scribblings on rain-smeared journal pages.

I believe there is nothing more important than knowing a place well. We cannot hope to preserve what we do not know. We need to know, and delight in, the details. We need the activist and the scientist, the passionate artist who can paint the story and the naturalist who can sing the praises of small bugs. We must learn what we can and cry for that which is unknown and unknowable and which may be lost forever.

❖ Songs of Timberline ❖

In Boston Basin, as in timberline forests throughout the western Cascades, a deep and persistent winter snowpack sets the ecological stage for the year's activities. Along the basin's lower edges timberline forests are composed of Pacific silver fir, while its upper edges form forest islands of mountain hemlock that interfinger with subalpine meadows. These beautiful parklands just below timberline are unique features of northwest mountains, better developed here than anywhere in the world.

Shelley's research project was concerned with the composition and distribution of plant communities in the subalpine parklands of Boston Basin. No matter what the weather, she would leave camp early each morning to sample new sites across the basin. Sometimes I watched her disappear into the blowing mists, a small figure clad in blue raingear moving slowly uphill. Her methods were simple: find, identify, sample, count, measure, write notes over and over again. Her schedule only varied with summer storms, the foot of snow that collapsed her tent on the fourth of July, and my entreaties to her to join me in the valley on my days off.

What Shelley learned that summer fascinated us both. The transition from mountain forest to subalpine meadow is dramatic. In Boston Basin the first glimpse of the upper meadows is spectacular. After climbing steeply through silver firs encrusted with gray tendrils of moss and lichen, we turned a corner and suddenly could see the entire basin spread out before us. Forest turns to meadow within a span of fifty feet. Trees are replaced by grasses, herbaceous flowers, and small shrubs. Lush meadows of alpine phlox, Davidson's penstemon, false hellebore, Sitka valerian, mountain lupine, partridge foot, fan leaf cinquefoil, and glacier lilies cover the slopes. A half-dozen small streams cascade over rock slabs while sheer faces of rock and ice float in mist and sunlight 3,000 feet above.

Subalpine meadows occupy an ecotone between the montane forests at lower elevations and the alpine tundra above. Timberline, caused by a complex interaction of ecological factors, including snow distribution and accumulation, topography and wind, is a special place where dramatic shifts in plant communities occur over very small areas. Subalpine meadows are characterized by deep, late-melting snow which insulates the plants during the winter and provides abundant meltwater during the summer. The depth of snow accumulation, and thus the duration of snowpack, influences soil moisture, soil temperature, and the length of the growing season. Leeward slopes and basins accumulate snow throughout the winter. Because snow persists into late summer in these sites they provide ample water but a very short growing season for plants. The accumulation of heavy snow damages woody plants, keeping the meadows free from trees. In contrast, ridge tops and windward slopes are exposed to the full force of winter winds which strip them clear of snow after it has fallen. With insufficient snowpack to recharge soil moisture, these sites are susceptible to drought throughout the growing season. Plants in these high alpine areas bloom early in the spring when water is available.

Two years of work finally led Shelley to describe eleven different plant communities in the rich environment of Boston Basin. She then simplified them into five broad categories, relating to habitat types and the timing of snowmelt. Lush *mesic meadows* cover a large area of the basin on deep, well-developed soil, often honeycombed with marmot burrows. In this habitat, higher ground melts out by mid-June, while swales hold snow as late as August. *Wet meadows*, created by meltwater from high snowfields, have a high water table throughout the summer. Shelley found that snowmelt in these communities is late, in mid-July or August, and the ground is muddy throughout the summer. In striking contrast to these wet meadows is the vegetation that occurs on the glacial *moraines* that dissect the basin. These steep, rocky features, remnants of alpine glaciers that covered the basin as recently as 100 years ago, are dry throughout much of the summer. Snow melts early from moraines and they are often snowfree by mid-June. We noticed that vegetation is sparse, especially on the steep, inner slopes of the lateral moraines. Large slabs of exposed *bedrock* extend across the center of the basin. Smoothed by retreating glaciers, the snow melts by the end of July, forming cascading streams that course across the polished rock. Plants are unable to gain a foothold in the bedrock and Shelley would return from a day of scrambling having found only isolated plants growing in small cracks and depressions that collect silt and water. There were also distinct *creekside* communities throughout the basin with their own rich assemblage of wildflowers.

Above the meadows we discovered the alpine world. This is where I went to climb and roam, and where Shelley and I went exploring on my days off from "work." We found the dominant life forms of the peaks to be lichens and small cushion plants: low-growing, prostrate plants such as Tolmie's saxifrage, crowberry, Douglasia, and spreading phlox. Growing low allows these cushion plants to stay in the warmer, more sheltered microclimate near the ground. On the most exposed summits, crustose lichens often represent the only growth.

In all the days we spent wandering the basin we saw relatively few large animals. The warning whistles of marmots and pika alerted us to the arrival of a hiker, coyote, or eagle. Birds were the most visible animals and the songs of horned larks, water pipits, and rosy finches often woke us from our bivouac on the rocky talus. Insects were far and away the most common creatures in the high country. It took awhile but we began to look beyond the mosquitoes' whine and the deerflies' bite to small and colorful worlds of wonder.

Lupine

In the center of each palmate leaf
mist has gathered
one small drop of rain.
Below
one blue butterfly
slowly opens its wings.

I came late to the love of butterflies. They were always around me, fluttering through green meadows, floating across ridges, and disappearing when the fog rolled in. I did not notice them for too many years. When the sun was out I was always on the move, too busy to watch for small insects among the flowers. Now that I have learned to look, I find them everywhere; flying at the edge of memory, they call me to mountain meadows.

I am drawn to small butterflies, and of all the little ones, those that sing to me most are the gossamer wings in the family *Lycaenidae*. The gossamer wings are a large family made up, in the Cascades, of three groups: the blues, the coppers, and the hairstreaks. They are the warblers of the butterfly world. At first they make some sense. Blues are generally blue, coppers are most often the color (and size) of a new penny, and hairstreaks have tiny hairlike tails. But—and this is what I love about biology—these insects have an attitude. There are blue coppers, tailed blues, and tailed coppers, and copper-colored hairstreaks and blues. You have to love them. There are about thirty-six species in the North Cascades, and I may never get them straight. Males and females differ markedly in color and in structure, while females have the six legs common to all insects, male gossamer wings have reduced forelegs and therefore appear to only possess two pairs of legs. With delicately banded antennae, brilliant colors on the dorsal surface of their wings, and soft hues intricately patterned with tiny spots and thin lines, their names reflect their stunning colors: silvery blue, immaculate green hairstreak, purplish copper, spring azure, lustrous copper.

What can small blue butterflies tell us about the future of the North Cascades? Most people would say, "Not much." But if all of us, or even most of us, actually took the time to *see* these small jewels, what changes would it make in our view of the world? Is butterfly watching merely a romantic pastime, a dream of old naturalists roaming through sylvan glades, naming butterflies after goddesses and figures from mythology? Or is it another vital *linking* that connects us to place and, thus, to home?

Butterflies surround us in the summer meadows. They dance through dappled clearings in the darkest forests and follow the openings along small streams and rivers throughout the Cascades. Theirs is a world of many-legged creatures waiting to be discovered.

Headwaters

With cupped hands
I bow and drink
Each day
a different stream
Many times
from the same river
And once,
the sea.

If the mountains comprise the body of the North Cascades, the Skagit River is its heart. The North Cascades is a land of rivers and the Skagit is one of the great rivers of North America. Born in mist and rain and nurtured in wilderness, the Skagit watershed is the largest river basin in Puget Sound, contributing over thirty percent of the freshwater and thirty percent of the salmon that flow into our inland sea. But while the Skagit is born in wilderness, its wildness is shrinking.

Wilderness is a gift that civilization gives to itself only once. When it is gone, it is lost forever. Words and pictures pale beside its fading memory. It is only because of the work of many individuals, organizations, and agencies that we have wild rivers and wildlands left in the Pacific Northwest. To imagine the future of the North Cascades we must imagine the future of wilderness. It is a challenge we must face *today* so that our children will be able to discover the magic and power of this green land for themselves.

As we move into the next century, places like the North Cascades are critically important. There are few places left where we can learn about the natural world in its original, unaltered state. These scientific values of wilderness become more important as we realize how much we have lost. We must share the lessons we learn from wildlands. Wilderness also provides opportunities that are essential to certain types of learning. Wildlands offer a preeminent outdoor classroom, places where the lessons we learn about ourselves are as important as lessons about food chains or alpine plant adaptations.

What future do I want for my home? Most of all I want the songs that whisper from these green mountains to keep singing. For that to happen we must keep listening. I worry that we will be left with only the larger parks and wilderness areas to roam in. Wildlands lose something when they exist within limited boundaries. We need a broad spectrum of wild places, from large, protected mountain parks and wilderness areas to greenways and nature corridors connecting our towns and cities. We need small backyard spots for butterflies and garter snakes, and places close to home for our children to explore. We need management directed at all levels of diversity, from the largest predators to the smallest pollinators. And we need an informed and educated public, people who care deeply and passionately about particular places, women and men and children who know these places intimately and care for them as they would care for their own home.

I look toward a future where there is a place for wilderness and biological diversity, a place for families and communities to live sustainably and well on the margins of wild landscapes, alongside rivers and forests, taking what we need and not allowing our greed to rob our children of the unique experiences we have shared. If we begin with love and knowledge and appreciation of specific wild places we can create a new vocabulary for talking about wildness and wild nature. I am looking for a place where the land sings to me and I sing back, my voice faint beside the creek's roar.

Walking into the Mountains

Walking into the mountains
in the rain
deeper and deeper
everything is green.

❖ Teaching in the Rain ❖

I have seen the future and it is wet and green. All winter the mountains have sung to themselves in low, muffled voices. In springtime their voices are louder. The sound of falling water, snowmelt streams breaking free from ice-fast earth, cascades from peak to valley. The group, some ahead of me, some far behind, moves slowly, silently. It is not the silence of quiet communion with the wilderness, but rather the footsore slogging of exhausted students. Our camp is miles away; our discussion on forest succession ended as gray clouds descended to the ground. We move without speaking. I think of the many forms of water: clouds and rivers and lakes and rain and sleet. I am wet and cold and tired. I am also teaching.

Once, when I was new to this business, I sat in the winter darkness of a Wyoming cabin with some of my closest friends, educators with more experience than I may ever know. Ed Grumbine's voice rang clearly from the darkness beyond the fire. "You can't teach in the rain!" That was years and miles removed from this green river valley deep in the North Cascades, but once again his words return.

As a naturalist I pride myself in being outside in all seasons and weathers. As a teacher who spends more time outside than in the classroom I am often asked, "How can you teach in the rain?" My answer is, "There is no such thing as bad weather— only inappropriate clothing." But of course the question goes deeper than that.

I *can* teach in the rain. But I teach differently, *learn* differently. Rain is an integral element of this wilderness place, and the place changes you. It reaches out and grabs your attention, demands to be noticed. In the North Cascades rain is one way the wilderness says, "You're not in the classroom or the city anymore."

Rain is the signature of the North Cascades; it makes the land. Glaciers, mountains, rivers, and the inland sea we call Puget Sound are all molded by its wet embrace. If you come here you are going to get wet. If you teach here, sooner or later you will find yourself walking through a dripping forest with your socks down around your ankles.

My work with North Cascades Institute has shown me that teaching outdoors in the Pacific Northwest means accepting the rain as an essential element and, more importantly, accepting what the land is teaching you. The crux of teaching, and learning, in wilderness is using the power of place. Let the rain teach. Let wildlands speak for themselves.

The elements of wilderness education are time, place, people, and something to talk about. The art lies in putting these elements together, then trusting yourself and the students enough to stand back and watch what happens. Immerse a small group of students in a powerful natural environment, give them something to sink their teeth into—be it alpine ecology or old-growth forests—mix thoroughly, and let simmer for a few days, a few nights under the stars. The experience is deep, powerful, and lasting.

Teaching in the rain involves more than just teaching. Living in the rain is hard: wet clothes, wet sleeping bags, soggy granola, field guides that either fall apart or swell to twice their original volume. We can learn from the earlier native inhabitants. Did they stay inside their longhouses sitting around a smoky fire, or did they put on their cedar-bark capes and go out to face the wet? After two or three days the rain stops being an outside force. Its presence is invasive—another being living with you, close to your skin. It becomes as familiar and natural as the wet jacket that clings soggily to your back.

Each time I am out with students and clouds roll in from the southwest, sink toward the ground, and begin spitting at us, I relearn the same lessons. First I look for signs of clearing, delaying projects "until the weather changes." Eventually there is nothing left but to continue. We gear up and move on toward the day's lesson. This is a good time to learn the lessons of microhabitats, to hunker down in protected crannies, and watch alpine saxifrages hiding from the wind.

Teaching in wilderness is powerful. Teaching for wilderness is infinitely more so. It is the only way we can retain wild places like the North Cascades for our children. Teaching for wilderness requires listening to the voices of the land. If we listen well, the land will change our lives. It has changed mine. Rain is one of the essential ingredients of place. A basic tenet of ecological truth in the Pacific Northwest is that the land is the way it is—in shape, smell, texture, sound—because of the rain. It sings sweetly to the cedars. Our job is to learn to listen to its song.

SAUL WEISBERG is a naturalist, writer, and educator who has been exploring and teaching in the North Cascades since 1976. He is co-founder and Executive Director of North Cascades Institute, and has been a climbing ranger, fire lookout, tree planter, and biologist. He lives in Bellingham with his wife, Shelley, and their two daughters, Hannah and Emily.

Sitec and Tomorrow in the North Cascades

SCOTT BRENNAN

I awoke to a roar that died and then returned. The air I breathed was frigid but I was warm as I rolled onto my back and pushed my hood from my face.

I had never seen such stars.

In an old story, stars were holes shot through a ceiling of night. From my bare, rocky bed, I saw bright heaven through those holes. A faded band of light, the Milky Way's far arm, glowed above me like threadbare cloth under a full moon.

There I was, almost a mile and a half high in North Cascades wilderness. Settling onto my back, I pulled taut the drawstrings on my jacket's hood and turned my head from left to right and back again, to wonder at the sky, which was filled with stars at all points of the compass. Neither haze nor city lights reflecting off polluted air dimmed my view of heaven.

And then there was the wind, my constant companion that night. It rushed across the deep, black lake upon whose shores we slept, up a sloping rock shelf, and across my bed. It flowed out the lower end of the lake and rattled through beds of tiny heather plants along the shore.

I lay in the murk of half sleep at a place I had found after a 15-mile walk. I was dizzy and unaccustomed to the thin air. Slowly, I remembered how I had come to this place so near the sky, so far from home. I shivered as I remembered that this place I had come to love, the protected core of the North Cascades, was slowly losing its soul.

Often, I retreat to such places to reflect on the lessons of the past, the folly of our daily lives, and the uncertainty of the paths we choose for the future. That starry night was a time for such reflection, and a time for making real the scientific abstractions that had lately defined my life. On that night, I contemplated the possibility of places being alive and possessing souls.

The Nooksack people, who have made their home for centuries in the northwestern quarter of what we now know as the North Cascades, use the word *sitec* to mean "soul" or, literally, "life force." An ecosystem is, in many ways, a living thing with its own *sitec*. It is complex, dynamic, persistent over time, and defined by its unpredictability. And if anyone would argue that an ecosystem cannot be alive because it cannot die, I invite them to visit any number of places in the American West where we have efficiently converted nature to strip mines, strip malls, parking lots, highways, and waste dumps. Ecosystems die—piece by piece.

If earth constitutes the North Cascades Ecosystem's flesh, rivers its lifeblood, and mountains its skeletal scaffolding, then the animals and plants comprise its *sitec*, or soul. Clearly, scientists tell us, the ecosystem's *sitec* is slowly slipping away. And, according to aboriginal stories common to many Native tribes of the Pacific Northwest, there is but one, inevitable consequence of soul loss.[1]

"The *sitec*, or soul is considered to be so light that it is easily dislodged from its owner," wrote scholar Sam Gill in his 1992 *Dictionary of Native American Mythology*. "Untreated soul loss is fatal. Death is usually slow, starting with unusual behavior. . . ."[2]

The North Cascades Ecosystem, a roughly circular area to the east of Seattle, Washington and Vancouver, British Columbia may be one of the few places in North America that is still home to all the species present when Europeans first settled this continent. Its *sitec* is still mostly intact, but of late, many small changes, much "unusual behavior," has been detected in this living system.

This remarkable place is the wild backyard to the fastest growing city in Canada and one of the fastest growing urban areas in the United States. This odd juxtaposition of wildness and urbanity has brought the biodiversity crisis home to the residents of the northwestern United States and southwestern Canada.

In late 1995 a small story appeared on the inside pages of newspapers around the world. In my hometown paper, *The Bellingham Herald*, it appeared under the headline, "30,000 Species Face Extinction, UN Study Says."[3] The article reported the startling results of a research project sponsored by the United Nations. Humans are rapidly destroying habitat around the world, according to the study, and this has sped the extinction of plants and animals a thousandfold.[4] While we all seem to know that animals and plants are becoming extinct in the far corners of the world, what we do not recognize is that they also may be disappearing from the Pacific Northwest at record rates. We do not know this for certain because too little money is available to those who would study this crisis. Our leaders are more concerned with short-term economic and political matters than with extinction. This reminds us that extinction presents a scientific and a social quandary.

Recent scientific studies have found that dozens of species are about to disappear from the North Cascades. National Park Service scientists have found that in the North Cascades, as throughout the world, existing parks and preserves are not enough to protect species which have survived there for hundreds of thousands of years.

North Cascades National Park caretakers spend half the park's annual $5.1 million budget on road, trail, and building maintenance, according to the park's wildlife biologist Bob Kuntz. Resource management, the business of caring for the plants and animals in the park, receives about one-tenth of the park's annual budget.[5] This limits the park's ability to protect its plants and wildlife, Kuntz told me, and many species are in trouble in the North Cascades.

Seven of the North Cascades' salmon and steelhead runs are on the brink of extinction,[6] and the gray wolf, peregrine falcon, bald eagle, and spotted owl are considered threatened there.[7] Species which are at risk of extirpation, or may already be gone from the park complex, include the wolverine, bighorn sheep, fisher, marten, lynx, moose, American white pelican, Rocky Mountain elk, trumpeter swan, sandhill crane, osprey, great gray owl, Pacific Western big-eared bat, North American lynx, cascade frog, spotted frog, northern goshawk, harlequin duck, bull trout, and barred owl.[8]

The state of Washington is monitoring the following at-risk species in or near the park: golden eagle, flammulated owl, common loon, Vaux's swift, pileated woodpecker, and western gray squirrel.[9] The National Park Service lists fifty-seven plant species found near North Cascades National Park as endangered, threatened, or sensitive.[10]

To those who argue that the disappearance of these creatures is simply a "natural process," and that it has no effect on our lives or our economy, I can say only this: while we seldom see the direct economic benefits of grizzly bears, wolves, and flammulated owls, we undoubtedly benefit from the systems to which they belong. Our health and the well-being of our descendants depend upon clean air, clean water, and quiet, wild places where each can be alone. A healthy, untrammeled system provides great spiritual and aesthetic rewards as well. Indeed, when Christ faced his greatest challenge, when he survived his most difficult days on Earth, he did not choose a city, or even a church as his sanctuary. He instead spent his defining days in wilderness.

Chaos theorists, statisticians, and corporate lobbyists will attack the idea of a healthy ecosystem as unscientific, unsound, and fanciful. But to those of us whose idea of integrity is defined by the continued presence of those creatures present during European settlement of the American West, the critics' arguments seem shortsighted, narrow, and foolish.

Arbitrary borders, as well as ignorance, threaten the native plants and animals in the North Cascades, Bob Kuntz told me, and North Cascades National Park's northern edge is evidence of this problem. At the United States–Canada border protected forests give way in many places to enormous clearcuts. Pristine rivers turn to muck-choked gullies as they cross the border. Similar nonsensical borders mark the boundaries between Forest Service and Park Service land in the United States and between protected areas and forestland in Canada.

This divided home is one reason the region's native animals and plants are in so much trouble, Kuntz and other scientists believe. The lines humans have drawn on the land do not match the patterns nature has established over thousands of years. Some places remain wild but roads, clearcuts, and new human settlements divide and isolate the native species.

In the early 1990s members of about a dozen Canadian and U.S. environmental groups decided the time had come to fix what was wrong with the way we use public lands in the North Cascades. They called themselves the Cascades International Alliance.

The Alliance asked for the creation of an international park in the North Cascades. Besides a new name for the place, the Alliance wanted the federal and provincial land managers to manage first and foremost for biodiversity protection. Logging, mining, and other activities must only occur after we have made sure we are doing enough to protect all native species, Mitch Friedman, an Alliance leader, told me.

According to Friedman's explanation, protection and use of the ecosystem can be compatible, but the protection of habitat and biodiversity must come before logging, mining, and grazing. Timber and hydropower are what scholars and economists call "renewable resources." That means, under most circumstances, that what we use today can be replenished tomorrow, or in a decade, or perhaps in a century. They are resources we can use without using up, if we are careful. Biodiversity, on the other hand, is not a renewable resource.

We used up the passenger pigeon, and nearly used up the American bison, bald eagle, and blue whale. We are on our way to wasting the grizzly bear, countless kinds of birds, and plants which might someday provide a cure for cancer or AIDS. It seems a straightforward, even an economic, argument that whatever cannot be replaced should not be used up. This belief is implicit in the Alliance's definition of ecosystem management.

The North Cascades, for me, is a place in which to reflect on the meaning of our relationship with the land. It is a place from which to learn from the past, study the present, and hope for the future. It is a place that generates questions and provides an escape from the numbing abstractions of land management and ecological science.

The most important question we can ask about the North Cascades Ecosystem, whether we favor protection, intensive use, or some combination of the two, is simply, "What is the meaning of this place?" This is what I asked myself as I stared from my warm cocoon into that near, wild, night heaven.

I learned a great deal about how we interact with the North Cascades Ecosystem while I studied the park proposal. I have learned a great deal more by walking through the heart of the ecosystem, sleeping in its high places, and enjoying the gifts it offers those who visit on its own terms. No single place has taught me more about our relationship to the nonhuman world than the damp, deep-green forest of the upper Baker River.

Ecosystem integrity and biodiversity, which I first learned of by reading textbooks and scientific journals, became real to me during a day-long walk along the upper Baker River in midwinter. This river, along with that high ridge upon which I awoke under the stars, has taught me the meaning of the vision some of us share for the future of the North Cascades. In one day on the river I learned a great deal about the motivation of the park proponents and of those who would restore wildness and integrity to the North Cascades Ecosystem.

The upper Baker River begins as countless trickles on the western flanks of the Picket Range in the heart of North Cascades National Park's northern half. It flows south and west from the Pickets toward Mount Baker. It rolls beneath the lee side of Mount Shuksan's imposing 9,127-foot greenschist summit and into civilization—the Baker Lake reservoir behind the black concrete hulk of Baker Dam. Sean Cosgrove, an Alliance volunteer and university student, and I left Bellingham for the upper Baker at 7:15 in the morning on January 23, 1995. For more than an hour we drove through farmland, private forests, and federal and state clearcuts whose stumps were often as big as small cars. We were on the trail at 9 A.M.

Sean had moved to the Northwest from Utah four years earlier and had worked as an intern for the National Parks and Conservation Association (NPCA), an Alliance organization. He has since been the coordinator of the Environmental Center on Western Washington University's campus in Bellingham and a grassroots organizer in the national movement to save unprotected ancient forests. He cares greatly for salmon, bears, wolves and wilderness.

Sean believes humans should be much better neighbors to large predators such as the wolf and grizzly bear. He argues for big wilderness, unbroken wildlands that would allow grizzly bears in Alaska to walk, unmolested and unhindered by humans and their inventions, to Colorado, to Mexico. He wants to help the wolf, salmon, and lynx return to their historical range. He wants us all to realize and eliminate the hubris which defines our relationship with the other residents of Earth.

He doesn't believe humans should hold any special position in the hierarchy of living things. If at all, he says, we should demonstrate our supposed superiority through acts of compassion and restraint, not through the wholesale conversion of the natural world to dollars, board-feet, and kilowatt hours. His beliefs, along with those of other supporters of the international park, remind me of Gottfried Wilhelm Leibniz's insight into such matters. "It is certain that God sets greater store by a man than a lion," Leibniz wrote. "Nonetheless, it can hardly be said with certainty that God prefers . . . a single man to the whole of lionkind."[11]

Sean had written several articles for the Cascades International Park newsletter to explain the park proposal. He joined me on the trip up the Baker to explain his reasons for supporting the international park and to simply spend a day outside. We parked at a four-foot-high heap of plowed ice and snow near the road's end and checked our packs for lunch, hats and water. We hiked the last, snow-covered mile of Forest Service Road 1168 and passed through a flat, open camping area near the river.

The snow was 2 feet deep in places and firm as styrofoam block. Hoary frost covered the snowpack. It hadn't snowed there since it last rained, and it hadn't rained for weeks. It was the cold, hard snow of a midwinter drought. It squeaked beneath our feet.

We followed the broad trail through a frozen swamp. A cliff face was close by on the left. Sword ferns grew from the wall, and icicles hung from the moss beneath the ferns. My breath floated in front of me in white clouds and my vision blurred as I stepped through it. Cedar and hemlock of all ages lined the path and the Baker ran low and gray as steel to our right and below. Boulders, 10 feet high, had fallen from a cliff sometime since the last ice age. Foot-deep moss covered them. Trees 8 feet in diameter lined the path. The moss glowed green; the tree trunks were a solemn brown. My toes ached from the cold.

There were no clouds. The river, 30 yards wide, rattled in its bed. The water sang in winter bell tones. It jumped in its rapids like grease in a skillet, popping, splashing, throwing shards of daylight into the dark forest. Water swirled through pools, clear as molten crystal. An hour later we walked from the forest onto open ground. It was swampy again and we looked beyond to an icy beaver pond. The water level had fallen since last thaw and the ice hung magically above it.

Thick mist rose from the snow. Sublimation—when snow turns directly to vapor at temperatures below freezing—had wrung the moisture from the snow. Steep red cliffs rose to our left and a glacier, smoothed by winter snows, met the sky across the valley and up a steep, forested ravine to our right. Three rock pyramids waved banners of morning mist as they roughened the skyline above the glacier. We walked across a steep hill and into deep forest and passed a paper sign tacked to a young cedar. "NPS Boundary Marker."

When we walked into the park and its federally protected wilderness, we came ashore onto an island of protection in a sea of clearcuts. Green earth, green forest, green mind, green spirit. Snow in plots beneath the sky. Luxuriant mosses beneath heavy canopy. Ferns growing from dead trees.

Suddenly, willows. Sulphide Creek and its crib, the south face of Shuksan. Shuksan's glaciers looked like marshmallow creme, slathered on the mountain's back steps. From the west, Shuksan is a photogenic mountain. Its hanging glaciers and symmetrical summit pyramid have graced numerous calendars and car commercials. From the east, our view, it is a broken mountain, its gray spine shattered and thrust into the sky. From the north, it can be deadly.

A few months earlier, as an especially hot, dry summer was ending, the north side of the mountain had released one of its victims. In 1991 Gary Gray, a university student, talented photojournalist, and accomplished mountaineer, died in an icefall on that side of the mountain. While my friend Hugh Dougher, wilderness district ranger in North Cascades National Park, was recovering Gary's body with the assistance of the park's helicopter pilot, Gary's mother stood a few miles away, looking up at Shuksan from the base of the Mount Baker Ski Area. She watched the helicopter and men working from it, but did not know they were looking for her son's body. She had simply chosen that day to return to the mountain to contemplate its harsh beauty and utter indifference. Shuksan is that kind of mountain; the North Cascades, that kind of range.

"Thank God for the parks," Sean said as we stood in late afternoon sun at the confluence of Sulphide Creek and the Baker River. "Thank God for the Wilderness Act."

At that time and place, it was difficult to disagree. We stood inside North Cascades National Park's Stephen Mather Wilderness in Shuksan's shadow at the joining of two wild rivers. We also stood at the junction of times that have been and times that will be.

Four or five sets of footprints marked the rock-hard snow. Quarter-inch-long cones, petals splayed, covered the snow in places.

"Hemlocks," he said.

They helped me keep my footing, like sand on an icy walk. There was no sound but the river's.

Farther up the Baker, a gray ouzel dipped and dove, hunting his lunch and shedding water from his teflon wings. The fat bird, about the size of a robin, dove and rolled like a seal, or an otter. He worked the river like a fly fisherman, but with everything in reverse. He dove beneath the surface to hunt insects with his beak. He flew upstream and rafted down, dipping and diving rather than working gradually upstream. His work was smooth, a quiet dance. We stood, knees stiff in the cold, watching him raft around a bend and out of sight.

"I want to see grizzlies fishing from the banks of this river," Sean said. "I want to walk around this corner and see a pack of wolves bringing down a deer."

We had spent the morning walking, staying warm and talking about the future of protected places. Neither knew what the future held but we had seen the 1994 elections move antipark and antiwilderness representatives into key positions on the Congressional committees responsible for places like this.

We talked a bit about the past, how the Baker must have changed when it was dammed and how this pristine upper stretch of river would be perfect for salmon spawning, as it was free of clearcuts and their silty runoff. The gravel looked ideal and lush forest shaded its channel.

Above the mouth of the Baker on the main stem of the Skagit, thousands of tourists gather every winter to watch bald eagles feed on the salmon still spawning there. As we walked upstream, Sean asked, "Have you seen any eagles this morning?"

I hadn't; eagles knew better than to fish above dams having no fish ladders. The black front of Baker Dam is impenetrable and indifferent to the salmon shadows that gather and bruise their bodies against its base.

We sat on a flood-stranded log and watched the river, the forest, and the sky. When a high, gray gauze of clouds began moving across the sun we decided to head home. We walked downstream on snow-covered gravel bars.

It was just above the confluence of the Baker River and Sulphide Creek that we found it. At first it looked like a gray rag, partially buried in snow. I stepped closer and saw silver flecks and a few bones resting at the bottom of a shallow depression in the snow.

We scraped the frost away and realized that the gray rags had once been a huge fish. Its gill cover, or operculum, was as large as my hand and the few remaining vertebrae and ribs hinted at a fish at least three feet long, maybe more. It was a salmon, apparently carried here by a bird whose wing beats had swept away the snow and whose talons had pitted the ground around its meal.

"Did the bird carry this fish here all the way from the Skagit, just to eat it?" Sean asked.

"I wouldn't think so, but how else would it end up here?" I answered.

We stood staring for a while and wondering at what was left of the fish before we headed home in silence. In an hour the gravel bars led us to a dead end. A wide stretch of river blocked our way. We had walked onto a pea-gravel peninsula exposed by winter's low water. We headed back upstream, hopping frozen rivulets and ice-choked

Old growth along the Sauk River

channels. As we reached the north shore we found a second fish trapped in a slough that had apparently been an active channel during flood stage.

A 2-foot-long salmon missing its head and tail rested beneath a thin layer of ice and 3 feet of acid-clear water. Its flesh had faded to white and begun to dissolve, returning nutrients to the bacteria and fungi that would feed insects and, in turn, its own young.

As we stood and watched the moldering fish we wondered how it had come so far, beyond a dam and back into wilderness. Baker Dam is at least 100 feet high—black, mossy, and brutish—and it has no fish ladders. Two weeks later we learned that salmon do indeed return to the upper Baker to spawn. Their return is artificial, by way of trucks, nets, and pumps, but, as Sean pointed out, humans had a lot to do with their disappearance from the river thirty-five years ago.

Even though they had not come on their own and their appearance here was as natural as their cousins' presence in the Seattle Aquarium, something seemed right about the river and its mountains: Shuksan, Icy, Cloudcap, and Ruth receiving their fish. And something seemed amiss, incomplete in the bear's absence.

Weeks later I asked Mitch Friedman, the leading proponent of biodiversity-based management in the North Cascades, why the bear mattered.

"Grizzly bears have a right to exist there and we want grizzly bears there," Friedman said. "That is the bottom line."

Friedman also explained that, as the ecosystem's largest predator, the bears probably played an important role in its processes. Bears might help till the soil as they dig for food and they likely keep other predators, such as coyotes and black bears, in check. They might also distribute salmon carcasses as a form of fertilizer as they drag them from the rivers, he said. Friedman admitted his arguments relied more on possibility and hope than on data, but I heard him out.

"Will the North Cascades turn into a parking lot if the grizzlies are gone?" he asked. "No, but there are other subtler changes, some of which we can predict, some of which we can't. That would be nice to avoid."

Most land managers say they must cooperate with their neighbors to do their jobs. They also say that science is a vital part of all effective management. Lately all of them have been talking about ecosystem, or big-picture, management. So everyone agrees that cooperation, science, and ecosystem management are compatible, important, and desirable. But few make the protection of biodiversity, including the great bear, their number one priority. Few are working to assure the grizzly bear and the salmon a place in the world of our great-grandchildren.

Critics argue we cannot protect species or control ecosystems and therefore should not even try. The systems are too complex, they tell us. And extinction is inevitable, change is natural, and ecosystem health nothing more than a sentimental notion. Whether these critics are right or wrong, there is an important lesson to be learned from another branch of science which has long dealt with the management and protection of such complex systems.

Medical professionals know that the human body is a vastly complex and inherently unpredictable bundle of systems, often impossible to control or protect. But they agree sometimes, perhaps all the time, that protection and restoration are worth a try. And we all agree with them when they tell us there is a difference between healthy and sick, living and dead.

We should use scientific principles, data, and action, therefore, to protect biodiversity in the North Cascades. Yes, it is a complex system. No, we do not understand it fully. Yes, we will make mistakes. Some species will become extinct despite our best efforts, just as some patients die despite the finest medical treatment. We should, I believe, act rapidly on the best available data and we should work ceaselessly to increase our knowledge of ecosystems and their components even as we begin treatment.

As I lay thinking under the stars I struggled with the meaning of all the debate about ecosystem management, ecological integrity, and the future of the North Cascades Ecosystem. To my left, about ten feet away, Lori Zatz, a park ranger and friend, slept in a six-foot-long tent. The tent's yellow sides flapped in the flood of cold air. Somewhere in the darkness to my right, Hugh Dougher and Mary Jane Lavin slept in tiny tents.

Hugh and Lori are rangers in North Cascades National Park. Hugh is a native of Pennsylvania's Dutch country and a Park Service veteran. Lori is a seasonal Park Service employee who grew up in Philadelphia. She has spent two summers living in the park's backcountry, meeting visitors and helping them in their times of need.

Mary Jane Lavin is a special agent with the United States Fish and Wildlife Service. She investigates illegal wildlife trade and tracks people who buy and sell endangered animals, their fur, hides, teeth, bones, and internal organs. All three are law enforcement specialists. All three, in different ways, guard the human and nonhuman inhabitants of the ecosystem.

The night before, we had shared a pasta dinner and a dessert of cinnamon liqueur. At sunset we had shared silence and a view of an empty, steep-sided valley below our camp. It is worth mentioning that the names of the particular places we visited are unimportant for several reasons. First of all, as my friend Chip Dennerlein, a former director of Alaska's state parks system, told me recently, "It is not *where* these places are, but *what* they are that is important." Indeed, our circuit of valleys and ridges could have happened in any of a dozen places in North Cascades National Park and the lessons I learned would have been the same. Further, it is said that in many aboriginal cultures when a person had lost his soul, his *sitec*, and death resulted, no one spoke his name again. It is mainly in deference to the *sitec*, the vanishing plants and animals of the North Cascades, that I withhold the names of the places in the rest of this story.

My traveling companions and I had camped on the lake's rim at the head of a forested valley. We watched the stream drop from the lake and wind toward a distant river, a half day's walk away. At dusk the stream had turned to a leaden blue thread as it wandered through meadows and disappeared into dense forest. We watched for signs of people in the valley bottoms below our perch.

The four of us had met about 36 hours earlier at the park's wilderness district office in Marblemount to prepare for a long, off-trail patrol of a seldom-visited part of the park. I had been excited to spend days in the backcountry with rangers, to watch them work and to learn more about the park and its place in the ecosystem.

Mary Jane and I had driven together from Bellingham to Marblemount. As we traveled, she told me stories about tracking criminals who traffic in the body parts of endangered species around the world. She has trekked through the jungles of Guam and posed as an upscale shopper in search of that hard-to-find fabric knit from the wool of the world's most endangered wild goat. But all in all, she told me, she preferred the meticulous research and thinking also required of detectives. Wilderness patrols such as this were the exception rather than the rule. She was particularly interested in finding poachers responsible for stealing endangered duck eggs within the park. Thus she justified the time she was about to spend outside.

We met Hugh at the ranger station and, after the requisite gear shuffling and food check, were on our way to the mountains. We drove an hour or so east on the North Cascades Highway and stopped at an unmarked, nondescript, wide spot in the road. "A friend of mine has been camping here for decades," Hugh said. "It's a perfect spot to spend the night before an early morning start." That perfect spot, on Forest Service land, is about to be developed as a car and RV campground. And so it goes.

We were on the trail near a gravel-spur road at seven o'clock the next morning. In the first half hour we passed from a Park Service parking lot, across a state highway, into Forest Service land, and finally into North Cascades National Park.

The trail disappeared beneath rank vegetation in the meadows and avalanche chutes but was clear and broad where it wound through old-growth groves. At each patch of slide alder I paused, looked upward, and imagined the power the cliffs, thousands of feet above, unleash through the winter.

At the park boundary, perhaps 2 miles from the trailhead, an avalanche had escaped its old chute the winter before and blasted through a stand of 500-year-old trees. It had taken the wooden sign marking the park boundary with it. Hugh found a few remnants of the sign under freshly bucked log rounds lining the trail. A huge, healthy fir, 3 feet thick at its butt, had exploded in the slide. The scattered shards of wood and bark reminded me of fallen cornstalks after a late summer storm. The ancient trees' frailty in the face of the slide reflected the ephemeral nature of even the ecosystem's oldest and largest residents.

As we walked down drainage toward the confluence of our creek and one of its many tributaries, we dropped into a notch between peaks that stand over 7,000 feet tall. The first high peak we passed rose sharply on our left to its pyramid-shaped, 7,600-foot summit. Steep, forested slopes broken by gray cliffs and bright green clearings rose from both sides of the trail toward the sky.

The valley floor was mostly forested. Its rims were rocky. Meadows, perhaps old fire scars, marked the skyline with odd patches of pale green. Thin veins of snow clung to the highest and deepest ravines. We were headed from the North Cascades' basement and its flowing water to the catwalks and buttresses of its high country.

As we followed the flowing water, Hugh listened carefully to his two-way radio. A call came in from the Golden West Ranger Station in Stehekin, the small village at the head of Lake Chelan. There had been trouble there the night before with a black bear. The bear had been hanging around town for a while looking for food and scaring tourists, Hugh told me. We talked a bit about bears and people in parks and the interesting situations that arise when hungry bears meet sloppy campers.

Someone suggested relocating the bear. Hugh disagreed, likening relocation to "firing a guy from his job and dropping him in the middle of a strange city without food, money, shelter, or family to fall back on." He said relocation is seldom better than simple execution for the bear. People should change their behavior to protect the bear, he said. Our talk soon moved beyond "town bears" and to stories about "real" bears, grizzly bears. Lori had seen a half-dozen bears that summer, usually a mother and cub, foraging near the streams or stepping quickly across the trail ahead of her. They were all black bears.

Grizzly bears lived throughout the North Cascades before European settlers arrived in the region and began traveling, mining, ranching, and homesteading in the river valleys. But for all practical purposes, "Griz," as Hugh called the animal, is gone from the North Cascades.

A federal research team found that in 1993 the public land within the Greater North Cascades Ecosystem could once again support a viable grizzly bear population. The grizzly bears, longtime residents of the range, are still out there, according to the same government report. As early as the 1850s European explorers reported grizzly bears on the north fork of the Nooksack River near Mount Shuksan. The grizzly bear is also present in the stories of the Upper Skagit and Swinomish tribes although it was more common in the territory of the Thompson and Methow tribes on the east slope of the range.[12] The great bear is *sitec* embodied, utterly wild and utterly vulnerable, "so light that it is easily dislodged from its owner," as Gill wrote.

The bears began to disappear from the range after European fur trappers arrived in the early 1800s. They became even less common after miners and ranchers settled in the region's river valleys, including the Methow, Skagit, Twisp, and Okanogan. These valleys were likely the bears' favorite places, their preferred habitat. Conflicts were common and miners killed bears to protect themselves and their property. Settlers cleared forests and built roads and homes, driving the bear from much of its range.[13]

From the beginning of European settlement until 1983 there were 234 reported grizzly bear sightings in the North Cascades. After a five-year study lasting from May 1986 to November 1991, the Interagency Grizzly Bear Committee (IGBC) concluded that some grizzly bears remain in the North Cascades. "We have documented the presence of a small, resident, widely distributed and reproducing grizzly bear population in the North Cascades . . . ," the committee wrote in its final report.[14]

The Committee ranked twenty-one grizzly bear observations between 1964 and 1991 as "class one" sightings—sightings either confirmed by a biologist or by a photograph, carcass, track, hair, or other sign. They also verified two sightings which were captured on videotape and identified a track and a food cache as those of a grizzly. Based on this meager evidence, the team concluded that between ten and fifty bears remain in the ecosystem. They called the numbers "an educated guess."[15] Critics of their work have called the numbers a tally of supersmart "stealth bears."

Bob Kuntz, the park's wildlife biologist, told me there may be some bears in the ecosystem, but that the report's numbers may be misleading. "You could say grizzly bears are still here, but they're not," he said. "We have them, but there's not a viable population out there. We need to augment, we need to bring bears into the system if we're going to have that."

The IGBC also found that the North Cascades provides "excellent habitat and foods to support a viable grizzly bear population," and Kuntz agreed. The team reported that there is enough space in the North Cascades for the bears to make a comeback but the bears there are an isolated, "island" population.[16]

Grizzly bears hold a special place in the history of the American West. They haunt native legend and pioneer lore. They are, some say, the hallmark of wildness and ecosystem integrity. Hugh told me that no one he knows has ever seen a grizzly in the North Cascades.

Still, I half-expected to see one tearing into the loamy, streamside soil or fishing at a pool on the creek we followed that day. Bear stories, like ghost stories, have a way of conjuring their hairy, toothy subject matter at every bend in the trail. But not even an overactive imagination brought us any bears during our hike to the park's high country.

At the confluence of the two creeks we turned east and began ascending a second valley toward a high lake and a pass beyond that. We stopped for lunch at the pass and sat in the shade of some trailside trees.

Lori and I had not met before that day but she was friendly and easy to know. We talked a bit about the pass, her camp there, and her work. The day before she had written her first ticket, a citation to a fisherman who had neglected to buy a license.

All backcountry rangers in North Cascades, I learned, are law enforcement officers. Gun, badge, two-way radio, you name it. If, at this used-up end of the twentieth century, you want to be a real park ranger, a wilderness ranger, you must first become a cop.

We headed west from the pass toward a named peak, about 5 miles distant. As we left the pass, the trail, and the last signs of civilization, talk turned to bears again. I suppose our departure from the trail had something to do with it.

We planned to visit places no one on the park's staff had ever visited. We would camp in drainages where, perhaps, no one had camped in a decade or more. We were, as much as is possible in the lower forty-eight states in 1995, leaving the beaten path. And with images of wilderness and wildness came images of grizzly bears, the North Cascades' *sitec* manifest in flesh, fur, and fang.

I have never seen a grizzly bear in the wild and I have only knowingly shared the woods with five black bears in my life. But the open benches on the back side of the ridge we traversed, their shallow tarns, luxuriant mosses, and dense stands of stunted firs seemed the perfect backdrop for bears. We talked more about grizzlies than anything else on our first day out.

Hugh enjoyed regaling us with his bear stories. "I have three specialties," he said, "law enforcement, search and rescue, and bear management."

Hoping to learn something more about bears from an expert, I asked Hugh how he handled bears like the one that had visited the park campground the night before, especially mothers with cubs.

"Well, the best thing to do is separate the cubs from the mother and then tree the cubs," he said. "You just get a good run at the cubs, make a bunch of noise, and they go up the tree and the mother doesn't know what to do."

I was fairly shocked and Hugh, as I would realize many times over the course of the next few days, was enjoying my gullibility enormously. He smiled, shook his head and moved on.

We followed a bare, open ridge system but stayed on its flanks to avoid the cliffs, loose rock, and nasty pitfalls that congregate on ridges. We traversed broad, marshy meadows linked like steps on an enormous, ramshackle staircase. Between each meadow we scrambled up a rocky step. As we passed a wet meadow and a shallow, warm pool on one of the benches Lori told me she had talked with the ranger who patrolled this area before she took the job in 1994.

"He worked here for seven seasons," she said, "and he told me that if there were grizzly bears anywhere in this park, this was the place. The open, marshy meadows, scattered stands of trees, and the well-guarded ridges and valleys just look like they would be great grizzly habitat." She told me she would like to think grizzly bears were still out here, but that she had little reason to believe they were.

I studied the thick, fibrous stalks of the plants growing on the swampy steps and imagined their fat, white roots would make great grizzly food. Huckleberry bushes grew on the higher and drier areas around the pond. The distant river, decades ago, would have made good fishing. Grizzly bears den on high, exposed ridges where heavy snow insulates them and the steep slope prevents water from filling their dens and waking them during winter thaws. I looked toward the ridge on our right and studied its steep flanks. I thought we had found a fine place for bears.

By three o'clock I was exhausted. We had been walking with heavy packs for eight hours and it was close to 80°F. I had been drinking about a quart of water an hour but still felt dehydrated and too hot. At the base of the last step before we reached a high plateau, we came upon a lake with no name at an elevation in the six thousands, as I recall. We stopped and swam. The water was cold and refreshing.

We dressed, hefted our packs, and began climbing the final step between us and the top of the ridge. As we neared the top I stopped and looked back at the lake. Our ascent had been so steep we seemed to stand directly above it. The shallows near shore were bright turquoise. The center of the lake was black and apparently bottomless.

We stopped at the top of the step above the lake for lunch. We sat on a rocky hummock near the middle of a rolling plateau the size of a supermarket parking lot. Snow covered half the plateau. Two ponds held half their winter ice. They would be dry by September, Hugh said.

I leaned back onto warm, smooth stone and listened carefully to the sky. Silence. No wind, no birds, no traffic. Across the small, slushy tarn an unbroken snowfield sat on the back of a knobby peak. The peak had no name and was little more than a rough spot on top of the ridge, but from my vantage point it seemed high and distant.

We finished our lunches and stood, groggily, to move toward that night's camp. The sun was low in the sky and we followed it. A 7,900-foot peak cast a shadow over our route. We dropped from the snowy plateau into a hanging valley. The valley was shaded by the ridge until afternoon and then in sun only for a few hours before the looming peak's shadow slipped over it. It was full of deep snow. We skied to the valley floor on our boots.

From the mouth of this hanging valley I looked up toward the sun and studied the black mountain. Its steep, shadowy north face stood above tomorrow's route. Hugh and Lori made a few nervous jokes about hotshot climbers gearing up for the north side of the peak and reluctant rangers following in helicopters. The peak's north side reminded me of the underside of broken asphalt—rough, dirty, and ugly.

204 ❖ *Scott Brennan*

After staring at the shadowed peak for a few minutes I looked down. We stood at the mouth of the hanging valley and I could see treetops and then whole trees and meadows below. I couldn't tell how steep a drop we stood above but the ground disappeared behind some slanting slabs covered with loose gravel and a few larger flakes. I looked beyond the lip and realized we stood at the edge of a natural amphitheater.

To our left, the ridge's impassable flanks wrapped around the head of the valley. Directly across the valley (we stood at its rim, somewhere near midvalley) green, red, and orange meadows were pocked with bare rock and clumps of stunted firs. Our side of the valley was mostly shaded and held several acres of late summer snow. At the head of the valley a round rock knob stood in sharp relief against the sky. Snow melted and trickled downward in a dozen streams which met as the valley flattened. Directly in front of us and 1,200 feet below, the streams had collected themselves and we could hear water flowing down. I imagined bears all over again.

Evening light softened and deepened the valley's colors. It was a warm, vibrant, welcoming place that opened before us in dramatic counterpoint to the black peak on the western horizon. Someone checked a map for the valley's name and read it aloud. Given breath, it had a magical quality. I realized it was the first time any of us had spoken for quite some time.

Lori and I immediately decided the place needed exploring. It had to be the grizzly's stronghold and, because it had a name, so must it have a story. Old sheep pens, a ruined cabin, a cave converted to a hermit's rest, tools, or perhaps even books left behind by a forgetful or hurried shepherd or prospector surely sat somewhere down there. We had not seen the valley from the creek trail, although its mouth was near the lake and not far from the pass.

Lori remembered that the drop at the end of the valley was so steep and the forest so dense that it would be impossible to see into the valley from the heavily used trail below. It is close to a popular backpacking route but, as we would learn later, almost impossible to enter.

We were tempted to find a way down into the valley but the steep, blind slopes, loose rock, and the setting sun scared us away. We turned toward the sun and climbed up once more and out of the hanging valley.

In an hour we came upon another lake, almost a thousand feet higher than the last but much larger. The unnamed lake sat in a basin below the black peak. We stepped carefully across braided streams covered with rotten snow bridges, and looked for a flat, dry place to make camp.

At the south end of the lake, near its outlet, we found a flat, rocky ledge. We each carried a sleeping bag and a shelter. Hugh and Mary Jane and I each carried a bivouac sack, a waterproof sleeping bag cover. Lori carried a tiny tent. We found room for four bodies and carefully scattered our beds along the ledge. During dinner we weighted our bags and sleeping pads with rocks the size of softballs and still worried they would blow south toward the distant river. And that is how I came to my bed beneath the stars.

After I awoke in the wind I studied the sky. I stared at the black interstices between the most obvious stars and when I had stared long enough, fainter stars appeared in the gaps. After another fifteen or twenty minutes a third set of stars, the faintest I have ever seen, appeared between the others. For the first time in my life I studied a night sky with more stars than space.

I drifted off to sleep somewhere between my second and third round of stellar interpolation and had a dream that still returns, although with decreasing frequency, nearly nine months later. In the dream, I rise high above that high camp, floating up a mile and then ten and then fifty. From my cold, remote dream locale I look down into the undiscovered valley, a tiny pocket in the barely discernible geologic fold that is the ridge we followed.

The park complex's backcountry, the adjacent Okanogan and Mount Baker–Snoqualmie National Forests, are inky black. A few faint lights of remote cabins glow at the park's edges.

Just south of the ridge, inches away it seems, the lights of a remote settlement shine brightly. A glow in the west catches my eye. Some nights it is much stronger than others. I stare down and to my left into Seattle, Everett, Tacoma, and Olympia. I follow the glowworm streak of Interstate 5, the international highway trailing north, to the bright smudge of Vancouver, B.C. The city's haze always dulls its lights. My eyes adjust to the brightness of the city as I search for landmarks, for individual points of light.

I look away to find again the undiscovered valley below, but the urban glow has tightened my irises and I fail to see the ridge, the valley, or the faint lights of the outlying cabins.

I look north and see the glow of the tiny community of Newhalem near the three dams on the Skagit River. Farther north the darkness of North Cascades National Park and the Forest Service's Pasayten Wilderness yields to the lights of the Canadian border towns of Hope, Chilliwack, and Manning Park. To the southeast of these intrusions into the darkness I see the shine of Twisp, Okanogan, and Winthrop. Farther south still, Wenatchee and its sprawling fringe glow against a backdrop of night.

I am watching the future unfold below me. How far will the lights spread into the dark wilderness, the ecosystem's wild heart? How far will we let development encroach on these remnants of the ancient system? I wonder if that pocket of green beneath me will ever see grizzly bears again. I wonder if we will see fit to make room for other species at some cost to our overly simple economy or if we will instead insist that dollars are the only things that matter.

I realize that the great bulwark of parks and wilderness is crumbling in the face of extinction's erosive force. I realize, too, that parks and wilderness are not forever. They are subject to changing values, political whim, and shortsighted greed. But extinction is forever. And today we are making important decisions about the way we will treat such places and their suffering natives tomorrow.

We, or our descendants, may someday begin a new era of biological steward-ship through ecosystem management as the Alliance has suggested. Or we may allow species and systems to disappear forever. Only a thousand or a hundred thousand mornings will tell which path we will ultimately follow.

I awake from this dream to gray dawn and an uncertain future. It is a brightening morning, but hazy. I am inside a cloud. The sun has just risen but it hides behind a fat Engelmann spruce. The spruce's branches split dawn into a dozen rays that light the thick mist like diamond dust. Hugh and Mary Jane crawl from their bivy bags, kneel in the mist, and then stand as the sun rises over the low peak to the east. Lori sleeps quietly.

On that day we broke camp and skirted the lush, hidden valley out of respect and a sense of urgency. But we wondered what it held and what it would hold in the future. For the duration of our trip we searched for signs of the grizzly but failed to see even the faintest hint that we had crossed paths with the North Cascades' *sitec* embodied.

A month later I returned to that valley. Lori and my wife joined me. We spent two days and a night there and failed to find any sign of grizzlies. We were profoundly disappointed.

I realized that despite the seeming perfection of the place as bear habitat, despite government reports, and despite all our hopes, the grizzly was on its way out, fading toward extinction in one more corner of its former range. The valley is too disconnected from the rest of the bears' shrinking home. Perhaps it is too small, its forage too sparse. Perhaps too many hikers have visited the place for it to be a suitable home any longer.

I realized during our return visit that if we do not decide soon whether we value the continued existence of bears, wolves, salmon, flammulated owls, osprey, lynx, big-eared bats, harlequin ducks, and bull trout more than we value short-term economic gains, the decision will be made for us when these creatures disappear forever.

No scientific experiment can help us make this decision. We will decide on the basis of our beliefs about our place on the planet, our knowledge of its systems and of ourselves, and our vision for the future.

We, the greediest species, will run up against limits. It seems obvious we should learn restraint. By making room for other species today, we have some hope of making room for our own tomorrow.

SCOTT BRENNAN was born in Aberdeen, Washington and has since lived in all four corners of that state. In early 1996 he moved, with his wife, Meagan, and dog, Kai, to the "other Washington" where he is the Executive Conservation Fellow of the National Parks and Conservation Association. He received his BS and MS degrees in environmental science from Western Washington University's Huxley College of Environmental Studies.

Landscape of Potential

MITCH FRIEDMAN

❖ Bears of Mystery ❖

Winston could have had it all. A new and spacious mountain home with countless hidden valleys and rich in every seasonal habitat and food plant. He could have been, in Neil Young's words, "Mother Nature's silver seed flown to a new home in the sun." But he left, silver seeds and all. What need did Winston the Grizzly Bear have that the rugged and diverse North Cascades landscape could not fulfill? Perhaps he had a longing for his Coast Range home or a frustration with the bad press that grizzlies suffer in Washington. Whatever his reasons, Winston followed some unknown sensory map to his original range, rejecting the ecosystem that needed him.

Winston was captured near Pemberton in 1992 by Bob Forbes, a British Columbia Wildlife Branch biologist, then transplanted to the valley of the Lower Pasayten, too near the U.S. border for the comfort of Washington's wildlife officials. He wandered the Cascades country on both sides of the border for a season or two, visited Hozomeen, denned out the winter somewhere around Cheam Ridge, then crossed the spring flows of the mighty Fraser River bound for home. It is possible he left a legacy of offspring with Coast Range genes to bolster the stagnant North Cascades

208

grizzly stock. More likely, Winston the Bear, like a cadre of bear biologists, failed to even encounter another member of his species. Maybe that's the reason he left.

I have spent my share of days in Cascades grizzly bear habitat, scanning in vain for an encounter. Not a single native species is known to have gone extinct in modern times here, though the grizzly and others are on the edge. The landscape is enriched for me just by my knowledge of its wholeness, if not by firsthand experience with every species. I have explored so many valleys, passes and meadows—Bald Eagle Creek, Snowy Mountain, Jackman Ridge, dozens of others—where I could have seen sign or maybe even a bear, but none was present. I am hardly alone in this regard. For a decade, the Washington Department of Fish and Wildlife employed an accomplished and capable bear biologist, Jon Almack, to document and authenticate sightings and to endeavor to trap and fit a grizzly with a radio collar. Through 1995, when budget politics slashed his program, Almack never trapped or even saw a Great Bear, for which some blame may rest with funding and bureaucratic shortfalls. But the dismal reality remains: this haystack is not yielding its needles. Plenty of sightings have been recorded, including incontrovertible evidence such as grizzly tracks (as far south as Mount St. Helens) and distinctively grizzly food caches.

I recall a hot, late-1980s summer day packing out of the Chilliwack Valley watching berry-colored drops from a leaky plastic bag, stuffed with our day's unseemly bounty, drip onto my friend Victor's calves as he led up the trail. Was it griz or black bear plop that we delivered to Almack? In an agency freezer in Sedro Woolley sits a whole mound of iced scat awaiting the money and motivation for analysis to key out its bear bowels of origin. So long as the sightings are of scat, track, or even ravaged carcass, rather than a crystal-clear photo or a collared bear, skeptics remain as to the very existence of Cascades grizzlies.

Bears of mystery are these. Ed Grumbine calls them "ghost bears." We know they are up there, Almack thinks maybe ten to twenty on the U.S. side, but they have a knack for secrecy. It is probably their reclusiveness that has allowed these bruins to survive a long era of human depredation. This meager population will require more than reclusiveness to survive the decades ahead. If the B.C. side of the ecosystem has as many bears as the U.S. side (which it may, thanks to Forbes' yeoman effort to transplant five or so from the Coast Range), the total grizzly population is maybe thirty for this giant expanse of wildland. If we can assume the population has been at or near this level for several decades, then almost certainly the population is afflicted with the consequences of genetic inbreeding depression. These bears may lack reproductive vigor or could be experiencing a range of health deficiencies. Without a miracle or the human-assisted transplantation of perhaps dozens of crosstown bears to invigorate the gene pool, the Cascades will descend to the bloated ranks of ecosystems without grizzly bears. It will become a place where wilderness has lost its howling and growling qualities and where the term *ecosystem* ought to be modified to recognize a conspicuous absence, a less than wholeness, of missing volumes in nature's archive of place.

❖ Bear Politics ❖

Enhancing the Cascades' grizzly population with bears from elsewhere, a process biologists call augmentation, is a charged issue. It is a program which would be difficult to fund in today's budget picture and difficult to implement at this time when bear numbers have dwindled across their range, leaving no clear "donor populations." The idea also suffers from loud, if curious, opposition. Every year a new rumor surfaces, such as the one about grizzlies being air-dropped near Darrington or another about seventy bruins being prodded by Almack out of a semitrailer near Concrete.

Antifederalists fear creation of a giant, elitist park, its borders enforced by man-eating bruins. Ranchers tremble at the restoration of grizzly appetites they labored a century to eradicate from "their" range. Backcountry horsemen carry on about how bear recovery will necessitate trail closures, an allegation which is not supported by the record of management in Yellowstone and other grizzly ecosystems. Even urbanites seeking nirvana or weekend relief in the meadows, lakes, and peaks of high country submit letters to editors about their safety concerns should the bear population rise to historic levels. Too often absent from these salvos, both credible and creative, is an appreciation of the trade-offs involved. It is easy to speculate how more bears could conceivably put a dent in one's herd or hike. What seems to be lacking, as bear advocate Doug Peacock has pointed out, is an appreciation for the positive things we have lost since leaving the cave and domesticating the wild.

A 1994 state-wide poll revealed that fifty percent of Washington residents support government efforts to recover grizzlies, compared to thirty-six percent opposed. Still, those who fear nature as red in tooth and claw have been more vocal, and the Washington Legislature passed a bill in 1995 that prohibits the state from participating in any process for augmenting grizzly bears. This is not a clinching obstacle to augmentation, but it does underscore that achieving a responsible recovery program will require the building and mobilization of public support.

It is worth exploring why people should want a North Cascades grizzly population enough to pay taxes to support recovery and to perhaps make minor sacrifices in recreation habits. One reason is that the tide of extinction is still rising for this species. The North Cascades has only one of five populations in the lower forty-eight states. Of these, only two, Yellowstone and the Northern Continental Divide, have more than a few dozen bears. Of further concern, populations across British Columbia and Alberta are in steady decline due to encroaching oil and logging roads in bear habitat and continued trophy hunting pressure. The Great White North no longer exists. If we fail to protect grizzlies in the North Cascades, we cannot assume that a short trip across the border will reconnect us with this part of our heritage. We must recognize that this ecosystem, while not pristine, is truly among the last, vast wildernesses of the continent.

Would it still be wilderness without the Great Bear? I think so. It would certainly still be beautiful country and a somewhat natural ecosystem without the gray wolf. Maybe also without lynx, wolverine, fisher, spotted owl, giant salamander, Pacific yew, and Nooksack spring chinook. Wilderness is a subjective concept, not an absolute, and the human mind has proven remarkably adaptive. Ecosystems can also be adaptive and resilient and withstand the loss of some species, depending upon the species and its role. But at what point is a line crossed? When is it no longer a "healthy ecosystem" or a vignette of American heritage? We no longer find grizzlies (or bison or even much tall grass, for that matter) on the prairies, yet Earth keeps spinning on its axis. However, it is a rare American who feels no remorse for the taming of the great prairie, its wildlife and peoples. If only the receipts from *Dances with Wolves* could be transported back in time, a lot of wild plains country could be purchased for preservation.

The fact is our heritage is important to us. We see evidence in polls, in market research, in electoral choices, in vacation destinations—Americans care about their birthright. Sure, we voraciously develop and cultivate portions of it, but we do so with the trust and expectation that other places will be kept whole. Some of us live to visit these places; others simply feel warm and fuzzy to know they still exist. Most of us would be willing to make a reasonable sacrifice to assure there are blue whales in the oceans and grizzlies in the mountains and that some places remain natural. The dilemma of the often-heard debate over local interest versus national interest is where these wild places and beasts shall be. The North Cascades, in my opinion, should be very high on that list. People who want to hike or horsepack without grizzly bears have plenty of options—about ninety-eight percent of the contiguous states meet that criteria, whereas this is among the last few places where an ecosystem may be truly conserved. Grizzly bears are a part of this ecosystem.

❖ Bear of a Challenge ❖

Apart from the politics, grizzly recovery will still not be easy. While augmentation would help prevent extinction in the next few decades, it alone would not assure a sustainable bear population. Computer simulations suggest that a viable, self-sustaining population for most species may comprise as many as several thousand individuals. For a species like the grizzly bear, which requires up to hundreds of square miles per individual home range, there is an obvious need for habitat expanses that seem contrary to the trends of spreading civilization. Not only is the North Cascades among only five places in the Lower Forty-eight where grizzlies exist, it is among a small handful of landscapes where remnant, non-viable bear populations could exist. This fact is reinforced when standing atop Tomyhoi Peak on the United States/Canada border, looking at the undulating rows of ridges extending in every direction like waves in a sea. Without Highway 20, built in the late 1960s, this landscape would contain the largest roadless area in the Lower Forty-eight. It has as much public land and more protected wilderness than the Northern Continental Divide Ecosystem of northwestern Montana, which is the last great grizzly stronghold in the country. Still, recovery of grizzly bears, like maintenance of ecosystem integrity on a large scale, entails more than great expanses.

Allowing that the grizzly bear is not confined to a particular rare habitat, its real limits are set by security. Security means freedom from people with guns. For the most part, this need can be met in the North Cascades and in many other Lower Forty-eight ecosystems. While scarcity of undeveloped, low-elevation valleys, providing snowfree habitat in spring, may be a problem, the real limiting factor on security is roads. A recent report by Northwest Environment Watch tallied at least 700,000 miles of roads in British Columbia and the Northwest states, which include 330,000 miles of logging roads. This is likely a great underestimate, since little information is available on logging roads in British Columbia or on U.S. private timberlands. Alone, the three U.S. national forests in the North Cascades have well over 10,000 miles of logging roads, reaching redundantly into valley after valley, crisscrossing endlessly up slope after slope. Many are old, poorly built, and of little or no use today. They channel or slide silt into streams and obstruct the natural movements of myriad species. In the floods of the Thanksgiving 1989 storm, and again in the fall of 1995, the Mount Baker–Snoqualmie National Forest experienced dozens of culvert blowouts and road-caused landslides that did heavy damage to streams and will cost tens of millions just for road repair. As long as these roads remain, so will the threat of watershed damage. The long process of revegetating these old roads, recently begun by the Forest Service, is necessary to any recovery strategy for grizzly bears and the ecosystem as a whole.

Even if thousands of miles of antiquated and destructive roads were removed from the North Cascades, another feature would be essential to achieve a viable population of grizzly bears and a healthy, self-sustaining ecosystem. The North Cascades must be linked, by way of habitat corridors, to adjacent large ecosystems. Until North America's wildland ecosystems are linked in this manner, where sub-populations of animals and plants are connected into a larger network, many will be isolated and too small for healthy predator-prey relationships and other ecological processes.

Linkages between large ecosystems are a daunting prospect. Such landscape-scale linkages must be wide and wild enough to provide security and habitat for the reclusive and specialized species which most need population connectivity at this

Evergreens on Sehome Hill

scale. These corridors must frequently cross productive lowlands to link mountain-ous areas which, along with deserts, constitute most American wildlands. Those lowlands are, in many cases, developed with highways, reservoirs, and rural agricul-tural uses, if not actual towns. To link the North Cascades to the Columbia Moun-tains Ecosystem will require crossing the Okanogan, Kettle, and Columbia River Valleys, with orchards, tree farms, roads, and homes dotting the path. A link to the Coast Range will include protecting threatened forests in the Siska and other water-sheds, crossing the settled Fraser floodplain, and restoring habitat in the lower Nahatlatch Valley. Linking to the Central Cascades involves spanning Interstate 90 and making sense out of the checkerboard of private/public ownerships, a legacy of century-old land grants to rail barons. Planning for establishment of these corridors must begin now, even if such plans cannot realistically be carried out for decades or possibly centuries.

Who said it was going to be easy? But in this inspiring landscape, there remains cause for optimism. The North Cascades has a brilliant conservation history. While British Columbia has been characteristically slow in its conservation efforts, with two small parks and a smaller recreation area, the U.S. government has been relatively generous on the Washington side. Citizen movements have brought establishment of North Cascades National Park and its associated two recreation areas, designation of seven wilderness areas, reductions in Forest Service logging programs, and more administratively reserved areas than anywhere else in the Northwest except the Olym-pia Peninsula. Even on some state lands, conservationists have battled the timber industry to a stalemate in recent years. Washington's largest expanse of state forest—the 150,000-acre Loomis Forest—sits on the eastern margin of the North Cascades Ecosystem, and about a quarter of the block remains roadless, providing valuable habitat for lynx, grizzly bear, and other rare wildlife.

Forty years of conservation struggle and success have laid a foundation for important challenges ahead. The Loomis State Forest and Okanogan National Forest are both making plans for putting roads and clearcuts throughout the larg-est unprotected natural areas in Washington and Oregon. The 104th United States Congress changed laws which, for twenty-five years, Americans have relied upon to protect the environment. Mining interests are in line to apply for permits to dig for and chemically process minerals on dozens of claims in the Okanogan country. Livestock grazing continues to damage land and streams. Forestry on private indus-trial lands is barely worthy of the word as clearcuts continue to spread like mange through maturing second and third growth in the foothills. Despite these continuing issues, conservation victories have been achieved against enormous odds and oppo-sition, and can be again. Ecosystem conservation in the North Cascades is a possi-bility, if not a trend.

❖ Bear Markets ❖

The North Cascades may be reaching its stride to become a model ecosystem for the twenty-first century, a place where the example is set for tempering the relationship between modern Western economies and wild ecosystems. The economy of the West has dramatically changed over the last two decades. It is now highly urbanized, even more than the population east of the Mississippi. A higher proportion of Westerners lives in cities and suburbs than Easterners! But in both the urban and rural West, resource extraction has decreased in economic importance, overshadowed by other economic activities. Perhaps the biggest factor in this transition is nature, which provides a lifestyle, healthful air and water, and recreation opportunities which attract footloose retirees, fax commuters, and E-mail entrepreneurs.

From a window in the building which houses my office, I have a novel view of Bellingham. The background is beautiful Bellingham Bay, framed by Lummi and Orcas Islands and wooded Sehome Hill. The foreground is a decades-old Georgia-Pacific pulp and paper mill, with logs piled on the side and plumes emanating from a dozen stacks. The mill is a remnant from when towns like Bellingham depended on timber jobs. But Bellingham, and the whole Puget Basin, has grown steadily for over a decade even as federal and state logging rates declined sharply and many timber mills closed.

The contrast between the old and new economies is everywhere in evidence. The Washington Department of Wildlife estimated that in 1991 wildlife hunting and viewing generated 42,000 jobs and 2.3 billion dollars of economic activity in the state. But environment has larger indirect effects. People old and young are visiting and moving to the West for its quality of life. Corporations are siting in places they would not have dreamed of ten or twenty years ago because they have found they can reduce labor costs. As Tom Power, chair of the Economics Department at the University of Montana, describes it, a quality environment is an important and substantial part of the wage, so the actual paycheck can be smaller and still attract good work. Incredibly, the counties and communities experiencing the greatest and most diverse growth are those nearest to protected wilderness. If salmon and bull trout are eliminated from streams due to logging and road washouts in their upper watersheds, these communities will lose something far more valuable than the local sawmill is producing.

North Cascades communities, from Princeton to Chilliwack, B.C. and from Twisp to Darrington, Washington, can adjust to and perhaps thrive upon policies which remove destructive logging roads, restore forests, streams, and habitat corridors, and protect wildlife and fish. The quintessential Northwesterner in this landscape of potential is one who uses and treasures wilderness but provides for his or her family without degrading its value. Hopefully this person may be educated to vote for the land and water, or at least to not demand continued federal subsidies for its exploitation.

I have experienced wilderness expanses which comprise healthy ecosystems. My memory traverses windswept Rocky Mountain ridges in northernmost British Columbia, where not a distant horizon has been touched by road, a land more traveled by wolves than people. And I have explored the remote wildlands of the Russian Far East, where brown bear, tiger, wild boar, leopard, and salmon come together in a landscape so wild that natural fire patterns are still evident. But these are places the modern economy is preparing to savage, repeating the injustice of colonial parasitism to yield riches for transnational corporations based thousands of miles away. Landscapes at risk, in need of political miracles, are wild only because civilization has not yet made its challenge. What is so unique about the North Cascades Ecosystem is that the very opposite is true: it has survived the rape-and-run state of economic growth and exists today as wilderness embedded in, and perhaps defended by, a modern urban society dependent on its natural health. The opportunity exists for the North Cascades to be a healthy, diverse, and wild landscape, despite its nearness to so many busy people. The challenge is to make it so.

❖ Out of the Clearcut, into the Condo ❖

The thing we have most to fear is that we have jumped out of the clearcut and into the condo. The economic and cultural factors which may save the ecosystem from extractive industries come with their own set of perils. The first question is whether the change is too late in coming. Dozens of salmon stocks, particularly coho and spring chinook, are at risk of extinction across the Northwest. Several are in North Cascades rivers. Low-elevation ancient forests, including the famous west-side rainforests and the majestic Ponderosa pines of the east side, are gone from private lands and are scarce and heavily fragmented on public lands. Tree farms are being replaced by upscale houses and agricultural lands converted to shopping centers and condos. We are paving the logging roads and running sewer lines through irrigation ditches.

More people, more cars, more buildings, less habitat. Some refer to the sprawling urbanization of the Northwest as californication, and only careful management of growth can prevent the pattern of destruction that countless places have experienced from San Jose, California to Bellevue, Washington. But in the roughneck libertarianism of the 1990s, growth management seems little more than a political organizing opportunity for developers and their private property bully squads.

In the 1980s, Washington grew by over 700,000 people (almost 400,000 from just 1988 to 1990) to a total of over 5 million, and the population is projected to hit 6 million before 2010. More than a million housing permits have been issued in Washington over the last three decades, and about 30,000 acres of wildlife habitat are being lost per year. While it is imperative we protect our mountain wildlands, it is equally important we manage the growth in the valleys. The 1995 floods, exacerbated by fast-draining clearcuts in the uplands and faster-draining roofs and parking lots in the lowlands, wiped out as much as ninety percent of wild salmon reproduction in the Nooksack River.

Just because the new resident makes his living logging data instead of trees, his home on the creek 20 minutes from town by car still contributes to sprawl, lowland habitat fragmentation, problems with air quality, waste treatment, and water allocation. We cannot have a healthy ecosystem "up there" without taking care at home. New residences are leaving too little water in the Methow River to meet the needs of salmon, and homes creeping up the Tulameen, Twisp, Chewuck, Entiat, Chilliwack, Sultan, and a dozen other North Cascades rivers will do more harm to wildlife than could an army of poachers. Deer and elk winter range is fragmented, cougar are displaced, snags needed by woodpeckers are cut for firewood, and salmon streams are culverted. With more and more people choosing rural counties like Chelan, Skagit, and Okanogan for their homes, the impacts of new roads and buildings on streams and forests—not to mention the impact of people and pets directly on wildlife—are spread wide and deep. While the North Cascades Ecosystem is likely not in the state of collapse facing other areas, elements of the ecosystem are clearly threatened.

The North Cascades landscape is subject to the same swirling changes and conflicting futures which engulf the entire West. This is a time of economic and demographic change, with the population and its livelihoods shifting like the sands on a dry beach. The changing society is demanding changes in politics and government, with wild electoral shifts reflective of overall dissatisfaction. People want government services, including environmental protection, but seem to not care for the government that can deliver them. Americans are demanding both the high-tech future and the pastoral past at the same time. How will American politics look when, or if, it settles down again? Will it protect the land?

The changes seem to indicate new opportunities for protection of North Cascades wilderness, but also more pressure on the valuable lowland habitats most impacted by residential growth. Certainly the public interest cries increasingly for conservation, but special interests including timber, ranching, and mining—those Charles Wilkenson refers to as the "Lords of Yesterday"—still call a lot of shots. Deep change may only come when community powers such as media, chambers of commerce, and real estate interests reframe their perspective to understand that nature, unmolested, is not their antagonist but their wellspring.

In a hotel cafe a couple years back, I was conversing with a rural North Cascades county sheriff. I would not expect this man to be a member of a conservation group, but like a lot of timber town people, the sheriff enjoys the wilderness and has fond memories of time in the backcountry. He told me, to my surprise, that he would like to see protection for the large complex of roadless Okanogan country called The Meadows, where he had spent a lot of time in his youth. But his greatest concern was for his community. If it turned into a tourist gateway, like Gattlinburg, Tennessee or West Yellowstone, he knew he would have to leave.

To the sheriff, that meant the timber and ranching base of the economy needed to be preserved. But rural communities can no more expect to recapture their 1970 economies than the Rust Belt can expect to reopen those old steel mills. Whether former timber towns become tourist traps or healthy, diverse communities is ultimately in their own hands. But either way, the first step is to protect the land.

Mɪᴛᴄʜ Fʀɪᴇᴅᴍᴀɴ is a conservation biologist and founder and Executive Director of the Northwest Ecosystem Alliance, based in Bellingham, Washington. He is a widely published author and has edited two books on conserving the Greater North Cascades Ecosystem. He is a board member of The Wildlands Project.

Wild Speculations

JOHN C. MILES

The future of anything is difficult to predict, least of all something as complex as a landscape. Eighty years ago, nobody would have thought that 2,480,774 acres in the North Cascades would one day be included in a national wilderness preservation system—but that is how much there is today. No one had yet conceived of such a system. Only a handful of national parks had been established. In the fall of 1915 Stephen Mather, then Special Assistant to the Secretary of the Interior and soon-to-be director of the new National Park Service, met in Seattle with advocates for a Mount Baker National Park. Members from Bellingham's Mount Baker Club, The Mountaineers in Seattle, and Portland's Mazamas, all advocates for the park, attended the meeting. Everyone was enthusiastic about the park, the only disagreement being over whether Mount Shuksan should be included. Mather thought it should be in the park, but the Mount Baker Club argued it should be excluded "out of consideration for certain mining interests that would be involved."[1] A bill to create the park was subsequently introduced in Congress, but the United States' entry into World War I stifled its progress and no Mount Baker National Park came to be. Fifty-two years later a national park was approved in the North Cascades which included Mount

Shuksan but excluded the centerpiece of that earlier proposal, Mount Baker. And why was Mount Baker excluded? This time, compromises "out of consideration for" certain timber interests removed the mountain from park status.

In 1988 Congress designated most of North Cascades National Park part of the National Wilderness Preservation System and named it the Stephen Mather Wilderness, an appropriate way in the minds of some to honor the founder of the National Park Service. The gesture is ironic, for Stephen Mather was not an advocate of wilderness. The idea had not entered official discussion of land use in 1916. Some attending that Seattle meeting, like the Mount Baker Club, wanted a park for the commercial value it would bring to their community. Others, like the Mazama contingent, wanted to preserve the natural beauty of a place they had come to admire on climbs of Mount Baker. Mather and Albright sought to create national parks wherever they could, without compromising standards too much, in order to strengthen their case for a national parks agency and to develop a system of parks bureaucratically comparable to the United States Forest Service. To be fair to Mather, he loved natural beauty, believed in its preservation, and sought to create parks for many good reasons. But as an urbanite who loved motoring more than hiking, he was not out to protect wilderness as such, though in the end his work helped the cause of wilderness preservation. His penchant for developing national parks was one factor which encouraged emergence of the wilderness idea in national forests, which in turn led to passage of the Wilderness Act of 1964 and designation of the Stephen Mather Wilderness in 1988. History takes ironic turns.

Forces unforeseen by Mather and the others at that 1915 meeting produced the landscape we know today. After World War I the Forest Service discovered recreation and wilderness and used them to foil national park system expansion in the North Cascades and elsewhere. After a second world war the forces of economic expansion pushed roads into the North Cascades and other roadless places in search of timber and other natural resources, thereby reviving latent efforts to preserve values of wild nature. Part of the landscape became national park in 1968, and wilderness was designated in 1964, 1968, 1976, 1984, and 1988. The core of this mountain region was given as much protection from development as any piece of land in the modern world. The North Cascades became one of the greatest concentrations of official wilderness in the United States. But will park and wilderness designation protect the wildlife, beauty, and solitude of this place?

All national parks and wilderness areas have been products of compromise molded out of consideration for various interests. I can travel today deep into the North Cascades and find vistas unmarred by logging, but most views even from the deep recesses of park or wilderness are marred by the linear scars of clearcuts. Aircraft intrude into even the most remote cirques and valleys. Commercial jets coming and going from Seattle rumble constantly over the Alpine Lakes and Glacier

Peak areas. Military jets roar up mountain valleys, bursting over passes in explosions of sound so startling that people are literally knocked off their feet by surprise and fright. Animals and plants, their habitats decreased by development outside protected areas, struggle to survive.

Now that we have this official "wild" country we struggle with the challenge of managing it. Some say we should just leave it alone—let it manage itself. But can alpine meadows survive with ever-increasing numbers of visitors, all with the best of intentions, literally loving them to death? Others say we should do landscape planning and ecosystem management in places like this, and think about natural subdivisions of the landscape like entire watersheds. These may be excellent ideas, but how do we implement them across a landscape subdivided into national forest and national park, wilderness and working forest, federal and state, and public and private land? Slowly we are coming to the realization that we cannot engineer nature for our purposes as handily and certainly as we once thought we could. As knowledge has increased, so has uncertainty.

We talk much these days about landscape plans and ecosystem management. Our confidence in our management ability may be shaken but is certainly not gone. We still think we can use our science and technology to mold the world to our purposes, yet as failures occur we seem to be learning a measure of humility, albeit small. As I contemplate the future of this landscape, I am reminded of the ancient Greeks who worried about *hubris*, pride before a fall. They feared they would be punished for their arrogance, that *nemesis* would be the consequence of that arrogance, a revenge of nature (or the gods in that nature). Should we worry about that? We probably should, whether we advocate wilderness for this place or call for some other use.

Michael and I sit atop a huge flat-topped boulder we call Fire Rock. We watch a small fire we've built on the rock where it won't burn any soil and leave a trace of our presence. We tend a base camp here, which we call Albert Camp, for a group of college students who are scattered across the surrounding ridges in solo camps observing the land and themselves and reflecting on what they find. Many are alone in a remote place for the first time.

We are here, high on the shoulder of a rocky ridge on the eastern edge of the North Cascades, and from our perch we look southward across rolling hills, the eastern Cascades foothills, covered mostly with lodgepole pine. As darkness falls, we see a solitary electric light far to the southeast, a reminder of the outside. We are here for two weeks. Thrush whistles rise from the pines and firs as dusk turns to night. Coyotes wail and yap off to the south, and we talk quietly. Scattered clouds shade from pink to purple as the sun drops behind the ridge to the west.

A year ago Michael was up here for the first time. A blizzard blew down on the high country, and his group became disoriented trying to cross Horseshoe Mountain in the clouds and wind-driven snow. They missed base camp and nearly went down a deep gorge into Hell's Hole, a valley filled with huge boulders and nearly impenetrable stands of lodgepole pine.

"We need places like this to get lost in," he says. "We had a few bad moments, but we found shelter, got out the map, looked at the compass, and worked our way out. We couldn't control the storm, but could control ourselves, and we did. We thought it a great adventure."

A few days later we make our way along a ridge and spot a bear a mile away across the same gorge down which Michael's group had wandered in the snowstorm. The bear is on a south-facing slope tearing up a meadow in likely pursuit of golden-mantled ground squirrels. Black bears are common here, but this one wears a reddish-brown coat rather than the customary black. Could this, we ask ourselves, be one of the mythical Cascade grizzlies? It is too far away and screened by scattered trees to see very well, even with binoculars. Safely distant as we are from the bear, we badly want it to be a grizzly.

Later, back in camp, we return to Fire Rock, bask in the afternoon sun, and talk about what a grizzly would mean to this place. To us this bear is the ultimate symbol of wildness. If such a bear was over there eating squirrels, this landscape had just become more wild. Our experience of the place had changed. The risk of being here was greater, but the wilderness, and our experience of it, was more complete. When Indians traveled through these mountains in search of game, this was not wilderness. They had no such idea of the place. This was part of home, and they shared it with grizzlies and other hunters. White hunters, miners, and ranchers removed the bear (or so they thought), and now it may be returning. Michael and I agree this is good.

"Some of my friends, who love the backcountry and wilderness, don't agree with this view," says Michael. "They like their wilderness low risk. I think that's very ironic—and wrong. If the bear can live here, if the habitat for it is here, then it should be here. We can and we should share this place."

After dinner we make the rounds checking the soloing students. They leave a signal flag that tells us all is well. Sitting atop a block of lichen-covered rock, the highest point on the ridge west of camp, we watch the sun set over Cathedral Peak and other ridges to the west. I tell Michael how, a few years earlier, I tracked a cougar to this very spot. A light snow fell in the afternoon, and I crossed the track of the cat in the fresh snow. Following it, I found myself looking down from this rock at a solitary student sitting beside his tent. The curious cat had been twenty feet from him, had watched him, then moved on. I never saw the cat, and neither did the student, but it surely watched us.

I tell Michael how later, when I told the student what I had seen, he just stared at me, saying nothing. I wondered if he was angry that I had placed him in such a position. After a moment he said, "That's incredible. I wish I'd seen it. I don't even know anybody who has ever seen a mountain lion in the wild! It's like he said it was okay for me to be here in his territory." We talked about how this was the lion's home, and we were the intruders. The more he talked about it, the more excited he became. He said he was honored by the visit. He seemed to see no risk in it at all, which was the way I had seen it. The cat was curious, there were plenty of deer around to satisfy its appetite; this was a brief brush with the true wildness of this place.

I reflect back on how I was up here with another group of students when thunder rolled out of a clear sky. How could this be? we asked each other. No storm was in sight. Someone joked that it was Mount St. Helens blowing up far to the south, but it couldn't be—the mountain was 200 miles away. Muffled thunder continued off to the south as the group dispersed on their wilderness business.

A few hours later a Forest Service messenger walked into camp to tell us the mountain had blown. That evening I sat with my assistant on Fire Rock and watched the last rays of sun color the ash cloud which had climbed 10 miles high over the distant mountain. Darkness was nearly upon us, yet that cloud shown brightly over the southern horizon. The students, watching from their solitary camps, could not know what they were seeing. Alan and I talked in wonder about the inconceivable scale of what had happened, of how puny we seemed in the face of it. A cold wind howled through the whitebark pines and we seemed fragile creatures in a primal landscape. We watched until the color disappeared into the night darkness, and the wilderness seemed wilder than we had ever known it.

We carried on our work in the backcountry for a week after the eruption, coming together to talk about this vast and wondrous natural event. A week later, when we finally came out of the wilderness, we read of the eruption in different terms than we had been using. The eruption was, in human terms, a catastrophe, a natural disaster. People were dead and injured, property damaged, and forests literally flattened. In our mountain camp, what we had seen as cause for wonder we now saw as destruction and disaster. We experienced contrasting perspectives on this event.

Michael and I agreed the perspective on nature and ourselves which we have when in wilderness is very important. When we return to our daily routines we see the world, at least for a time, differently. We are reminded that nature is all around us and that we are fragile and not in control of everything. We are a bit more humble.

Historian Nancy Langston observes, "There are ways of living on the land that pay attention to the land, and ways that do not."[2] We have not lived in and around places like the North Cascades very long—we have been here in any numbers for little more than a century. And we have only just begun to pay attention to the land in any sense other than as a source of resources to fuel our civilization. We decided to protect wildness in the rugged core of these mountains because we found value in the beauty and inspiration found there. The decision was not difficult—the practical uses of these places were few. The natural defenses against human activity of weather and topography were too strong for much economic development. We thought we were not giving up much when we said, "Leave it as it is."

But the decisions become ever more difficult as there are more of us with more competing interests and values. Today, for instance, we are learning the importance of biological diversity and trying to protect species, but we cannot simply find places useful to spotted owls that are "throwaway" places for us and give them a reservation. They need what some of us want—remaining ancient forests with their big, economically valuable trees. The land seems to be telling us we need complexity and diversity for our own good as well as that of other creatures, but to have it we need to give up some profits and even some jobs.

Langston makes another point central to thinking about the future of this landscape. We have made mistakes resulting in fire, disease, and other plagues upon the land. We have created difficulties, she says, because we have often tried to force the land to fit our idealized visions of it. In these North Cascades, for instance, some of us have envisioned a place entirely free from human impact, a place where bears and wolves roam, where nature is as it was, a place where we can touch the nature of nature before we were present. Or, on the other hand, our vision has been a landscape of production and efficiency, where exercise of knowledge and technical ability allows us to forever take resources from the land without damaging it (or at least not damaging it much). We have been so obsessed with such visions, says Langston, that we have too often been blinded to information the land sends us. The truth is there are limits to what we can manage in either direction.

We find the same lesson here we found in contemplating the eruption of Mount St. Helens: humility. Spinning visions of the future we desire is dangerous business, not to be done casually. We can be so blinded by our desires and ambitions that we literally lose touch with reality. We can be so bent on bending nature to our aspirations, whether they be preservation or development, we stop listening to the land. Can we envision a human community here more humble in its views of what it can and should do on this land? Such a community will be better able to recognize limits of what it can manage on the land—whether the managers be scientists, foresters, environmentalists, politicians, or wilderness rangers. Such a vision—perhaps *dream* is a better word for it—will require deep rethinking of what we are and what nature is, but the self-examination is under way. As the naturalist David Raines Wallace has written, "If there is symmetry to evolution, the future will not see us dominating all other life as gods. It will see us becoming part of a greater organism which we cannot imagine."[3]

We draw lines across this and every other landscape as we try to impose the shapes of our visions upon them. We confidently say, "This is park and wilderness—that should be enough for the creatures that need wild places. The rest of the land will be for production." But as we listen to the land we come up with ideas such as *island biogeography* and *connectivity* and *fragmented landscapes*. As we study how the creatures we have relegated to these reservations are doing, we usually find the reservations are not big enough for them to meet their life needs. Quite possibly they will not survive in these reserves. So we must think about this problem differently. We must think on larger scales of space and time. We must think in terms of *watersheds* and *ecosystems* and *landscapes*. Haltingly, reluctantly, we try. We encounter resistance from those who still believe we humans are firmly in control. To them, all problems are problems of engineering. But we persist, and as we do our thinking forces us across the lines. We move across park and wilderness and state and national forest boundaries.

In the future we will not discuss the North Cascades in quite the way we do today, as though it were some clearly discrete geographic unit. We will instead speak of a region where storms off the north Pacific bring water to rainforests, where rivers gather in the mountains and flow to floodplain and estuary, where populations of animals must disperse across lands we own as individuals as well as collectively. We will talk of *systems* and *networks* and will see this mountain region as part of a place where we live with other creatures. Our backyards will be connected to our backcountry, and our planners and managers will think of all of these parts as one entity. The upshot will be that we will live *in* and *with* this place. We will be part of it and it will be part of us in ways we find hard to understand today. Boundaries will still be here, of course, but they will not be the barriers they are today. They will help people define their rights, as they do now, but will also help define responsibilities more than they do at present. The view across the physical world will not look very different than it does today, but the world of ideas that governs our relations with this place will be very different.

Each year I try to visit Albert Camp, to return for a few days to this wilderness place for solitude and reconnection. Barry Lopez writes that we must come to look upon the land "not as its possessor but as a companion." To do this, in his view, requires "cultivating intimacy, as one would with a human being. And that would mean being *in* a place, taking up residence in a place."[4] Albert Camp is in an official wilderness—no residences in the conventional sense are allowed. How can we "take up residence" in such a place?

When I am at Albert Camp I seem to open up to the world. The weather engulfs me. I hear the lilting song of the ruby-crowned kinglet, the buzz of the mountain chickadee, and the croak of the raven. Bear, cougar, wind, and blizzard remind me of my place in this community. Here I live more fully in the present. Something about this place opens me to my self and surroundings. Memories of time spent in the wilderness at Albert Camp are as vivid as any in life and are reminders of opportunities often lost in the crush of daily routine, especially the loss of connections to the world around me.

Such places not only seem to intensify connections with natural surroundings but also with people. Lacking the preoccupations of TV and E-mail, we interact with human companions, talk more, tell stories, share the experience of storm or spring day or encounter with a wild resident of the place. We have, in a sense, created this place by excluding distractions of modern technology. Here we can be reminded of some of the costs of building lives around the technological gadgets we all enjoy and depend upon. We return to them, of course, but for a while are reminded of what they are and what they do to our life experience.

Living at Albert Camp, then, is an interlude that allows me to see myself and nature through a different lens, to slow down and tend to the present and establish intimacy, much of that intimacy with a natural community. When I go home to the city, I do not leave that community, but move to another part of it. Perhaps that is the most important lesson I learn there.

Life at Albert Camp is instructive in another way. When I go there I am constantly aware of the need to minimize my impact on this pristine landscape. I want to have no impact, but since that is not possible, I try to offset my impact with good works—cleaning up other people's litter, removing fire rings, whatever. Do I feel this same responsibility and take this same care at home in the lowlands? Not as I should, yet that is where I truly reside. The need to care for my place in the lowlands must be at least as great as in the wilderness, so why do I not take the same pains down there? It must be that I value the wilderness place more, but if I do, I am a fool. And so it goes—this place where I only occasionally live forces me to think about responsibility for the place where I live most of the time. I come to see that I must live the same everywhere, that I am a resident of Earth and not of this or that separate *part* of the place.

Everyone in our crowded world certainly cannot find nature and wildness in vast protected places like the Pasayten Wilderness. Remote settings with bears and mountain lions are not the only places where we can learn the lessons I have learned at Albert Camp. We can find wildness, if we look, in our gardens, city parks, and in the landscapes that lie between the city and wilderness. Isn't that the point? The neighborhood park, the woodland down the street, the managed forest, and the local lake are all part of the same natural community, and if we open ourselves to these places, we can become intimate with them. If, in the future, we decide we will set aside a small portion of the landscape for such experiences, relegating everything else to shopping centers, parking lots, and housing developments, then even those places we set aside to be wild will be doomed. They will be crushed by visitors, loved to death, and the bear and cougar will perish. Only if we see this landscape as a living place, where we can and must live but within limits, will its future be one in which "wildness" will survive. When Henry David Thoreau wrote "In wildness is the preservation of the world" a century and a half ago, what he may have meant was that only if we recognize that we are part of nature, that wildness is a quality of place upon which we all depend, and that we bear the responsibility to nurture that wildness, will we prosper and sustain ourselves as members of the natural community. The future of this North Cascades landscape will reflect how well we incorporate this insight.

The aim of Stephen Mather's meeting in Seattle eighty years ago was to draw lines on a map which would transpose to a landscape and meet human goals there. His intention was to create a park, a "pleasuring ground for the benefit and enjoyment of the people" as Congress had stated in establishing Yellowstone National Park in 1872.[5] The intention was also, as specified in the act forming the National Park Service being drafted even as Mather spoke with the Seattle group, to "conserve the scenery and the natural and historic objects and the wildlife therein" and "provide for the enjoyment of the same in such manner and by such means as will leave them unimpaired for the enjoyment of future generations."[6] These aims seemed simple and straightforward in that simpler time. Today we know that putting boundaries around geography is not enough. Achievement of our goals on any landscape requires much more.

I am an admirer of Stephen Mather and the work he did. He led a defensive action on a bureaucratic front, continuing work which John Muir had begun and that would be carried on by Aldo Leopold, Sigurd Olson, and David Brower, among others. Whether or not Mather understood wilderness as we think of it today, his actions contributed to its preservation. But the time is past when even the best-intentioned could come together, inspired by a leader such as Mather, and divide up the "spoils" of an undeveloped continent. The task now is to work together as part of a greater community of the North Cascades. As recent rifts over spotted owls and international parks reveal, such cooperation will not be easy. But it must be done. Chickasaw writer Linda Hogan says, "In other days and places, people paid more attention to the strong-headed will of earth."[7] That is our challenge here and everywhere. Our history is one of believing that ours was the stronger will and that we could impose it upon all creation. Perhaps the humility we can learn in wild places such as the North Cascades will allow us to avoid *nemesis*. The crags and raven, the monkeyflower and glacier lily, the fir and hemlock will observe how well we do.

Notes

Keepers of the Beat, *Jon L. Riedel*
1. Colin Fletcher, *The Man Who Walked Through Time* (New York: Vintage Books, 1967).

2. J. Imbrie and K. P. Imbrie, *Ice Ages: Solving the Mystery* (Short Hills, N.J.: Enslow Publishers, 1979).

3. R. B. Waitt and R. M. Thorson, "The Cordilleran Ice Sheet in Washington, Oregon, Idaho and Montana," in S. C. Porter, ed., *Late Quaternary Environments of the United States, Vol. 1* (Minneapolis: University of Minnesota Press, 1983), pp. 54–70.

4. E. C. Pielov, *After the Ice Age: The Return of Life to Glaciated North America* (Chicago: University of Chicago Press, 1991).

5. S. R. Hicock, K. Hobson, and J. E. Armstrong, "Late Pleistocene Proboscideans and Early Fraser Glacial Sedimentation in Eastern Fraser Lowland, British Columbia," in *Canadian Journal of Earth Science* 19 (1982): 899–906.

6. J.J. Clague, "Late Quaternary Geology and Geochronology of British Columbia, Part Two: Summary and Discussion of Radiocarbon-dated Quaternary History," in *Geological Survey of Canada* Paper 80, 35 (1981).

7. Donald J. Easterbrook, "Stratigraphy and Chronology of Pleistocene Sediments," in D. A. Swanson and R. A. Haugerud, eds., *Geological Fieldtrips in the Pacific Northwest* (Proceedings from the Geological Society of America Annual Meeting, Seattle, 1994).

8. Jon L. Riedel and R. A. Haugerud, "Glacial Rearrangement of Drainage in the Northern North Cascades, Washington," in *Geological Society of America Meeting Abstract 8982* (1994).

9. Jon L. Riedel, "Existing Conditions of Reservoir and Streambank Erosion in the Skagit River Hydroelectric Project (Unpublished Report, North Cascades National Park, National Park Service, Sedro Woolley, Wash., 1989); and J. J. Clague, J. E. Armstrong, and W. H. Mathews, "Advance of the Late Wisconsin Cordilleran Ice Sheet in Southern British Columbia Since 22,000 Years B. P.," in *Quaternary Research* 13 (1980): 322–326.

10. M. B. Davis, "Quaternary History and the Stability of Plant Communities," in D. C. West, H. H. Shugart, and D. B. Botkin, eds., *Forest Succession: Concepts and Application* (New York: Springer-Verlag, 1981), pp. 312–353.

11. S. R. Hicock and J. R. Goff, "Geohazard Risk Assessment of the Klesilkwa Basin" (Report to the Skagit Environmental Endowment Commission, 1993).

12. J. H. Mackin, "Glaciology of the Snoqualmie-Cedar Area, Washington," *Journal of Geology* 49 (1941): 449–481; D. R. Crandall, "Surficial Geology and Geomorphology of the Lake Tapps Quadrangle, Washington" (U.S. Geological Survey Professional Paper 388-A, Washington, D.C.: U.S. Government Printing Office, 1963); S. C. Porter, "Pleistocene Glaciation in the Southern Part of the North Cascade Range, Washington," in *Geological Society of America Bulletin* 87 (1976): 61–75; R. B. Waitt, "Late Pleistocene Alpine Glaciers and the Cordilleran Ice Sheet at Washington Pass, North Cascade Range, Washington," in *Arctic and Alpine Research* 7 (1975): 25–32.

13. S. C. Porter, "Present and Past Glaciation Threshold in the Cascade Range, Washington, U.S.A., Topographic and Climatic Controls, and Paleoclimatic Implications," in *Journal of Glaciology* 18 (1977): 101–116.

14. R. B. Waitt, "Evolution of the Glaciated Topography of the Upper Skagit Drainage Basin, Washington," in *Arctic and Alpine Research* 9 (1977): 183–192.

15. N. M. Fenneman, *Physiography of the Western United States* (New York: McGraw-Hill, 1931).

16. S. C. Porter and G. Denton, "Chronology of Neoglaciation in the North American Cordillera," in *American Journal of Science* 265 (1967): 117–210.

17. S. C. Porter, "Pattern and Forcing of Northern Hemisphere Glacier Variations During the Last Millennium," in *Quaternary Research* 26 (1986): 27–48.

18. R. A. Daly, "Geology of the 49th Parallel," in *Geological Survey of Canada, Memoir 38* (1912).

19. Jon L. Riedel, "Chronology of Late Neoglacial Glacier Recessions in the Cascade Range and the Deposition of a Recent Esker in the North Cascade Mountains, Washington" (Unpublished M.S. Thesis, University of Wisconsin, Madison, 1987).

20. W. V. Tangborn, "Two Models for Estimating Climate-Glacier Relationships in the North Cascades, Washington, U.S.A.," in *Journal of Glaciology* 25 (1980): 3–21.

Who Walks on the Ground, *Bob Mierendorf*

1. For the only published account of Custer's notes and records, see Harry M. Majors, "Discovery of Mount Shuksan and the Upper Nooksack River," in *Northwest Discovery* 5, 21 (1984) and "First Crossing of the Picket Range 1859," in *Northwest Discovery* 5, 22 (1984).

2. Martin J. Sampson, "Indians of Skagit County," in *Skagit County Historical Series No. 2* (Mount Vernon, Wash.: Skagit County Historical Society, 1972).

3. See Harry M. Majors, "The First Crossing of the North Cascades," in *Northwest Discovery* 1, 3 (1980).

4. George Gibbs, "Tribes of Western Washington and Northwestern Oregon," in *Contributions to North American Ethnology* 1, 169 (1877).

5. G. P. V. and Helen B. Akrigg, *British Columbia Place Names* (Victoria, B.C.: Sono Nis Press, 1986).

6. Robert R. Mierendorf, "Chert Procurement in the Upper Skagit River Valley of the Northern Cascade Range, Ross Lake National Recreation Area, Washington" (Technical Report NPS/PNRNOCA/CRTR-93-001, North Cascades National Park Service Complex, Sedro Woolley, Wash., 1993).

7. Helmut K. Buechner, "Some Biotic Changes in the State of Washington During 1853–1953," in *Research Studies of the State College of Washington* 21 (1953); and Carl E. Gustafson, et al., "The Manis Mastodon Site: Early Man on the Olympic Peninsula," in *Canadian Journal of Archeology* 3 (1979): 157–163.

8. Most of the information about Holocene vegetation in this section is from Cathy Whitlock, "Vegetational and Climatic History of the Pacific Northwest during the Last 20,000 Years: Implications for Understanding Present-day Biodiversity," in *The Northwest Environmental Journal* 8, 1 (1992): 5–28.

9. Jan L. Hollenbeck and Susan L. Carter, "A Cultural Resources Overview: Prehistory and Ethnography, Wenatchee National Forest"(Paper written for U.S. Department of Agriculture, Forest Service, Pacific Northwest Region, 1986).

10. Whitlock, 5–28.

11. Gibbs, 220.

12. Henry H. Pierce, "An Army Expedition Across the North Cascades in August 1882," edited by Harry M. Majors in *Northwest Discovery* 3, 1 (1980): 68.

A Home for the Spirits: An Interview with *Vi Hilbert*

1. Vi Hilbert, *Haboo* (Seattle: University of Washington Press, 1985).

2. Janet Koder, ed., *Writings About Vi Hilbert* (Seattle: Lushotseed Press, 1992).

3. Annie Dillard, *The Living* (New York: Harper Collins, 1992).

4. Wayne Suttles, *West Coast Salish Essays* (Seattle: University of Washington Press, 1987).

5. June M. Collins, *Valley of the Spirits: The Upper Skagit Indians* (Seattle: University of Washington Press, 1974).

6. Nels Bruseth, *Indian Stories and Legends of the Stillaguamish, Sauks and Allied Tribes* (Fairfield, Wash.: Ye Galleon Press, 1977).

7. Her parents belonged to the Indian Shaker Church.

8. Her father was born circa 1880.

9. Ilabot Creek flows from the south into the Skagit between Rockport and Marblemount; Hamilton is 15 miles east of Sedro Woolley.

10. Baker Hot Springs north of Concrete, Washington.

11. Susie Sampson Peter, Upper Skagit tribe.

Beaver Is Greedy, *Charles Luckmann*
1. See Nch'i-wana, "The Big River" in Eugene S. Hunn and James Selam and Family, *Mid-Columbian Indians and Their Land* (Seattle: University of Washington Press, 1990), pp. 156–157.

2. David Wagoner, *Who Shall Be the Sun?: Poems Based on the Lore, Legends, and Myths of Northwest Coast and Plateau Indians* (Bloomington: Indiana University Press, 1978), p. 97.

Cascade River: 1974–1996, *Bob Keller*
1. Aldo Leopold, *A Sand County Almanac* (New York: Oxford University Press, 1949), pp. viii, 67, 216.

2. Simon Schama, *Landscape and Memory* (New York: Alfred A. Knopf, 1995), pp. 576–578.

3. Quoted in Rudolf Walter Leonhardt, *This Germany: The Story Since the Third Reich* (Greenwich, Conn.: New York Graphic Society, 1964), p. 161.

4. Skagit Co. Comprehensive Plan, section 2; Skagit Co. Planning Dept. Finding of Fact, American Alps Resort, Dec. 7, 1994, Appl. No. SPU 93-033; Robert C. Schofield, Hearing Examiner, Decision and Order, April 26, 1995; U.S. Forest

Service, Mt. Baker District, Jon Vanderheyden memo, January 20, 1994. The National Park Service, sensitive to "buffer" and border issues, remained silent during this dispute even though its policy is "to encourage and help people enjoy their natural surroundings free from the distractions of mechanized equipment and imposing structures" (NPS General Management Plan: North Cascades National Park, 1988, pp. 19, 23).

5. In Western Washington timber harvest as a whole increased seventy percent from 1950 to 1975, with record years in the 1980s up fifty percent over the 1975 rate. Numbers dropped with the recession of the early 1980s, rebounded in mid-decade, and declined again in the 1990s, but not below 1950 levels. See State of Washington, Department of Natural Resources (DNR), "Timber Harvest Summaries, 1975–93," and "Timber Harvest by Ownership, 1950–93" (WA DNR, Natural Resources Building, Olympia, Wash.). Forest managers currently cannot provide statistics by watershed: "The only way we track board feet is by county. We don't have any particular need for the watershed data" (Interviews, Jeff May, DNR; Ed Johnson, USFS; Keith Wyman, Skagit System Co-op; Jim Cahill, Skagit County Planning, January 17, 1996).

6. Gretchen A. Luxenberg, *Historic Resource Study: North Cascade National Park* (Seattle: National Park Service, 1986), pp. 72–81; Fay Davis, *Marblemount of the North Cascades* (Privately Published, 1988).

7. Larry J. Kunzler, *Skagit River Valley: the Disaster Waiting To Happen* (Privately Published, 1992). See pp. 22–23 for a chronology of discharge volume and river levels.

8. Estate of Claire Wilson, et al. v. Georgia Pacific and the State of Washington, Skagit Co. Case No. 86-2-00164-9 (Interview, Dean Brett, January 11, 1996).

9. The maximum clearcut on private lands is 240 acres, but different owners can log adjacent to each other. New cuts may begin after five years or if trees on harvested areas average four feet high; clearcuts of less than 50 percent do not require replanting. Most private land in the Skagit system is owned by The Trillium Corporation or Crown Pacific, successors to Georgia Pacific and Scott Paper.

10. Schama, *Landscape and Memory*, pp. 191–201.

11. State of Washington Department of Natural Resources, "Timber Harvest by Ownership, 1950–93."

12. Schama, *Landscape and Memory*, p. 574.

13. Alexander Ross, *The Fur Hunters of the Far West* (Norman: University of Oklahoma Press, 1956), p. 39.

14. Wendell Berry, "The River Bridged and Forgot," in *The Wheel* (San Francisco: North Point Press, 1982).

Sitec and Tomorrow in the North Cascades, *Scott Brennan*

1 Sam D. Gill and Irene F. Sullivan, *Dictionary of Native American Mythology* (Santa Barbara: ABC-CLIO, 1992).

2. Ibid. p. 275.

3. *The Bellingham Herald,* 14 November, 1995.

4. Ibid.

5. Fiscal Year 1995 Funding Report from North Cascades National Park, January 8, 1996; Bob Kuntz, North Cascades National Park Wildlife Biologist (Interview, October 26, 1995).

6. Scott Brennan, "Controversial Activist in Uproar over Park Plan," in *The Bellingham Herald,* 13 November, 1994, A:1.

7. USDI, National Park Service, North Cascades National Park complex, "State of the Stephen Mather Wilderness, 1994" (Sedro Woolley, Wash., 1994),4-4.

8. Ibid. 4-8.

9. Ibid. 4-8.

10. Ibid. 4-7.

11. Gottfried Wilhelm Leibniz, *Theodicy* (orig. pub. 1710), ed. Austin Farrer (London: Routledge and Kegan Paul, 1951), p. 118.

12. J. A. Almack, W. L. Gaines, R. H. Naney, P. H. Morrison, J. R. Eby, G. F. Wooten, M. C. Snyder, S. H. Fitkin, and E. R. Garcia, *North Cascades Grizzly Bear Ecosystem Evaluation; Final Report* (Unpublished Report, Interagency Grizzly Bear Committee, Denver, Colo., 1993).

13. Ibid.

14. Ibid. pp. 1–4.

15. Ibid. pp. 1–4.

16. Ibid. p. 21.

Wild Speculations, *John C. Miles*

1. Charles Finley Easton, "Mount Baker: Its Trails and Legends," Whatcom Museum of History and Art, Bellingham (Unpublished Scrapbook, compiled 1903–1930), p. 42.

❖ Notes

. Nancy Langston, *Forest Dreams, Forest Nightmares: The Paradox of Old Growth in the Inland West* (Seattle: University of Washington Press, 1995), p. 306.

3. David Raines Wallace, *The Klamath Knot* (San Francisco: Sierra Club Books, 1983), p. 132.

4. Barry Lopez, *The Rediscovery of North America* (Lexington: The University Press of Kentucky, 1990).

5. Statutes at Large of the United States, 17, 32, Forty-second Congress, Second Session, February 1872.

6. Statutes at Large of the United States, 39:535, Sixty-fourth Congress, First Session, August 25, 1916.

7. Linda Hogan, *Dwellings: A Spiritual History of the Living World* (New York: W.W. Norton, 1995), p. 120.

North Cascades Institute

All royalties from the sale of *Impressions of the North Cascades* are donated to North Cascades Institute, a nonprofit educational organization dedicated to celebrating the natural and cultural landscapes of the Pacific Northwest.

From a dream born around a backcountry campfire by a group of naturalists and educators, North Cascades Institute has grown to be one of the preeminent environmental educational programs in North America. Since 1986 the institute has nurtured a sense of wonder and place through powerful field-based learning experiences for children and adults.

❖   ❖   ❖

North Cascades Institute
Learning is the Ultimate Adventure!

Programs include:
Natural History Seminars   ❖   Watershed Education   ❖   Mountain School Elderhostel   ❖   Summer Mountain Camp   ❖   School Programs   ❖   Custom Workshops   ❖   Research   ❖   Educational Materials   ❖   Teacher Training

2105 State Route 20, Sedro Woolley, WA 98284-9394
(360)856-5700 ❖ E-mail: nci@ncascades.org ❖ http://ncascades.org/nci/

About the Author

John Miles has taught environmental studies at Western Washington University for twenty-five years, serving as dean of the Huxley College of Environmental Studies for eight years. He is a current member of the Washington Forest Practices Board, an executive editor of *The Journal of Environmental Education*, and editor of *Adventure Education*. An avid outdoorsman, Miles has traveled the North Cascades for nearly thirty years, climbing to many summits, serving for a decade in mountain rescue, and chairing the board of the North Cascades Institute. He is the author of *Komo Kulshan: The Story of Baker* and *Guardian of the Parks: The History of the National Parks and Conservation Association*. He lives in Bellingham, Washington.

Dale Hamilton has carried his sketchbook into the mountains for over twenty years, recording his impressions of the landscape he has come to know intimately. He has worked for the U.S. Forest Service and for Western Washington University, and has shown his work in various galleries over the years. He lives with his wife, Sheena, in White Rock, B.C.

Other titles you may enjoy from The Mountaineers:

LOOKOUTS: Firewatchers of the Cascades and Olympics, *Ira Spring & Byron Fish*
An inspiring history of the fire-protection lookouts built and manned over a thirty-year period, and of the people who endured formidable conditions to make them a reality.

JOHN MUIR: His Life and Letters and Other Writings, *Terry Gifford, Editor*
This second Muir omnibus, a companion to *John Muir: The Eight Wilderness-Discovery Books,* gives readers a fresh and vivid portrait of the world's most influential conservationist.

MONTE CRISTO, *Philip R. Woodhouse*
The complete story of the Monte Cristo region of the Cascades during the search for gold and silver in its fabled mines in the late 1800s and early 1900s.

SNOQUALMIE PASS: From Indian Trail to Interstate, *Yvonne Prater*
Colorful history of the Washington Cascades pass. Published in conjunction with the Mountains to Sound Greenway Trust.

STEVENS PASS: The Story of Railroading and Recreation in the North Cascades, *JoAnn Roe*
Covers the exploration and development of rails and roads to scenic and recreational areas in this region of Washington State.

EXPLORING WASHINGTON'S WILD AREAS: A Guide for Hikers, Backpackers, Climbers, X-C Skiers, & Paddlers, *Marge & Ted Mueller*
Guide to 55 wilderness areas with outstanding recreational opportunities, plus notes on history, geology, plants, animals, and wildlife.

HIKING THE MOUNTAINS TO SOUND GREENWAY, *Harvey Manning*
Recreational walks and all-day hikes along Puget Sound's I-90 corridor. Includes the history, founding, and future of the Greenway project.

THE IRON GOAT TRAIL, *Volunteers for Outdoor Washington, USDA Forest Service, & Mount Baker-Snoqualmie National Forest*
History-filled walking guide to the first railroad route across the Cascades.

100 HIKES IN WASHINGTON'S GLACIER PEAK REGION: The North Cascades, 2nd Ed., *Ira Spring & Harvey Manning*

100 HIKES IN WASHINGTON'S NORTH CASCADES NATIONAL PARK REGION, 2nd Ed., *Ira Spring & Harvey Manning*

100 HIKES IN WASHINGTON'S ALPINE LAKES, 2nd Ed., *Ira Spring & Harvey Manning*

THE MOUNTAINEERS, founded in 1906, is a nonprofit outdoor activity and conservation club, whose mission is "to explore, study, preserve, and enjoy the natural beauty of the outdoors. . . . " Based in Seattle, Washington, the club is now the third-largest such organization in the United States, with 15,000 members and five branches throughout Washington State.

The Mountaineers sponsors both classes and year-round outdoor activities in the Pacific Northwest, which include hiking, mountain climbing, ski-touring, snowshoeing, bicycling, camping, kayaking and canoeing, nature study, sailing, and adventure travel. The club's conservation division supports environmental causes through educational activities, sponsoring legislation, and presenting informational programs. All club activities are led by skilled, experienced volunteers, who are dedicated to promoting safe and responsible enjoyment and preservation of the outdoors.

If you would like to participate in these organized outdoor activities or the club's programs, consider a membership in The Mountaineers. For information and an application, write or call The Mountaineers, Club Headquarters, 300 Third Avenue West, Seattle, Washington 98119; clubmail@mountaineers.org; (206) 284-6310.

The Mountaineers Books, an active, nonprofit publishing program of the club, produces guidebooks, instructional texts, historical works, natural history guides, and works on environmental conservation. All books produced by The Mountaineers are aimed at fulfilling the club's mission.

Send or call for our catalog of more than 300 outdoor titles:

 The Mountaineers Books
1001 SW Klickitat Way, Suite 201
Seattle, WA 98134
1-800-553-4453; E-mail: mbooks@mountaineers.org